Coeds Ruining the Nation

MICHIGAN MONOGRAPH SERIES IN JAPANESE STUDIES

NUMBER 87

CENTER FOR JAPANESE STUDIES
UNIVERSITY OF MICHIGAN

# Coeds Ruining the Nation

## WOMEN, EDUCATION, AND SOCIAL CHANGE IN POSTWAR JAPANESE MEDIA

**Julia C. Bullock**

University of Michigan Press
Ann Arbor

Published in the United States of America by the
University of Michigan Press
Manufactured in the United States of America
Printed on acid-free paper

A CIP catalog record for this book is available from the British Library.

Library of Congress Cataloging-in-Publication data has been applied for.

First published September 2019

ISBN: 978-0-472-07417-4 (Hardcover: alk paper)
ISBN: 978-0-472-05417-6 (Paper: alk paper)
ISBN: 978-0-472-12559-3 (ebook)

*for Shane*

# Contents

Digital materials related to this title can be found on the Fulcrum platform via the following citable URL: https://doi.org/10.3998/mpub.9969367

# *Acknowledgments*

The first book feels hard, but you're writing to keep your job, so there's your motivation. The second is harder. The Sword of Damocles (otherwise known as tenure) no longer hangs over your head. People expect more from you in terms of leadership on the job. Family, friends, and pets all want a piece of you too. Will anyone notice if you don't keep writing? Maybe not. Meanwhile, all that other stuff beckons.

I couldn't have completed this book without the extraordinary forbearance of loved ones, the guidance and support of colleagues, and the kindness of vague acquaintances and total strangers. You know who you are. Or maybe you don't, but I'm still grateful. Please believe that, even if I somehow manage to omit your name in what follows, which can only ever be a partial remembrance of all the ways my life and work have been enriched by the community that feeds it and gives it purpose.

First and foremost, this kind of thing takes money. I've been fortunate to have access to generous research funds through both my home department of Russian and East Asian Languages and Cultures (REALC) and the Dean's Office at Emory College. I offer my deepest appreciation to Dean Robin Forman, Dean Michael Elliott, and Dean of Faculty Carla Freeman for investing in me and making this work possible. I also benefited early on from a Twentieth-Century Japan Research Award from the Nathan and Jeanette Miller Center for Historical Studies and the University of Maryland Libraries, in support of the Gordon W. Prange Collection; the award transformed this project in ways I can't begin to describe here. At the University of Maryland, Kana Jenkins, Eleanor Kerkham, Marlene Mayo, Yukako Tatsumi, and Amy Wasserstrom graciously welcomed me, provided advice and guidance on the use of the collection, and patiently answered an endless stream of questions and requests for information. In the final stages of revision, a year of sabbatical as senior fellow at Emory's Fox Center for Humanistic Inquiry (FCHI) provided the necessary time and space for contemplation, without which this project might not have come to fruition. At the FCHI, which has supported my work from the moment I arrived at Emory, I've been particularly grateful to Keith Anthony, Colette Barlow, Tina Brownley, Amy Erbil, and Walter Melion.

Colleagues in REALC supported and covered for me in numerous ways to help me get this project done, especially (but not exclusively) Juliette Apkarian, Cheryl Crowley, Julie Darby, Elena Glazov-Corrigan, Seth Goss, and Laura Hunt. Also at Emory, I've had the great fortune to have models of scholarship, teaching, and service to admire and embolden me to hang in there, not least of whom are Carol Anderson, Tonio Andrade, Matthew Bernstein, Stephen Crist, Lisa Dillman, Tim Dowd, Lynne Huffer, Scott Kugle, Jeff Lesser, Michael Moon, Mark Risjord, Pamela Scully, Karen Stolley, Don Tuten, and Elizabeth Wilson. The East Asian Studies writing group at Emory has been a continual source of inspiration, so I extend profound thanks for feedback and encouragement to Aaron Balivet, Eugenia Bogdanova-Kumar, Jenny Chio, Ryan Cook, Helen Kim, Sun-Chul Kim, Yu Li, Mark Ravina, Meredith Schweig, Maria Sibau, Amanda Wangwright, Amanda Weiss, Wei Wu, Shunyuan Zhang, and any past members whose names have slipped my mind.

Beyond Emory, I've also been blessed with colleagues, mentors, and friends along the way who have inspired me, shown interest in my work, and challenged me to make it better. Special thanks for years of collaboration, camaraderie, and guidance go to Marnie Anderson, Jeffrey Angles, Jan Bardsley, Rebecca Copeland, Peter Duus, Alisa Freedman, Sally Hastings, Noriko Horiguchi, Ayako Kano, Kitada Sachie, Vera Mackie, Mark McLelland, Mizuta Noriko, Barbara Molony, Jim Reichert, Ann Sherif, Setsu Shigematsu, Doug Slaymaker, Nancy Stalker, Bob Tierney, and James Welker. I'm deeply grateful to my editor at the University of Michigan Press, Christopher Dreyer, for his encouragement and support of this project. Two anonymous reviewers of this manuscript also offered vital suggestions and thoughtful questions that helped me to shape the book into its current form. Any remaining deficiencies are entirely my responsibility.

Family and friends have been a wellspring of encouragement, forgiveness, empathy, and patience. It's truly the mark of a loving spouse/parent/sibling/friend when someone keeps cheering you on even though they have absolutely no interest in your work but nevertheless want you to be happy with it. My parents, Marie and Jon, my sister, Arwyn, and my niece, Riley, continue to welcome me home in spite of missed birthdays, anniversaries, holidays, and other special occasions, and I'm forever grateful to them for their support. Over the years, Heather, Emiko, Tavishi, Jules and Steve, Paula and Charles, Dusty, Dave and Anne, Jon, Hilke and Chris, Steven, and countless others kept me entertained, fed, and (mostly) sane through the ups, downs, and sideway adventures of life.

And saving the very best of the best for last: This book is dedicated to my husband, Shane, who makes the good stuff in life that much better and the bad stuff less awful, who provides safe harbor in stormy times, and who inexplicably continues to put up with me.

# Permissions for Image Use and Quotations

Every effort was made to locate the original rights holders for approval to reproduce the illustrations listed below. Unfortunately, given the extraordinarily unstable nature of the publishing industry (and Japanese society, generally speaking) during the Occupation era, in most cases it was impossible to locate the responsible party. Most publications and publishing houses that produced these images no longer exist, and even in cases where I was able to contact a representative of the magazine, they were often unable to confer permission for various reasons. Exceptions are noted below, with grateful recognition of the following individuals who did respond to my inquiries regarding permission to replicate these works, whether or not they were in a position to grant it: Arai Akiko of Jiji Press; Sako Megumi of Jitsugyō no Nihonsha; Kawake Makiko of the Katsushika Ward Office, Tokyo; Kadokawa Rie of the Chūgoku Shinbun; and Hirose Satoru of Suiseisha.

Deepest gratitude also goes to the following individuals who responded to my request to reproduce lengthy quotations from their schools' newsletters in chapter 4:

Ōta Ryōji and Gotō Naomasa of the Kyoto Pharmacy University granted permission to quote from *Yakusōshi*.

Yoneda Satoko and Muta Hisatoshi of the Saga Prefecture Takeo High School Arts Division granted permission to quote from *Sazanami*.

Ogawa Yūka and Watanabe Takatsune of the Nagasaki Prefecture Shimabara High School Arts Division granted permission to quote from *Muhyō*.

# Illustrations

All illustrations courtesy of the Gordon W. Prange Collection, University of Maryland Libraries

# Introduction

When I ran into K-san from the Number Two Boys' class in the hallway, he was disagreeably agitated. "Ah, you scared me," he said, putting a hand to his chest, and after a moment seemed to remember the cause of his agitation. "Doi-san, I'm begging you, loan me your math notes. We have a test next period." Well, I thought, boys certainly are careless about these things. But rather than be annoyed I put myself in the place of an agitated friend about to take a test, and felt nervous for him. "I'll loan them to you, but we haven't yet done integrals or differentials or anything." "That's OK, as long as there's irrational equations and logarithms and stuff like that." I ran back to the classroom and brought him my notebook.

As I turned to go I said, "Don't pay attention to the handwriting. It's awful," but he was humming something as he slid down the banister so he didn't respond to that. Instead he said, "Doi-san, thanks. I'll bring you some American chocolate," using a rough colloquial expression. . . . "Hey, rough language is something you use when talking to boys. How rude!" I shouted at him from behind. For a moment he turned and looked at me with a strange expression, but he kept going. . . . Then the next moment I stopped short. I shouldn't have said that to him. I wondered what he thought about my remark. . . . I remembered hearing from my mother that men like to assert themselves and put on airs. And that a good woman, a good wife, lets them assert themselves and put on airs. . . .

You could say that this way of thinking was forced on women during the feudal era. But whatever you say about equal rights between men and women, isn't it kind of a shame to cause men to lose face in the name of a world of democracy and human rights? Today I learned a good lesson—to be polite when associating with the opposite sex and not to be careless in my speech, which should be good training for me when I go out into society.[1]

POOR MISS DOI. As if adolescence weren't confusing enough, she had the misfortune to come of age in interesting times. The year was 1949. Japan had just lost a devastating war and was occupied by a foreign power that had forcibly rewritten its entire legal structure in an effort to "civilize" what it saw as a backward and feudalistic country. Meanwhile, average Japanese were still struggling to feed themselves. Many were also homeless, a result of the crippling destruction of infrastructure during the final months of the war.

Imagine being an adolescent girl at a time like this. Parents, teachers, and other adults are most likely too preoccupied with the struggle for daily survival to be of much help as you navigate your way toward adulthood. And on top of the everyday tragedies and general awkwardness associated with puberty, you are forced for the first time into uncomfortably close proximity with an alien life form whose language, behavior, and psychology you are totally unprepared to understand: boys.

Miss Doi provides no information about her family status or home life, but we know that she lived in a small town in rural Ehime prefecture, on the island of Shikoku. When she penned this essay, her high school was in the process of converting from a single-sex to a coeducational institution, meaning that boys and girls were now to be educated in the same classroom with the same teacher according to the same curricular standards. This was part of a wholesale restructuring of the educational system that took place under the auspices of the Occupation. When coeducation was first introduced, many parents and teachers voiced strident concerns about the "moral problems" that would surely result from educating boys and girls together, in a society where young people had been kept carefully segregated from one another and inculcated with gender-specific norms and values. Students like Miss Doi were therefore among the first to experience coeducation and were forced to work out for themselves how to balance the Occupation regime's promises of "equal rights between men and women" against cultural norms that had historically relegated women to a subordinate position within a hierarchical model of gender roles.

What other "lessons" did the Miss Dois of Japan learn about gender equality as a result of this coeducational experiment, and how did these experiences impact relationships between men and women in the years and decades to come? This book is devoted to a discourse analysis of accounts of coeducation—many of them first-person testimonies written by young people who pioneered this "new system" of education—that were published in newspapers, magazines, school newsletters, and other print media from the

Occupation period (1945–52) through the early 1960s. Highlighting the experiences of schoolchildren and young adults during this period helps us to better understand the controversies that accompanied coeducation, because this cohort of young people began their educations under the "old" (sex-segregated) system of education and were then forced to adapt quickly to the new postwar coeducational context. Furthermore, they lived through this massive cultural experiment at a formative time in their own personal development, thus incorporating postwar transformations in gender and sexual norms into their own gender and sexual identities. Younger members of this group had enormous opportunities to capitalize on the changes in the educational system to rewrite their own destinies. Those who were nearing the end of their educational careers by the time coeducation was implemented likely benefited much less from these changes. But as we will see in the chapters to come, regardless of age cohort, all young people during this period faced the challenge of negotiating the precipitous chasm between past and present, a struggle that frequently brought them into conflict with their elders.

## THE PROBLEM WITH COEDUCATION

Japanese society had not always frowned at educating boys and girls together or at providing girls with a level of education that rivaled that of their brothers. Aristocratic women of the Nara (710–94) and Heian (794–1185) periods were highly literate, and the most important works of classical Japanese literature were written by women during this time.[2] Scholarship continues to unearth more evidence of women's literacy and literary production during subsequent eras as well,[3] even prior to the marked expansion of education during the Edo period (1600–1868) that extended opportunities for schooling beyond the ranks of the aristocracy. During this era, "education levels rose and institutional development increased, as evidenced by the sustained growth in the number of local schools (*terakoya*) and private academies (*shijuku*). Parents sought greater education for their daughters as well as their sons, which increased enrollments in these two educational insitutions."[4] In the Edo-period *terakoya*, or "temple schools," boys and girls were often educated in the same room with the same teacher, although "there were far fewer girls than boys, and the two groups were rigidly separated in seating arrangements."[5] Thus, prior to the Meiji Restoration of 1868, which marked the beginning of "modern" Japan, access to education for both boys and girls varied widely according to time period, social class, local customs, and geo-graphical locale.[6]

Values governing social roles for women and relationships between the sexes likewise depended on these contextual factors. During the Nara and Heian periods, aristocratic women engaged actively in love affairs, and elab-orate courtship rituals structured a great deal of the social interaction among members of this class.[7] As Karen Brazell notes, these customs continued to dominate relationships among members of the imperial court well into the Kamakura period (1185–1333): "In this rarefied scene, poetry was a staple form of communication. . . . It was unthinkable to write a letter without a poem, and it was a gross breach of etiquette for a lover to neglect to send a morning-after poem as soon as he returned to his own quarters."[8] While the Muromachi period (1333–1573) is often thought to represent a low point in the history of Japanese women, scholars such as Barbara Ruch and Caitilin J. Griffiths have illuminated the role of religious devotion and pilgrimage in creating opportunities for increased mobility and status for female adher-ents of Buddhism, even within mixed-sex groups.[9]

The expansion of the educational system in the subsequent Edo period seems to have offered women of all classes opportunities for greater social roles. "The increasing visibility of women from both samurai and commoner classes in the public role of teacher and school administrator shows that by the end of the Tokugawa [Edo] period, teaching had become a suitable oc-cupation for women as a gender group and not just for women of a certain social stratum."[10] While concerns for chastity may have restricted the lives of upper-class women, young women of the lower classes and those in rural areas had significantly more freedom of movement and association. As late as the 1930s, anthropologists John Embree and Ella Lury Wiswell encoun-tered permissive attitudes toward premarital sex in remote villages of Japan.[11] Sonia Ryang suggests that in some areas this flexible attitude toward chastity may have continued even into the postwar period.[12]

But as a general rule, beginning in the late 1800s, when a comprehensive modern educational system was first constructed, Japanese schools began segregating the sexes in order to educate them according to very different cur-ricula and expectations. Hirota Masaki describes this transition as follows:

> In the first years of the Meiji period [1868–1912], boys and girls were educated together in elementary schools for four years of compulsory education. But around the time of the 1879 educational directive that segregated boys' and

girls' post-elementary education, the number of schools that separated boys and girls in the later years of elementary education increased. This trend eventually came to dominate, and opportunities for experiencing equality between the sexes at school became limited to the first several years of elementary education.[13]

By 1898, the purpose of education for girls was explicitly defined as intended to produce "good wives and wise mothers" (*ryōsai kenbo*). This term was coined in the late 1800s to describe the role that Meiji leaders envisioned for women in the modernization of the nation. Women were thus exhorted to support their husbands' public-sphere activities and to nurture the next generation of imperial subjects. It is important to note that this ideal of femininity was not "traditional" (in the sense of ahistorical), but rather a modern invention that was as much a product of the rise of Japanese nationalism as it was a legacy of Confucian beliefs regarding women's roles in the family and society. As Kathleen Uno notes, Meiji-era leaders "came to cherish a vision of Japanese mothers as the socializers of the next generation of citizens needed to build and defend a strong Japanese nation-state. Education of girls to become wise mothers would ensure their future role as positive agents of national change."[14]

As the new national system of education developed to meet these needs, the "good wife, wise mother" model of femininity became increasingly important to the education of girls and was inculcated through a curriculum that focused heavily on acquisition of domestic skills. Meanwhile, boys were trained for professional careers according to a more rigorous set of academic standards. In tandem with this differential set of educational expectations, social intercourse between the sexes was increasingly monitored by parents and teachers and coded as problematic, particularly for adolescents. While compliance with the ideal of sex segregation varied according to location and family resources, with daughters of wealthier urban families being relatively more "protected" from contact with the opposite sex, it was increasingly assumed that girls of good reputation did not socialize unsupervised with males who were unrelated to them.

Societal injunctions against mixed-sex socializing among young people intensified in the 1930s as Japan geared up for total war. Japanese government policies reinforced this notion of separate spheres for men and women not merely through separate educational curricula for boys and girls but also through propaganda and censorship activities that increasingly promoted suppression of personal desires of all kinds in favor of national goals. Kyoko Hirano notes, for example, that in 1940 the Ministry of Internal Affairs banned "films describing individual happiness" and "films dealing with sexual frivolity" as detrimental to the war effort.[15] As Douglas Slaymaker and Mark McLelland have separately demonstrated, this government campaign to subordinate human needs for love and sex to the war effort was so pervasive that after 1945 there was a veritable explosion of publications devoted to expression of pent-up carnal desires.[16]

But government repression alone cannot account for the ideological shift toward separate spheres for men and women that reached its apotheosis during the Pacific War. In fact, many women embraced this essentialized model of gender difference based on complementary but mutually exclusive roles for men and women, precisely because it gave them an unprecedented role in contributing to national projects such as modernization and empire. Michiko Suzuki importantly notes the role that feminist writers like Hiratsuka Raichō and Takamure Itsue played in promoting a "mythologized" ideal of maternal love that worked hand in hand with state ideologies of nationalism and militarism, thus helping to undergird the war effort:

> The feminist agenda and the nationalist cause merged in lionizing women as valuable subjects able to participate in both the private and public spheres, reproducing and raising children but also working while men were at war. . . . Such convergence of female and maternal identities, as well as the erasure of self and the promotion of the state, constricted women; at the same time, however, it also enabled the articulation of a gendered Japanese identity that appeared powerful and unique.[17]

As we will see in chapter 1, this notion of mythologized motherhood was so seductive that it persisted in modified form well into the postwar period.

This emphasis on separate spheres for men and women had a particularly chilling influence on relationships between young people who entered adolescence during wartime. As one woman who was a schoolgirl during the war recalled:

> Real relationships with boys were strictly prohibited. Sometimes, when there were special festivals or ceremonies or that sort of thing, we would visit the local Japanese boys' school, but every time that happened we would get a

special little lecture first, telling us that we mustn't have private conversations with any of the boys, and we mustn't let our eyes wander unnecessarily.

In a small, close community like ours anyone who walked out with a boy was likely to meet someone who knew them, and then there would be a terrible scandal, and gossip at the *tonarigumi* [neighborhood association] meetings, and the story would probably get back to the headmaster. If that happened, he would call the girl into his study and give her a good talking to, and she would have to make a public apology or, if it happened more than once, she might be suspended from school.[18]

Thus, particularly for girls of "good" families, activities such as walking to school with a boy, sitting side by side with a boy, exchanging words or letters with a boy, or engaging in any sort of unnecessary communication with a boy were considered to be warning signs of degeneracy, and such behaviors were met with swift and merciless social retribution.

In spite of all of this, after the war young people transitioned to the new system of coeducation with remarkable equanimity. Certainly the experience of being in such close proximity to the opposite sex was uncomfortable and embarrassing at first for members of both sexes. There were misunderstandings, conflicts, and feelings of consternation, particularly for the first few weeks or months. But many first-hand accounts written by boys and girls who lived through this transition are remarkably upbeat and optimistic about the possibilities that this brave new world of "cooperation between the sexes" opened up to them. Adults, on the other hand, were often hostile or fearful at the prospect of the "moral problems" they were certain coeducation would cause. Parents in particular often viewed coeducation with grave concern as a potential cause of social chaos, imagining that the practice would wreak further harm on a Japanese society that was already unbearably rent by the physical and moral devastation of defeat.

Occupation-era debates over coeducation ultimately intensified into a fully blown moral panic that dominated the mass media of the early postwar period. While this study is limited primarily to discussion of print media such as newspapers, popular magazines, student newsletters, and other journalistic sources from 1945 to the early 1960s, the controversy over coeducation permeated Japanese media of all types during the early postwar period. This is evident, for example, from the influence of coeducation on literary fiction and film as early as 1947, with the publication of Ishizaka Yōjirō's *Blue Mountains* (*Aoi sanmyaku*).[19] The novel was subsequently made into a two-part film by director Imai Tadashi in 1949—the same year that coeducation was introduced on a broad scale at the high school level—to great acclaim. Though the young couple at the center of the controversy in this film attend separate, sex-segregated high schools, the furor their seemingly chaste courtship causes in their small rural town serves as eloquent testimony to the fears of social upheaval that coeducation occasioned at the time of its introduction (see chap. 5). While the film itself suggests this controversy is overblown, it was also made during the Occupation, a time when directors were strongly encouraged to portray such reforms in a positive light.

It is perhaps no surprise, then, that shortly after the end of the Occupation we see far more disturbing pop culture portrayals of the "moral problems" coeducation was thought to cause. The "sun-tribe" (*taiyōzoku*) craze in fiction and film of the mid-1950s is the most obvious and well-documented manifestation of this phenomenon (see chap. 6), though, interestingly, scholarship on this media frenzy typically fails to acknowledge coeducation as a proximate cause. So named after the novella *Season of the Sun* (*Taiyō no kisetsu*) by the literary enfant terrible Ishihara Shintarō, these "sun-tribe" tales of juvenile delinquency oozed with a violent sexuality that would seem to suggest the apocalyptic consequences of coeducation, given its perceived role in facilitating unfettered "association" between teenagers of the opposite sex. We see coeducation directly implicated in the film *Punishment Room* (*Shokei no heya*, 1956), based on another Ishihara novel in which a university coed is drugged and raped by a fellow member of her study circle. The young woman is targeted for this attack by an angry young man who resents her for publicly contradicting male members of the group during a debate over political theory, as if to punish her for daring to exercise the right to "equality of educational opportunity" to which she is legally entitled. In this sense, we may posit a direct line of descent linking the fervid hand-wringing over youthful romance in *Blue Mountains* to the paroxysms of erotic anarchy depicted in the *taiyōzoku* media products of the mid-1950s, which spawned even more nihilistic tales of depraved teenagers in the subsequent decade, as in Ōshima Nagisa's *Cruel Story of Youth* (*Seishun zankoku monogatari*, 1960).

## EQUALITY AND GENDER (IN)DIFFERENCE

As the central conflict of *Punishment Room* suggests, coeducation produced disturbing conflicts between prewar views of women's roles in society and the new guarantees of equality of opportunity enshrined in the postwar constitution. Did "equality" mean that women should be educated in the same way as men to pursue careers outside the home? Or was it more important to stress preparation for roles as wives and mothers in the domestic sphere? These questions became ever more urgent as the Japanese economy transitioned from the postwar recovery of the 1950s to the high economic growth of the 1960s. During this period, government and industry combined forces to promote a gendered division of labor that gave women full responsibility for the domestic sphere so that men could be free to concentrate on their responsibilities to the workplace.[20] Major media outlets excoriated female university students for "ruining the nation" by taking coveted spots at elite universities away from male applicants, only to "waste" their educations by becoming wives and mothers rather than career-track professionals upon graduation (see chap. 6).

In many ways this effort to return women to the home mirrored contemporary trends in the United States and elsewhere. As Mire Koikari notes, the Cold War ideology of "containment" sought a bulwark not merely against communism but against other potential "threats" to the integrity of democracy as well, such as transgression of gender and sexual norms. This produced a model of gender equality that was safely embedded within a "postwar cult of domesticity." Thus, under the auspices of the Occupation, Japan too became a "salient site for the articulation of Cold War containment culture."[21] Coeducation was introduced, debated, and ultimately co-opted toward this project of containment just as Japan was transforming itself from abject devastation to economic superpowerdom. Therefore, studying the effects of coeducation on early postwar Japanese society promises to reveal much about the relationships between ideologies of gender, educational reform, and economic growth in mid-twentieth-century industrialized nations.

I use the term "ideology" advisedly to highlight the socially and historically constructed aspects of the gender roles espoused both by the Occupation authorities and by the Japanese population they presumed to regulate. In describing good wife, wise mother as an example of such ideologies of gender, I build on the linkage suggested in Fukaya Masashi's seminal study of this discourse. He considers it to have been a "structural ideology" of Japanese modernity, connecting this model of femininity to other modern discursive phenomena such as the contemporaneous rise of nationalism and the concept of the nation as one body (*kokutai*) united by ethnic identity and a moral imperative to support national goals.[22] Thus, good wife, wise mother discourse became structurally interwoven with other national myths of identity and belonging, making it an essential thread of the political fabric of Japanese modernity. With this in mind, I believe it makes sense to speak of gendered discourses such as good wife, wise mother in ideological terms, in recognition of their status as constructs that possess disciplinary power[23] yet that are nevertheless malleable enough to be open to contestation or renegotiation.

I also find the conceptual framework of ideology to be useful because it highlights the way personal desires may be incited in the service of corporate interests, thus encouraging individuals to envision their own life narratives as consonant with national or institutional goals. Good wife, wise mother discourse found many ready adherents among Japanese women precisely because it offered them a meaningful role in the national project of modernization, discursively rendering them historical agents whose individual stories were interwoven with the national narrative of progress, even as it circumscribed their activities within a narrow sphere. After World War II, the Occupation regime attempted to counter this narrative with a competing ideology that promised women equality by giving them the same, rather than complementary, roles as men in the project of national rebuilding. The conflict between these two models of equality may therefore be understood as a contest between competing ideologies of women's value to the nation.

As we will see in the chapters that follow, much of the conflict that ensued when coeducation was first introduced revolved around this notion of "equality," which was understood differently by the Japanese than it was by the Americans. American Occupiers frequently assumed, consciously or not, that for men and women to be equal, they should be treated as the "same"— that is, have the same rights, responsibilities, and access to resources (including education). This often entailed a state of willful forgetfulness about the very real inequalities, sexual and otherwise, that remained in American society in spite of these ideals. The Japanese, by contrast, generally preferred to think of male and female roles as complementary yet different and viewed separate spheres for men and women as a means of maintaining social harmony. These presumptions undergirded the prewar sex-segregated system of education that was predicated on an assumption of innate and immutable gender difference, implying that the sexes might be equally valued but were still fundamentally different from one another and should therefore be trained for very different roles in society. This often entailed a state of willful blindness to the different valuation, in fact if not in theory, accorded to men's (paid) and women's (unpaid or poorly paid) labor.

In addition to bearing little resemblance to the realities they purported to describe, these ideologies of gender were also fraught with constitutive contradictions.[24] Prior to defeat in 1945, the Japanese had exhorted women to behave as guardians of home and hearth even as they mobilized them in significant ways for the war effort. After defeat, government bureaucrats resented and resisted Occupation efforts to impose gender equality provisions even as they indicated a basic agreement with many of these measures. For their part, the Occupiers were hardly united on the form and degree this equality should take, and many of the staunchest supporters of reforms that would give Japanese women a greater role in the public sphere nevertheless expressed private qualms about the effect this would have on their roles as wives and mothers. The introduction of coeducation to Japan therefore took place amid a host of unexamined assumptions and internal inconsistencies that resulted in unresolved conflicts between very different sets of gender and sexual norms—conflicts that remain unresolved, to some degree, to this day. Most recently, we see evidence of this conflict in Prime Minister Abe Shinzō's exhortation for Japanese women to "shine" in the public sphere, while taking on ever more responsibility in the home for the care of aging parents and the reproduction of the next generation.

## CONTRIBUTION TO SCHOLARSHIP AND METHODOLOGY

Analysis of debates over coeducation promises to yield important insights into the philosophical and psychological transformation experienced by Japanese people as they struggled to internalize (or contain) the societal changes wrought by the new postwar order. However, to date there has been no study in English on this topic. In Japanese, a few excellent studies of coeducation cover this period, but none of them provide the level of discursive analysis of underlying transformations in gender roles and sexual mores that this book seeks to provide. Hashimoto Noriko's *Danjo kyōgakusei no shiteki kenkyū* (Historical research on the coeducational system, 1992) delivers a comprehensive overview of the history of coeducation in Japan from the

Meiji period to the 1970s. But as a historical overview, it focuses primarily on factual details and does not give much attention to the underlying theoretical shifts in discourses on sexuality, gender roles, and norms of behavior that occurred particularly in the first two postwar decades. Uemura Chikako's *Josei kaihō o meguru senryō seisaku* (Occupation policies surrounding women's liberation, 2007) provides a careful study of the role of the Occupation regime in pushing for inclusion of coeducation into the 1947 Fundamental Law of Education (FLE). However, it is more focused on documenting the relationships between occupier and occupied than on discursive analysis of shifting values surrounding gender and sexuality in Japanese society, which is the focus of the present study. Koyama Shizuko's *Sengo kyōiku no jendā chitsujo* (The gender structure of postwar education, 2009) documents the backlash against coeducation and higher education for women from the early 1950s to the mid-1960s. However, it does not delve deeply into the Occupation-era ideological conflicts over norms of gender and sexuality that produced this backlash, as this book seeks to do. Thus, existing studies of coeducation in Japan have left several important lacunae in scholarship that this book seeks to fill.

Furthermore, *Coeds Ruining the Nation* is the first book in any language to exploit the extraordinary trove of Occupation-era newspapers, magazines, journals, and pamphlets housed in the Prange Collection at the University of Maryland in order to document and analyze the discourses of gender and sexuality surrounding coeducation.[25] The materials in this archive were collected by Occupation censors for the purpose of monitoring and controlling public discourse. Because everything published during this time had to go through this process of approval, the Prange Collection represents the most comprehensive sample of Occupation-era publications available anywhere in the world. It is not a complete collection—some issues of certain titles are missing, and other titles may have been lost or destroyed. Because the censorship apparatus took some time to begin its work and began to relax its oversight toward the end of the Occupation, the collection is most robust for the years 1946 to 1949 and sparse for the months prior to and after that time. Nonetheless, it is the most complete collection of Occupation-era materials available to scholars interested in understanding public discourse in Japan during this period, and the years that are well represented fortunately coincide with those when societal reforms such as coeducation were conceived and implemented. Finally, although we cannot discount the likelihood that writers practiced self-censorship so as not to run afoul of Occupation authorities, the censorship records in the Prange Collection suggest that writers at this time were relatively free to express opinions both for and against coeducation. This indicates that the publications in this archive offer a useful and reasonably representative sampling of public opinion on this topic (see chaps. 3 and 4).

A keyword search of the Prange Collection database for articles on the subject of *danjo kyōgaku* (coeducation) revealed 406 separate items dedicated to this topic. These included news articles, op-ed pieces, interviews and roundtable discussions, and images (particularly cartoons). These items appeared in a wide range of publications, from regional and national newspapers and general interest magazines to large-circulation magazines targeted to specific audiences (women, children, educators) and amateur publications such as newsletters created by schoolchildren and local voluntary associations. I collected and sorted all of these publications by type and also coded them according to whose perspective the contents purported to represent (students, teachers, parents, community leaders, private citizens, etc.). I then looked for correlations between these various perspectives and the views expressed about coeducation. Statistical data summarizing these findings are discussed in chapters 2 through 5, which are devoted to analysis of the Prange Collection materials (see below for chapter overviews). The publications discussed in chapter 6, which covers the post-Occupation backlash against coeducation as reflected in large-circulation magazines and newspapers of the early 1950s to the mid-1960s, were located through an analogous search of articles in the Online Public Access Catalog database of Japan's National Diet Library.

## SCOPE AND STRUCTURE OF THIS STUDY

This book is primarily a study of the discourses of gender and sexuality underpinning Japanese debates over coeducation in the Occupation and subsequent decade. As such, it is not meant to offer a comprehensive history of coeducation or of women's education in Japan, although I provide a brief overview of this history in chapter 1. Neither does this book take a position on whether or how coeducation might, generally speaking, be "better" or "worse" for women than sex-segregated education. Finally, while many of the arguments for and against coeducation discussed in this book echo similar arguments made in Europe and North America at the time coeducation was introduced in those areas, cross-cultural comparisons are beyond the scope of this book.[26] I am interested primarily in how gender roles had been constructed in Japan prior to the introduction of coeducation, how this new system challenged these norms, and how these challenges were handled on an individual and societal level in the years during and after the Occupation.

I argue that, whereas adults generally resisted coeducation and continued to object to it even as it was being implemented, most (but by no means all) students were quick to adapt to the new system and to see it as contributing positively to a newly democratic Japanese society. Parents and teachers, who were accustomed to the prewar sex-segregated system of education, were far more likely than children to view coeducation as a disastrous project that was doomed to failure because of perceived differences in academic ability between boys and girls and to insist that coeducation was likely to further disrupt an already fragile Japanese society by contributing to "moral problems." Young people thus faced a confusing set of mixed messages regarding equality of educational opportunity, with the Occupation regime promoting the notion that boys and girls should have access to the same level and type of education and with their parents' generation continuing to argue for sex-segregated education for gender-specific roles in society. In response, students' natural impulse was to attempt to reconcile these mixed messages into a new postwar model of equality that emphasized preservation of essentialized gender differences within a coeducational context. As the Occupation drew to an end and Japanese conservatives regained control of the government, the educational system increasingly adopted this "separate but equal" logic, preserving the appearance of coeducation yet continuing to value and reinforce "masculine" and "feminine" roles and behaviors so as to produce gendered educational outcomes.

Chapter 1 traces the rise and fall of the sex-segregated system of education prior to the Occupation, as well as the course of negotiations that resulted in official legal recognition of coeducation in 1947. Chapter 2 provides an overview of the implementation of coeducation that followed, as seen through coverage in regional newspapers across the Japanese archipelago. It also introduces the main objections raised by parents, teachers, and other adult members of Japanese society to coeducation—specifically, (1) the gap in academic preparation between boys and girls that resulted from the prewar sex-segregated educational system, (2) concerns about "moral problems" (expressed as a pervasive fear of adolescent sexual experimentation), and (3) anxieties regarding transgression of gender roles and norms of behavior that underlined this fixation on "moral problems."

These three categories of analysis structure the chapters that follow, which explore the way these objections were framed by adults and the way children responded to them as seen in comics (chap. 3), student-authored school newsletters (chap. 4), and student roundtable discussions published in mass-market print media (chap. 5). Chapter 6 traces the prevalence of these arguments into the 1950s and 1960s, as the increasing number of women gaining admittance to prestigious universities as a result of coeducation prompted a backlash against "coeds ruining the nation," as seen in both journalistic and entertainment media of the time such as fiction and film. The conclusion brings the discussion up to the present day, highlighting the resonance of these debates over gender and sexual norms for contemporary Japanese society, given a sputtering Japanese economy and an impending demographic crisis due to its low birthrate.

In telling the story that follows, I prioritize the voices of Miss Doi and her cohort precisely because they had the dubious fortune of coming of age in interesting times. Thanks to coeducation, girls of their generation had a tremendous opportunity to choose life paths that were likely unimaginable to their mothers and grandmothers. What a thrilling experience this must have been! And how terrifying this must have seemed to many, for the consequences of daring to exercise these new rights were severe. In choosing whether—or how—to respond to these challenges, they had to consider anticipated responses from parents, friends, and members of the community of both sexes. For those who did dare to assert themselves, how did they handle the backlash that would inevitably accompany their actions? For those who judged transgression of conventional norms of femininity a bridge too far, what anxieties might they have harbored about choosing the safer path? And how did these choices in the aggregate shape postwar Japanese society, as Miss Doi and her fellow "coeds"[27] enabled Japan's rise to the status of economic superpower in subsequent decades?

# CHAPTER I

## *From Sex Segregation to Coeducation*

The education of girls and women has been, throughout the history of Japan, based on the idea that women's chief object in existence is to become "good wives and wise mothers." There has been no widespread belief that women should be trained in academic subjects or have any knowledge of life outside the home. Since the [Meiji] Restoration, there have been notable exceptions to this idea in the several fine women's colleges, many excellent girls' high schools, and many outstanding mission schools. In general, however, the basic idea that men are more important than women and that the wife must subordinate herself first to her parents and then to her husband, has been the dominating theme in the training of Japanese women.[1]

WITH THIS LOFTY PRONOUNCEMENT, the Allies began their campaign to dramatically restructure the Japanese educational system to ensure "equality of opportunity" for both sexes. The quote, which begins the section titled "Women's Education" in the Occupation regime's report *Education in Japan*, is a telling indication of the low esteem in which the Occupiers held the "traditions" of their former enemy. It is also remarkably ahistorical, ignoring (for example) the substantial contributions of women to Japanese literature, particularly in the Heian period (794-1185), and projecting the good wife wise mother model of Japanese femininity—a decidedly modern phenomenon— back upon centuries of premodern Japanese history.[2] As Martha Tocco notes, the image of Japanese women as wallowing in ignorance prior to the modern period is a common and unfortunate misconception, given the fact that "the education of noble women had begun more than eight centuries earlier, and by the end of the Tokugawa period [1600-1868], the education of both samurai and affluent commoner women was a regular feature of the Tokugawa educational landscape."[3] And yet the Allies frequently marshaled indignation at the low status of Japanese women to justify their plan to de-mocratize Japan and rid it of "feudal" tendencies through a radical overhaul of its government and institutions. In fact, even before his plane had touched down in Japan in August 1945, General Douglas MacArthur, the Supreme Commander of the Allied Powers (SCAP), had identified elevation of the sta-tus of Japanese women as one of five cardinal objectives of the Occupation and a key cornerstone of democratic reform.[4]

As the opening quote implies, the Occupiers believed that true democ-racy required the equal participation of women in democratic institutions, both inside and outside the home. They understood the prewar Japanese educational system to have been profoundly unequal in structure, having relegated girls to a separate track of education designed to inculcate virtues of good-wife-and-wise-motherhood at the expense of "train[ing] in aca-demic subjects" and knowledge of the wider world, which were characteris-tic of education for boys. This was a problem for SCAP—the term used to re-fer not only to MacArthur but to the entire Occupation regime—not only because they expected women to participate in the democratic process themselves but also because they relied on women to inculcate their chil-dren with the democratic values they saw as necessary to "pacify" Japan and prevent future outbreaks of militarism. In the minds of some of these SCAP officials, coeducation—teaching boys and girls side by side in the same class-room according to the same curriculum—was the only way to ensure that girls received the equality of opportunity in education necessary for full par-ticipation in a democratic society.

The logic behind this assumption is outlined in an internal report titled "Co-education—Staff Studies,"[5] which recommended the practice "at all lev-els" of the Japanese educational system, along with a number of other "ob-jectives for improvement of women's education." After noting what they claimed to be widespread support among Japanese educators for this mea-sure, the writer of this report recommends the repeal of legal obstacles to its implementation, notably Article 51 of the Elementary School Law, on the following grounds:

> The pre-war publications of the *Mombusho* [Ministry of Education] and state-ments of the Mombusho until approximately last December, have implied that coeducation actually existed in the elementary schools. Such is not the case. In most schools the pupils are separated after the second or third year by Article 51 of the Elementary School Law which states,

If the number of the same school year of girls is sufficient to organize a class, classes of the said school year shall be divided for boys and girls. In the case of the upper classes, if the number of girls throughout each school year is sufficient to organize a class, it is also the same as above.

The regulation of the above clause shall not be applied when organizing classes of the lower first and second class children.

In short, except in country schools where there are few pupils, separate education of the two sexes exists by law beyond the first two years.[6]

This practice of segregating students by sex is implicitly understood here as a cornerstone of Japanese oppression of women and an obstacle to the objectives of equality and democracy espoused by the Occupation authorities.

In an apparent effort to influence the course of the upcoming negotiations over what would become the Fundamental Law of Education (FLE) of 1947, which legally "recognized" coeducation as a lawful practice, the report goes on to suggest "Action [to repeal Article 51] to be taken now. It seems unnecessary, if not undesirable, to wait for what will probably be a year or more before this becomes a 'fait accompli' in the ordinary course of law revision."[7] The document promotes coeducation with some urgency, along with a number of other recommendations, such as "equalization both of texts and of curriculum" for boys and girls, promotion of youth organizations for both sexes, and "curtailment of so-called Domestic Science courses" for girls so as to allow more time for academic instruction.[8] In doing so, the writer takes aim at many of the pillars of the good wife, wise mother style of prewar education in favor of a newly reconstructed system designed to foster equality of educational opportunity. However, the moral conviction with which this writer justifies these measures gives little hint of the conflict that would ensue when the Occupiers' demands for reform clashed with the fervently held ideologies of gender roles underlying Japan's prewar educational system.

This chapter will provide a brief overview of the rise and fall of the sex-segregated school system in Japan, from the beginning of the Meiji period to the era of Occupation reform, with particular emphasis on its ideological and practical consequences. It is intended to set the stage for the discussion in subsequent chapters of students' experiences in the Occupation period, when coeducation was first introduced and the chasm between prewar and postwar models of education had to be negotiated on a daily basis by young people who were the objects of this "new system" of education. I do not pretend here to provide a comprehensive overview of the history of education for women prior to World War II or an accounting of the intellectual achievements of the many talented Japanese women whose professional careers blossomed during this time in spite of the good wife, wise mother orientation of education for girls. Many scholars writing in English have already documented the opportunities provided to women through the sex-specific system of higher schools and colleges that developed at this time in Japan or through study abroad.[9] I am primarily interested here in setting the stage for the conflict between ideologies of sex-segregated education versus equal educational opportunity that arose in the immediate postwar period as a result of this prewar history of gender-specific training.

As fictive constructs, both sides' way of viewing gender roles failed to account for the significant diversity of feminine experience in Japan, in contemporary or historical perspective. These ideologies also masked the remarkable gap between the cherished ideal of gender equality in the American imagination and the actual experiences of American women, who were exhorted to return to the home so that their men could reclaim jobs vacated for military service during the war, even as the Occupiers preached the doctrine of "equality" to their Japanese subordinates. But these gaps between ideology and reality did not make the underlying beliefs any less compelling to those who harbored them.

Furthermore, unconscious assumptions of the "naturalness" of sex and gender norms on both sides remained largely unexamined, significantly complicating the process of Occupation-era reform and its postwar legacy for the Japanese educational system. As we will see in the narratives analyzed in this and subsequent chapters, both Japanese and Americans were prone to imagine the good wife and wise mother model of femininity as "traditional" and inherent to Japanese culture. Americans, raised with the assumption of equality of opportunity as part of the birthright of any "civilized" person, understood this expectation of women's roles as mired in "feudalistic" thinking and a wrongheaded idea sorely in need of correction for the sake of a peaceful and democratic Japan. By contrast, Japanese conservatives—whether Ministry of Education (MOE) bureaucrats, teachers, or parents raised with this cultural ideal as part of their "common sense"—tended to understand it as natural and inevitable that women's life course would revolve around the roles of wife and mother and consequently subordinate their own desires to the family and nation.

As noted in the introduction, this model of femininity formed a vital structural component of the fabric of modern Japanese society. Thus, the Occupation-era challenge to good wife, wise mother provoked intense anxiety and resistance from Japanese conservatives who felt this as an attack on the integrity of the nation writ large, at a time when so many other structural ideologies of Japanese modernity—the emperor system, the family-state, and so forth—were in existential crisis. Viewing good wife, wise mother and its American counterpart of equality-as-sameness as competing ideologies of gender thus helps to explain the virulence of the debates over coeducation and their centrality to understanding modern Japanese discourses of national identity and individual purpose.

## THE RISE OF GOOD WIFE, WISE MOTHER EDUCATION

In the early years of the Meiji period, the framers of the Japanese educational system had extremely ambitious and idealistic goals about the kind of modern society their nation would become, and their vision for the kind of educational system that would be necessary to support such national goals was correspondingly expansive. They began by sketching out a comprehensive system of schools that would provide every child, regardless of sex or family background, with the same basic education. (These plans were scaled back repeatedly over the following years in response to straitened government finances and popular opposition.)[10] This elementary level of education was followed by a complex and increasingly narrowing ladder of secondary and tertiary institutions that was intended primarily to prepare male students of ability with the necessary skills for national leadership. Ambitious boys continued on to middle school after the compulsory grades[11] of elementary school, followed by higher school and then university. There were also variant tracks that led from middle school to specialty colleges or higher normal schools (which trained secondary school teachers) and from elementary school to a variety of vocational institutions, including lower normal schools.[12] Beginning with the Education Law (*Kyōiku rei*) of 1879, girls were increasingly shut out of the elite track of middle and higher schools available for boys, leaving it mostly to private and missionary schools to fill the demand for girls' secondary education.[13] It was not until 1899 that the Girls' Higher School Law (*Kōtō jogakkō rei*) mandated that each prefecture establish at least one secondary school for girls.

Ironically, the early Meiji years of governmental neglect of education designed specifically for women allowed a small minority of talented and ambitious girls a window of opportunity to attain the same educational credentials as men, effectively opening the door to early (and unofficial) experiments with coeducation beyond the elementary level. Because there were as yet no similar institutions designated explicitly for girls and because the Meiji government had not yet thought to bar them from institutions designed primarily for male students, a few young women in the early Meiji period were able to gain admittance to secondary and tertiary schools, establishing themselves in professional fields.[14] Some of these women became leaders in women's education who helped to establish private colleges for this purpose in the following decades. For example, Yoshioka Yayoi (1871–1959) braved parental opposition and harassment by male colleagues to graduate from medical school in 1892; she would later establish the first medical school for Japanese women in cooperation with her husband in 1900, in spite of governmental obstruction and ridicule by the general public. This groundbreaking institution, which would become Tokyo Medical College for Women, was finally recognized formally by the Japanese government in 1912 and would go on to cultivate generations of female Japanese doctors.[15] However, even the most prestigious tertiary institutions for women's education were held by the government to the rank of "specialty schools" (*semmon gakkō*), which were legally defined as inferior to the universities designated specifically for men in terms of quality and prestige.[16]

In spite of these early experiments with coeducation, as the twentieth century approached, the Japanese government became increasingly invested in promoting education specifically for women while simultaneously controlling and regulating its contents, and this small window of opportunity for exceptional women to attend the same institutions as men soon began to close. Koyama Shizuko links this sudden government interest in women's education, after more than twenty years of neglect, to the rise of nationalism that accompanied Japan's victory in the Sino-Japanese War of 1894–95. By the 1880s, there were already rising social concerns about the level of foreign missionary involvement in the education of Japanese women. As Japan turned its attention to imperialistic adventures beyond its borders, the importance of educating its masses to support and contribute to state goals became increasingly urgent. Educators and political leaders began to argue that education for girls, as well as boys, could play an important role in ensuring Japan's national success. Koyama characterizes this new approach to women's education as follows:

> The knowledge gained by education enabled women to give their private support to men's work and to promote awareness of national life and the workings of the state. The desirability of women using their knowledge to support men in their work is particularly interesting, since during the Edo period [1600–1868], the main requirement for being a good wife was docility toward one's husband and parents-in-law. Here, by contrast, a more active role was expected of the wife. It was no longer acceptable for women to remain "stupid"; they were now expected to receive an education and to use the knowledge gained to help their husbands. This, indeed, was what being a *ryōsai*, a "good wife," meant.[17]

The resultant system of secondary education for girls, as mandated by the Girls' Higher School Law, emphasized a three- or four-year curriculum based on general education subjects—Japanese (*kokugo*), history and geography, basic math and science, drawing, and music—along with instruction in "morals" (*shūshin*) and domestic arts such as sewing. This was in stark contrast to boys' higher schools, which lasted five years and taught a more intensive curriculum with specialized instruction in math and scientific fields (natural history, physics and chemistry, and sometimes law and economics) as well as courses that did not exist in the girls' curriculum (e.g., literary Chinese, or *kanbun*) or were treated as optional (e.g., foreign languages).[18] The goal of this differential system of education was to produce men who could lead the nation in the public sphere and women who had just enough education to be supportive of men's goals and ably manage the household in their absence. In other words, women were expected to cultivate themselves as good wives and wise mothers whose primary obligation was to the domestic sphere, capable of contributing to public life but mainly through their support of men's activities rather than through professional careers in their own right.

As we will see in subsequent chapters, the ideological underpinnings of this good wife, wise mother system of education stressed an idealized form of complementarity in sex roles that remained influential in the postwar decades, in spite of Occupation-period reforms that sought to promote equality of educational opportunity.[19] As it developed in the first few decades of the twentieth century, good wife, wise mother discourse was founded not so much on traditional Japanese sex roles but rather on a combination of pseudoscientific "knowledge" of sex differences and imported Victorian morality. In the aggregate, these imported ideas assumed a host of fundamental biological and psychological differences between men and women that were understood to be innate and immutable, thus justifying the "natural" division of labor in the public and private spheres along gendered lines.[20] As Koyama notes, this logic differed from Edo-period notions of sex difference that presumed men to be superior to women, in the sense that men and women were now, at least in theory, thought to be "equal," though fundamentally different from one another:

> The developers of the *ryōsai kenbo* theory rejected equal rights (*dōken*) for men and women. They also rejected the view of holding men in respect and women in contempt [*danson johi*]. Rather, they asserted the equal status of men and women (*danjo dōtō*). . . . [B]ecause men and women are completely different both physically and psychologically as well as in their respective roles, they are seen as having equal, mutually reinforcing, value. On the other hand, for them to intrude on each other's territory is seen as a rejection of "masculinity" and "femininity" and as the embodiment of the undesirable "equal rights."[21]

Koyama also makes the important point that while early twentieth-century Japanese proponents of good wife, wise mother discourse stressed the "equal status" of men and women in theory, in fact, men's work outside the home was valued in economic terms while women's work inside the home was not, thus implicitly rendering women's contributions to society inferior to those of men through their dependence on the economic support of husbands and fathers.[22]

But what I would like to stress here is what lies underneath these distinctions in terminology. The "equal rights" rejected by the framers of good wife, wise mother discourse in the early twentieth century are rendered in Japanese as 同権, a compound formed by the ideographs for "same" (同) and "rights" (権). Arguments that men and women are fundamentally different from one another thus provided the rationale for denying women the same rights as men in the public sphere. It was on this logic that women were denied the right to vote or to run for office, the right to attend public meetings, and the right to receive the same education as that of men. As will become evident in subsequent chapters, this logic persisted even after women were legally granted these rights by Occupation reforms, in the fantasy of complementary sex roles that were in theory equal but not the same.

## TAISHŌ-ERA CHALLENGES TO THE SEX-SEGREGATED SYSTEM

In spite of the dominance of the good wife, wise mother model of education prior to 1945, the Taishō period (1912–26) saw some early experiments with coeducation, along with more public roles for women in Japanese society. This section will explore the emergence of a small but vocal group of progressive educators during the first few decades of the twentieth century who actively lobbied for coeducation at a time when it seemed that such change might be possible, before the resurgence of militarism and nationalism of the late 1930s ground all such projects to a halt. While these progressives were ultimately unsuccessful in their quest for reform, they did lay the intellectual groundwork for support for coeducation among some sectors of the Japanese public during the postwar period, when this cause was taken up by Occupation staffers.

In what follows, we will see that these progressive narratives of coeducation, which were focused on cultivation of individual talents and abilities regardless of gender, were fundamentally at odds with the logic of the good wife, wise mother style of education. Early twentieth-century education reformers rejected the logic of separate spheres for men and women as unequal and potentially harmful and presented coeducation as a method of helping young men and women learn to understand and cooperate more effectively with one another. They argued that in a modern industrialized society where men and women were increasingly mixing with one another in the workplace, and in public space more generally speaking, it made no sense to try to isolate the sexes from one another until they reached adulthood. As we will see in the next section, the arguments they forwarded in favor of educating boys and girls together are strikingly similar to those promoted by Occupation staffers, thus anticipating the debates that would take place prior to the drafting of the FLE of 1947, which formally "recognized" coeducation for the first time in Japanese history.

Experiments with coeducation during the early decades of the twentieth century were facilitated by three important sociohistorical trends: (1) rapid industrialization after World War I that exerted intense pressure on the Japanese labor market, leading to the creation of new categories of jobs for women; (2) the rise of a burgeoning feminist movement that sought new roles and freedoms for women in Japanese society; and (3) the introduction of progressive pedagogical theories that stressed education as a means of individual self-actualization, as opposed to education for the purpose of producing an obedient workforce in service to the modern industrial state.

World War I spurred the development of Japan's industry, given its strategic position as supplier to the nations allied against Germany. Japan's entry into the war on the side of the allies likewise garnered it lucrative territory and spoils. In the wake of these developments, Japan's domestic economy flourished, creating new categories of white-collar employment that required increasing levels of education. Some of these occupations came to be designated as specifically feminine. "The rapidly expanding modern industry required increasing numbers of women not only in the factories, but as office workers, telephone operators, teachers, and receptionists,"[23] along with department store "shop girls," "elevator girls," and "bus girls."[24] Women were preferred for many such jobs particularly since prevalent wage discrimination allowed employers to pay women less than male employees, on the understanding that their participation in the labor market would be temporary and contingent on their single status. It was widely assumed, by employers and female employees, that young middle-class women would work for a few years before "retiring" to become housewives and mothers and so did not need to be paid a living wage. On the other hand, many of these occupations required a higher level of education than the compulsory six years of elementary school, and therefore increasing employment opportunities for women resulted not only in more female students completing the compulsory minimum but also in increasing demands for women's secondary and higher education.

Opportunities for women's employment were not limited to young, unmarried women, however—married women too were increasingly encouraged to work part-time or take in piecework. As Koyama Shizuko notes, in the late 1910s the parameters of good wife, wise mother discourse were progressively widened to allow for women's economic participation as a form of patriotic service:

Women's participation in this kind of paid work was not simply to reap economic benefit. Rather, it was thought that there was a moral benefit to nurturing a will to work in women, which was perceived to be positively connected with the development of society and the nation. Part-time work or piecework was promoted not just as a preferable alternative to engaging in full-time work. Rather, part-time work and piecework were promoted in the context of rationalizing housework and promoting women's participation in society as much as possible.[25]

This resulted in a reformulation of good wife, wise mother ideology that understood women as "not limited strictly to the household; they were expected to shoulder some social duties as long as they did not conflict with their domestic duties or diminish their femininity."[26] Sally Hastings further underscores the somewhat paradoxical effect of these transformations:

The widely-held assumption in Japan . . . that men and women operated in separate functional spheres had multiple and contradictory effects. On the one hand, this assumption justified the development of women teachers and medical professionals. At the same time, it problematized the presence of women at work outside their own homes. As state officials believed that women's bodies and women's work were essential to the health and prosperity of the nation, they allowed, sometimes even encouraged, women to exercise what were regarded as feminine functions in public institutions. That is, state anxieties about women's bodies and women's work . . . as well as political ideologies and measures such as pro-natalism and eugenics . . . resulted in the creation of public professional functions for women.[27]

In effect, these new roles for women outside the household were reinscribed as feminine and newly understood as compatible with women's roles as good wives and wise mothers, in the sense that they were now seen as supportive of national goals and therefore consistent with women's primary function as nurturers of the family-state. This remarkable capacity of good wife, wise mother discourse to adapt to new societal demands of women would help to ensure its persistence well into the postwar period, in spite of Occupation-era efforts to promote a model of equality of opportunity intended to ensure the same rights and responsibilities for both women and men.

The early twentieth century also witnessed the rise of a feminist movement that promoted a more diverse range of ideas about the role of women in Japanese society. Female educators like Hani Motoko and Yosano Akiko (see below) pushed for women's equal right to higher education and to em-

ployment outside the home. Socialist women like Yamakawa Kikue were particularly active proponents of work as a path to financial independence for
women. The rise of women's organizations like the New Women's Association, founded by Hiratsuka Raichō and Ichikawa Fusae, as well as publications such as the journal *Seitō* (Bluestocking) that gave women a venue to
express their opinions on a host of issues affecting women's social status,
rights, and responsibilities all contributed to an intensified social dialogue
that sought to negotiate new roles and opportunities for women against conventional assumptions of their domestic obligations.[28]

This increasing willingness to challenge the status quo prompted some
ambitious women to seek entrance to university in spite of formal and informal barriers to the admission of women. Women had effectively been barred
from university-level institutions because the higher schools that normally
served as preparation for university entrance were themselves closed to
women. However, beginning in the 1910s, some university administrators
began to warm to the idea of admitting a limited number of women. While
the two top-ranked imperial universities in Tokyo and Kyoto could afford to
be highly selective, the regional imperial universities in Sendai, Kyūshū, and
Hokkaidō attracted far fewer applicants. In some years they faced challenges
in filling their freshman classes, so the idea of making up the difference by
admitting a few female students was an attractive financial proposition for
these schools.[29] This prompted the creation of a new policy to open up admission to graduates of specialty schools (*semmon gakkō*) or those possessing
a middle school teaching license, provided that they also passed the entrance exam.[30]

In 1913, Tōhoku Imperial University admitted its first three female students on the justification that their middle school teaching licenses from
Tokyo Higher Women's Normal School and Japan Women's University provided them with comparable credentials to the higher school education required of male applicants. Over the subsequent decades, the Imperial Universities in Kyūshū (1925) and Hokkaidō (1930) followed suit, along with
private institutions like Tōyō Daigaku (1916), Dōshisha (1923), Aoyama
Gakuin (1928), and Meiji Daigaku (1929).[31] By 1920 about one hundred
women were enrolled in universities throughout Japan, although they were
not officially recognized as such by the MOE. Other schools, importantly
including the imperial flagship universities in Kyoto (1919) and Tokyo
(1920), began allowing women to audit lectures but did not grant them degrees. Women auditors were also denied privileges extended to regularly

enrolled students, such as library access and contact with professors. This system was short-lived, with some schools withdrawing even these limited opportunities beginning in the late 1920s. Women's enthusiasm for this system also began to wane as they realized that they would not be able to earn the credentials that men did even if they successfully completed their programs of study.[32]

Dissatisfaction with the limited opportunities for university education available to women prompted some to begin to organize to promote coeducation. Beginning in September 1920, female university students began gathering to share information on topics related to "women's problems" (*fujin mondai*) and women's education. These gatherings soon blossomed in the early 1920s into more activist demands for equal treatment and status, leading to the formation of the Female Students' Alliance (Joshi Gakusei Renmei). Many of these women were students at Nihon Daigaku, which had begun admitting women in 1920 and had a particularly large number of women students.[33] In 1924, in addition to those at Nihon Daigaku, female students at Waseda and Tōyō Daigaku began participating as well. The same year they visited the MOE along with a group from the All-Japan League of Private University Students (Zenkoku Shiritsu Daigaku Semmonbu Gakusei Renmei Iinkai) to petition for women's eligibility for regular student status. This petition was refused, as was a subsequent petition filed in 1925.[34] Other women's groups also took up the cause of higher education for women, including the aforementioned New Women's Association and the Kansai Women's Alliance (Kansai Fujin Rengō Taikai) in 1922.[35]

As a result of this increased demand for women's higher education, as well as the influence of the burgeoning feminist movement, from the 1910s to the 1930s feminist women and progressive male educators increasingly criticized the sex-segregated educational system, speaking out in support of coeducation. Meanwhile, conservative pundits feared that the mingling of the sexes that would occur under a coeducational system would invite moral turpitude, particularly at the middle school level, when students were in the throes of puberty. Echoing the good wife, wise mother discourse, they also openly worried that such an environment would blur the boundaries between the genders, such that boys would become more "feminine" and girls would become more "masculine" as a result of mutual influence. To this notion, proponents of coeducation argued that men and women were increasingly mixing in society anyway thanks to women's increasing participation in the workforce, and it was unnatural to isolate them from one another during their youth. They stressed that giving young people the opportunity to develop mutual understanding at such a formative age might actually alleviate the kind of social and moral problems that conservatives feared.[36] (As we will see in subsequent chapters, the very same arguments for and against coeducation resurfaced in the postwar period.) This debate raged into the 1930s, when the tide of conservatism and repression of progressive ideas following the Manchurian Incident of 1931 increasingly made it difficult to champion liberal causes.

During this two-decade period when coeducation was actively promoted, a number of private individuals experimented with coeducation outside the structure of the public education system. For example, in 1921 the feminist poet Yosano Akiko joined forces with painter Ishii Hakutei and educator Nishimura Isaku to open the Bunka Gakuin, an artistically oriented "free school" at the higher school and university level that was devoted to cultivating individual character rather than training students for any particular occupation. It began with thirty-three female students and admitted its first four male students in 1923. The curriculum was just as rigorous as contemporary middle schools for boys, and students were encouraged to see each other and themselves as independent individuals rather than gendered subjects.[37] In 1923, MOE staff came to check out the experiment and were shocked to see boys and girls studying together. The visiting officials criticized this, but Ishii defended the school and evidently intimidated the ministry staff enough to silence them for awhile—presumably because of his stature in the art world and the pedigree of his students, many of whom hailed from very wealthy families.[38] However, by the time of the Pacific War, sentiments against this kind of experimental education deepened due to a rising tide of moral conservatism and militarism, and they were forced to close down the school.

The New Education (Shinkyōiku) movement also rose to challenge the overwhelming focus of mainstream public schools on instilling patriotism and gender role training, by proposing coeducation among a host of other pedagogical innovations. In 1923, one of the leading lights of this New Education movement, Noguchi Entarō, set up an experimental coeducational school called Children's Village Elementary School (Ikebukuro Jidō no Mura Shōgakkō) in the Ikebukuro neighborhood of Tokyo.[39] A survey of educators conducted around this time revealed that most approved of coeducation at the elementary level but not at the middle school level, citing the potential for moral problems that might occur if girls and boys mixed freely, along with perceived differences in the character and process of development of the sexes and differences in the anticipated responsibilities of both upon maturity.[40] As we will see in subsequent chapters, while on the surface these references to moral problems typically suggested fears of premature sexual experimentation, they also concealed anxieties about the potential for co-education to erode gender norms and role distinctions.

Noguchi countered these objections by explaining that the purpose of the New Education movement was to allow each student to develop accord-ing to his or her own potential and abilities, which meant making only basic knowledge courses mandatory and providing many opportunities for stu-dents to take electives and progress at their own pace. In other words, he em-phasized the primacy of individual differences among students over sexual difference and argued that education should address the former by catering to each student's unique set of aptitudes and inclinations.[41] Furthermore, in contrast to the highly stratified system of public education devoted to chan-neling students into clearly defined occupational strata from the earliest years of schooling, Noguchi emphasized the importance of helping young people to develop as individuals, not simply preparing them for a specific occupa-tion. While the public educational system required extensive training in home economics for girls and provided them with less rigorous academic preparation for advanced study in comparison with boys, Noguchi proposed making domestic science courses elective and available to young women as part of a range of coursework options.[42] Many of these arguments about the purpose and content of education for young people dovetailed neatly with arguments raised by Occupation reformers in the postwar period.

But although enthusiasm for progressive educational reform in intellec-tual circles was strong, efforts to translate these new ideas into policy changes yielded mixed results. While there were some tentative steps in the direction of reform prior to 1945, none of these effectively dismantled the logic of the good wife, wise mother system of education for women. For example, in 1917, the government established a Provisional Education Committee (Rinji Kyōiku Kaigi) as a deliberative body that was directly responsible to the cabi-net for reviewing the existing educational infrastructure and making recom-mendations for reform. Its formation coincided with a wave of support among educators for the creation of universities for women, at a time when educated women had begun to clamor for more opportunities to attain a level of education similar to that of elite men. Although the committee did take up the problem of women's education, conservative voices dominated the proceedings, and deliberations proceeded on the presumption that the purpose of such education was to prepare women to be wives and mothers of the nation. Proposals to create university-level institutions for women were defeated amid concerns that higher education would damage the health of young women and delay the age of marriage, thus "obstructing the reproduction of the race."[43]

Another wave of policy reform initiatives in the late 1930s raised important questions about equality of educational opportunity, but these reform efforts seem to have been more concerned with economic equality—that is, enabling more men from the lower classes to attend higher schools and universities—than with gender equality. In 1937, Prime Minister Konoe Fumimaro established an Education Council (Kyōiku Shingikai) to discuss proposals for educational reform across the board. In 1939, the council did make some recommendations for reform that were designed to improve access to higher education for women, but these were nevertheless predicated on assumptions of gender-specific education designed to train most women for domestic roles. Proposals submitted by the council sought to create a system of education for girls that would more closely parallel the existing structure for boys.[44] Rather than maintaining the existing status of "higher girls' school" (kōtō jogakkō), which was designed to provide a terminal level of education yet operated at the boys' middle school level, it proposed renaming these five-year schools as "girls' middle schools" (joshi chūgakkō), which would serve as parallel institutions to the middle schools for males. These would be followed by a three-year college prep course (kōtōka) that would be known institutionally as "girls' higher schools" (joshi kōtō gakkō), which would represent a feminine counterpart to the higher schools for boys. Completion of the girls' higher school would then constitute the requisite level of preparation necessary for entrance to universities to be created specifically for women as an alternative to mainstreaming them into historically male universities.[45] Because of the exigencies of wartime that followed Japan's attack on Pearl Harbor in 1941, none of these reforms were actually enacted.

While Hans Martin Kramer considers these proposals to have signified high-level support for equality of educational opportunity in gendered terms, it is important to note that the goals of education for women and the descriptions of curricula for the new types of schools outlined in these proposals nevertheless indicate that this new system was still designed around inculcation of appropriately feminine training for gender-specific outcomes. For one thing, the reform of the middle school level of education for girls outlined in the committee's "Outline for Reform of Higher Girls' Schools" (Kōtō Jogakkō Kaizen Yōryō) is entirely phrased in terms of *ryōsai kenbo*–style ideology.[46] Section 2 of this document, titled "The Purpose of Higher Education for Girls," explicitly states: "The aim of higher education for girls is to provide ordinary higher education that is most important for girls and to train women who form the core of the nation as loyal and pure subjects through cultivation of the imperial spirit and womanly virtues."[47] The goals of such training as articulated in the proposal center around the production of a compliant and maternalistic model of femininity in the service of the state, exhorting schools to train girls to strive for "preservation of the family customs unique to our nation," "cultivation of [students'] self-awareness as mothers of the next generation," "cultivation of the firm principles and elegant feelings [*shinjō*] that are special characteristics of our country's women," "strengthening of practical training to deepen a spirit of diligence and self-sacrifice," and "recognition of the correlation between the household economy and the national economy toward cultivating a spirit of thrift."[48] Furthermore, the structure of the proposed "girls' higher school," which in theory was supposed to parallel the elite higher schools for boys, includes a division for domestic science (*kaseika*) in addition to coursework in home economics and related fields to be included in the divisions of arts and sciences as elective subjects.[49] So while in theory the council's proposals may have been thought at the time to provide equality of educational opportunity for women, they nevertheless seem to have been embedded in many of the same assumptions of gender-specific training that underlined the good wife, wise mother style of education. As we will see in the next section, these assumptions were carried over into the process of educational reform that took place during the Occupation as well, as MOE bureaucrats sought to minimize the extent of reform by retaining as much of the prewar system of education as possible.

## NEGOTIATING COEDUCATION IN OCCUPIED JAPAN

In this section, we will trace the intricate web of negotiation between the Occupiers and their Japanese counterparts that ultimately produced the FLE of 1947, which formally "recognized" coeducation for the first time in Japanese history. In what follows, we will see that the negotiations that ultimately produced the FLE were significantly complicated by a profusion of discourses regarding the nature and extent of gender equality that should be incorporated into the law, not to mention how that equality should be achieved. As a general rule, Occupation staffers tended to assume that "equal" meant "same"—in other words, that women should be extended the same legal rights and responsibilities as men. Japanese bureaucrats, on the other hand, tended to want to preserve as much of the prewar good wife, wise mother model of femininity as possible, yielding a "separate but equal" interpretation of equality that emphasized gender complementarity and distinctly different roles for men and women in society.

Having said this, the two sides were hardly monolithic or internally consistent in their views. This lack of agreement over the nature of equality for women resulted in an "agreement" over the language of the FLE that was underlined by very different assumptions as to what this equality would mean in practice. Consequently, subsequent efforts to implement coeducation provoked intense debates over the goals and effects of the new system of education that were not resolved by the end of the Occupation and continued to bedevil Japanese educational policy well into the postwar period.

As Uemura Chikako has shown, while General Douglas MacArthur and other top Occupation officials in theory espoused equality for women as a goal from the very beginning, progressive women within the Occupation who lobbied for greater opportunities for Japanese women in fact had to struggle against the more conservative views of their male colleagues regarding women's proper role in society.[50] High-ranking male members of the Occupation tended to see the cause of women's equality in instrumental terms; for them, the desirability of "women's emancipation" was predicated on an understanding of women as a conservative and stabilizing force in Japanese society. MacArthur in particular assumed that if Japanese women were given the right to vote and be elected, they would act as a counterweight against what he perceived as the Japanese tendency for fanaticism and would facilitate Japan's transformation into a peaceful and democratic nation.

These views were predicated on rather conventional notions of American femininity that were defined by women's roles as wives and mothers within the domestic sphere and limned with fears of the development of a "women's bloc" that would allow women to work together to advocate for social change. MacArthur specifically warned against this type of feminist solidarity, for example, by exhorting the newly elected female Diet members to work with the male representatives rather than together in single-sex pressure groups.[51] And yet because the Occupation brass delegated much of

the work of drafting policies regarding Japanese women to lower-ranking female staffers, these women were in fact able to work together with Japanese
women (and some sympathetic male colleagues within the Occupation)[52] to
push initiatives intended to ensure women's equality in fact as well as in law.
This was achieved in part through the creation of the very sort of women's
"networks" decried by MacArthur himself.

On the other hand, even among female Occupation staffers, attitudes toward the extent and kind of equality to which Japanese women should aspire
were somewhat conflicted. This was in part due to the values that these
women brought with them from the United States, which themselves were
inflected by the peculiarities of American gender dynamics during World War
II. During the war, women were called upon to fill in gaps in the labor force,
both in and out of uniform, that were left by men drafted to serve as combat-
ants on the front lines. Many of the female Occupation staffers who were
most active in pushing for equal rights for Japanese women were among the
cohort of American women who had pioneered new roles for women in their
own country—in the military (in the form of officer positions within the
women's auxiliary corps) and in academia (by serving as university professors
and deans at their home institutions). They attempted to replicate the same
kinds of opportunities within Japan for Japanese women, even as they admitted to mixed feelings regarding the conflict this posed with women's roles
within the home and family. As one female Occupation staffer put it:

> It is very difficult to extol women and constantly work for their equal repre-
> sentation in government, etc., and at the same time to avoid "exalting
> women to excess." Personally, I hate even the thought of a real matriarchy. I
> believe that men and women have their separate contributions to make to
> the world, and that the contributions of both are needed for a peaceful and
> well-integrated civilization. They must work together.[53]

Ironically, by spending the first few postwar years in Japan as part of the Occupation, these women were insulated from the conservative turn witnessed in their
home country at this time, when women were increasingly exhorted to return
to the home to make room for male GIs who were legally entitled to job and
university placements upon return from the front by virtue of the GI Bill.[54]

The Japanese side too was neither monolithic in its views nor divided
neatly along gender lines. Occupation reformers received crucial support
from Japanese progressives of both sexes who helped push for a more radical

version of equality of opportunity. For example, Nambara Shigeru, the president of Tokyo University, who played an important role as advisor to the U.S. Education Mission to Japan (see below), actively lobbied mission representatives for more liberal reforms than they initially intended to make, including coeducation.[55] Likewise, Yamamuro Tamiko, a female MOE staff member, worked closely with staffers from the Civil Information and Education (CI&E) section of SCAP to promote coeducation at the local level through public awareness campaigns.[56]

On the other hand, top male MOE bureaucrats tended to espouse the notion of equality for women in theory while resisting or attempting to sabotage policies intended to produce such equality in fact. For these men, equality was an acceptable goal so long as it was actualized through women's conventional roles in the family. This way of understanding equality (byōdō) in separate but equal terms is illustrated by a remark made by Liberal Party representative Miura Toranosuke during the course of a Diet discussion of one of the gender equality provisions in the 1947 revision of the Japanese constitution:

> It goes without saying that the husband and wife should be equal in marriage. Men and women are equal and have equal rights, but I believe that they have different responsibilities (shokubun) within a home. The woman has responsibilities as a housewife within her home, and the man has his responsibilities as a man. So I believe that in maintaining a home, each one should respect one's own role. I do not think that this would prevent equality between husband and wife. I don't know if my metaphor is appropriate, but if we compare [marriage] with a tree, the wife is the roots that hold the tree from below the ground, and the husband is the branches above ground. . . . I believe we can maintain the Japanese family system and equality of the sexes quite well along this line [of thinking].[57]

As Kyoko Inoue notes, Japanese government representatives during the Occupation were acutely interested in preserving the integrity of the Japanese family (ie) system, which subordinated women and younger males to the authority of the male head of household.[58] These representatives therefore were highly motivated to interpret the equality promoted by Occupation reformers in such a way as to preserve the prewar gender hierarchy of Japanese society. Inoue argues that, as understood by Japanese government representatives, equality did not necessarily imply social equality. Rather, it meant that each person had the ability to fulfill the duties and responsibilities of his or her social position. These ideas were quite compatible with social inequality. The Japanese thus interpreted the expression "equality of the sexes" to mean men and women were essentially equal in their ability to fulfill their respective roles in the family. This, of course, was much different from what the Americans had intended—that women have, or should have, equal rights.[59]

So while Occupation reformers tended to understand equality as mandating the same rights and responsibilities for men and women, male members of the Japanese government tended to assume that equality could be accomplished through preservation of separate spheres along gender lines.

MOE representatives seem to have brought the same separate but equal vision of equality into negotiations over the text of the FLE. This much is evident from the educational policies enacted by the ministry after the Japanese surrender but before the Occupation began acting in any concerted way to guide the process of reform. For the first few months of the Occupation, the ministry seems to have devoted a great deal of time and attention to divining the intentions of the foreign invaders and determining how to respond to those wishes as they understood them. In some cases this involved preemptively instituting reforms "designed to forestall more radical action by Allied authorities."[60]

For example, on December 4, 1945, on its own initiative, the Japanese government issued a cabinet-level order entitled "Guidelines for the Reform of Education for Girls" (Joshi Kyōiku Sasshin Yōkō), with the avowed aim of "promoting mutual respect among men and women and equal opportunity of education for girls and boys, and equalizing the contents of education."[61] It listed a number of generalized instructions for reform, with the first being to abolish regulations that barred women from attending universities on an equal footing with men. It further proposed allowing graduates from certain ministry-designated women's specialty schools to apply for admission to historically all-male universities. For the time being, graduation from such designated women's schools would be considered as equal to graduation from the elite higher schools for boys, which under the prewar system was requisite for entrance to university. Graduates of girls' higher schools (kōtō jogakkō) would also now be allowed to apply for admission to college prep academies. Finally, the order recognized the need to elevate schools deemed worthy from the ranks of existing women's colleges to the level of women's universities, thus placing these institutions at least in theory on the same level as historically male-dominated elite universities.[62]

Other provisions were designed to raise the level of girls' higher schools to that of boys' middle schools (*chūgakkō*) by restructuring the curriculum and improving methods and content of instruction. The order proposed equalizing the curricula by requiring the same number of hours of instruction per week and employing the same textbooks at both types of schools. Other types of institutions that had historically been sex-segregated, such as the wartime youth schools (*seinen gakkō*) for men and women, should likewise be equalized in terms of rigor and structure. Finally, lectures at universities and higher specialty schools (*kōtō semmon gakkō*) should be opened to female auditors, and extension courses at such institutions should likewise be created for the cultivation of the general female public.[63]

While these proposals might seem to represent a seismic shift in attitude on the part of the Japanese government regarding the value of women's education, upon closer scrutiny, the December 4 directive was not as radical as it might seem. First of all, the order only proposed coeducation at the university level, a process that (as noted above) had in fact begun by 1913 with the opening of first Tōhoku University, and then several other prestigious imperial and private universities, to women applicants.[64] While the number of women who were in a position to take advantage of this opportunity during the prewar period was rather small, this was also true of Japan in 1945, when the cabinet issued its December 4 "reforms," so the measure merely gave official sanction to a practice that had been initiated several decades earlier. The most momentous aspect of this particular reform was that it opened the doors of Tokyo University and Kyoto University, the two imperial universities that had so far resisted this trend of allowing female applicants, to women for the first time. (Women had in fact previously been allowed to audit lectures at these prestigious schools, though not to receive credit for their studies.) Finally, although the order sought in theory to "equalize" secondary school standards for both boys and girls, it simultaneously tried to preserve the sex-segregated system that had historically fostered educational inequality, raising the distinct possibility that such separate but equal accommodations might remain unequal in fact if not in law.

MOE directives and other documents issued between September and December 1945 likewise suggest that while the government might have wanted the Occupation forces to see its December 4 order as a bold attempt to rectify gender discrimination in education, its true intentions were likely far less grandiose. Certainly ministry personnel gave lip service to the goal of raising the level of education for girls to that of boys. In a written explanation of the September 15 change in policy dated September 29, 1945, Vice Minister Omura Seiichi gave cursory attention to the problem of women's education, lamenting that the level of such education had historically been kept low and confined to the domestic realm and would therefore need to be reformed to reach the democratic goals set for the country.[65] In a separate section of the document written by Maeda Tamon, the education minister only briefly touched on the topic of education for girls to say that it was still under consideration but provided no specific information about what policies were being considered.[66] He responded exactly the same way a month later in a speech given at a conference hosted by the Tokyo Women's Higher Normal School (Tokyo Joshi Kōtō Shihan Gakkō) on October 15 and 16, briefly mentioning the topic as one of many that was "under consideration" before moving on to other points.[67] So while MOE officials clearly perceived a need to voice support for the "reform" of women's education, they offered little in the way of ideas for substantive reforms in their public statements prior to the December 4 directive.

Official documents issued by the MOE during this period also suggest a ministry that is doing its best to preserve the gender-segregated structure of education under the guise of "reform." For example, Proclamation #213, issued on October 14, 1945, ordered schools to provide supplementary coursework in fields now deemed strategically important—primarily science, math, and foreign languages (namely, English)—by the end of the school year the following March.[68] The guidelines provided to educators in this document are differentiated into boys' middle school (chūgakkō) and girls' higher school (kōtō jogakkō) versions, indicating that at this point the MOE still intended to preserve the gender-segregated educational structure.

Furthermore, the document clearly articulated sex-specific differences in expectations of mastery for these supplementary subjects. While boys' schools are instructed to provide four to five hours of math and physical science education per week, standards for the girls' schools are phrased in terms of one to two hours per week in science and math (risūka) and two to three hours per week in home economics (kaseika).[69] In other words, the majority of "scientific" education for girls was still routed through mastery of gender-specific tasks and knowledge intended to produce competent wives and homemakers, not to prepare girls for advanced study in these fields. If the intention of the ministry were truly to catch the girls up to the boys by remedying historic deficiencies in academic rigor at girls' schools, then this would seem a poor way of attaining that objective. In fact, the same directive explicitly lists subjects considered important for girls as including "duties of a housewife," "[care/construction of] men's clothing," "childcare," and other skills considered necessary for "careers" as wives and mothers.[70] So in spite of the ideals espoused in the ministry's December 4 agenda for reform, it is unlikely at this point that the MOE truly intended to support coeducation at all levels of the Japanese educational system or even to equalize education for boys and girls in the sense of providing the same academic preparation to both sexes.

Discussions the following spring during the visit to Japan of the U.S. Education Mission, which was tasked with offering recommendations on reform of the educational system, illustrate that the mixed messages offered by American proponents of coeducation and their Japanese allies created further confusion about the degree and extent of equality that postwar Japanese women were to enjoy. Recognizing the dearth of education specialists among Occupation staffers, the CI&E section of SCAP had begun making plans almost from the moment of its inception to invite a panel of experts to advise it on education reform.[71] As a result, twenty-seven North American educators were empaneled after a long process of selection by State Department personnel, in consultation with the MOE, to visit Japan in March 1946 and make recommendations for restructuring and reorienting the Japanese educational system along more democratic lines. This group, known as the U.S. Education Mission and headed by New York State Commissioner of Education George Stoddard, represented a variety of U.S. educational institutions, geographic regions, and fields of specialization, but none had any specific knowledge of Japan or its educational system. Furthermore, they were given a mere three weeks in Japan to get up to speed before getting down to the business of drafting their recommendations.

Because of this lack of basic knowledge of the system they were entrusted with reforming, they were highly dependent on briefings by Occupation staffers, as well as the advice of the Japanese Education Committee (JEC), selected by the MOE to assist the foreign "experts" with their work. This committee was composed of high-ranking Japanese academics possessing similar qualifications to their counterparts on the Stoddard mission. It included prominent progressive Japanese educators such as Nambara Shigeru, president of Tokyo Imperial University, as well as two female presidents of women's colleges, Hoshino Ai of Tsuda College and Kawai Michi of Keisen Women's College. After the Americans left, the JEC was transformed into the Japan Education Reform Council (JERC), which was tasked with the responsibility of crafting specific proposals to implement the recommendations of the mission.

Advice provided by the JEC proved decisive in influencing the final version of the mission's report. Upon their arrival in Japan, the Stoddard mission was given a series of briefings and lectures by CI&E staff and JEC members, who presented their case for various kinds of reforms. In the briefing titled "Women's Education in Japan" given on March 14, 1946, by Captain Eileen R. Donovan of CI&E and in speeches that followed by Hoshino and Kawai, all three women pushed for aggressive reforms to ensure Japanese women equal educational opportunity with men. Donovan explained that the Japanese educational system had historically sought to prepare girls to become good wives and wise mothers and highlighted the inequities that resulted from this focus on gender-specific role training. She stressed the historic exclusion of women from most elite institutions of higher education, as well as from important policy-making bodies such as the MOE. She also noted the pervasive lack of respect for women's intellectual abilities and the resultant lower expectations that teachers and principals communicated to female students. She indirectly critiqued the recent reforms proposed by the MOE, suggesting that in spite of the apparently progressive slant of their recommendations, the ministry was still rife with an inveterate conservatism that rendered actual implementation of these reforms unlikely:

> The old laws are in the process of revision and now women are eligible to take the entrance examinations for universities. The plan as outlined by the Mombusho [MOE] is "to alter or cancel the regulations which prevent women from entering men's schools, to put co-education into operation in universities as well as to establish women's universities." The university and the Mombusho men with whom we have talked shake their heads and say: "very difficult."[72]

In her speech that followed, Kawai likewise highlighted the fact that the prewar educational structure had relegated Japanese girls to an inferior level of academic preparation. She also implicitly challenged the gendered division of labor that this model of education facilitated, declaring that "the era of men working [outside the home] and women cleaning [inside the home] is past" and suggesting that men and women should instead share both roles.[73]

On the other hand, rather than rejecting the logic of good wife, wise mother entirely, both women attempted to reframe the concept so as to reconcile it with the model of equal opportunity promoted by the Occupation. Donovan's remarks, for example, stressed the importance of equality of educational opportunity to women's successful performance of their new responsibilities as active citizens of a democracy, arguing that giving them the same education as men would be necessary to make informed decisions when voting. Thus, for the sake of the country's future (including that of their own children), the Japanese understanding of good wife, wise mother would need to be broadened to include this expanded public role for women. Likewise, Kawai suggested that the problem was not so much the concept of good wife, wise mother itself but that women's cultural and intellectual development had been retarded by a prewar system of education that had failed them. She noted that while it was "correct" to guide women in the direction of becoming good wives and wise mothers, society should properly respect them in these roles, implying that affording them the same level and type of education as men would help achieve this goal.[74] Thus, these presentations might understandably have left the impression that the good wife, wise mother model of sex-segregated education was reconcilable with the new postwar embrace of equality of educational opportunity.

In fact, this conflation of the two concepts was ultimately reflected in the language of the U.S. Education Mission report itself, which shied away from a wholesale endorsement of coeducation in favor of a somewhat qualified promotion of the practice to the extent that it did not fundamentally challenge Japanese values regarding gender norms. The Stoddard mission submitted its final report to SCAP on March 30, 1946. The report recommended what is frequently described as a "6-3-3" system, with six years of primary school, three years of lower secondary school, and three years of upper secondary school, with the first nine years being compulsory and the final three "open to all who desire to attend."[75] As the primary goal of the Americans was to establish a more equitable system of education that would underpin its efforts to remake Japan as a democratic nation, many of the recommended educational reforms are phrased in terms of promoting equality of opportunity. This is stated explicitly in the report's declaration of "Basic Educational Principles": "Educational opportunity, commensurate with individual ability, should be equally available for all persons regardless of sex, race, creed or color."[76] The document goes to great lengths to stress the inclusion of women on an equal footing with men in all aspects of the educational process, both as teachers and as students. Most of the time, the authors tend to use gender-inclusive terms such as "men and women" and "boys and girls" to emphasize the democratic thrust of these recommendations. One interesting exception to this rule may be found in the section titled "Higher Education" (part VI), where university professors are envisioned exclusively in masculine terms.[77]

But while the phrase equality of educational opportunity appears frequently throughout the report and in other SCAP documents, the precise meaning of this term is never clear. Furthermore, it is used in such a wide variety of contexts that its meaning seems to shift unpredictably from one passage to another. Does this mean that all students should receive the same education? If not, how is equality of opportunity to be ensured? The following passage, while presumably attempting to clarify this point, succeeds in muddying the waters considerably:

> Equality does not imply a dead level of uniformity. Some differences between pupils are properly ignored by the democratic school, such as those of religion, race and social status. Equal educational opportunity should be provided for all, in spite of any prejudices which may be found in the adult population. The democratic school, however, through its testing program, and in other ways, seeks to discover the intellectual level of its pupils and adjusts its program accordingly. It tries not to make demands on pupils which they are unable to meet, and further, it broadens its offerings to provide educational experiences for those of differing intellectual abilities. Similarly, it seeks to adjust its program to pupils of different interests, to those from rural and from urban areas, for example.

> Intellectual differences between the sexes are found to be practically non-existent where boys and girls are educated in the same classrooms. The experience of growing up together is believed to be both natural and helpful. Segregation within the school for such activities as sports and physical education and, when desired, for certain manual activities, presents few difficulties, once it has become standard practice.[78]

It is likely that the drafters of the report meant this passage as an implicit rebuke to the uniformity and standardization of the prewar educational system, given that they rail against this approach to education elsewhere in the document.[79] But for many Japanese at the time, who took it for granted that intellectual differences could "naturally" be found between men and women, this wording might well have justified the separate tracking of boys and girls into different educational programs. As if in anticipation of this response, the Stoddard report specifically states that "intellectual differences between the sexes are found to be practically non-existent where boys and girls are educated in the same classrooms."[80] However, the fact that Japanese boys and girls historically had *not* been educated together was cited by some opponents of coeducation as a reason why that system should not be implemented. In fact, they argued (not unreasonably) that suddenly throwing boys and girls together into the same class and holding them to the same set of standards would actually put girls at a disadvantage, given their relative lack of academic preparation.

Furthermore, rather than challenge the historically gendered division of labor that reinforced and justified separate educational standards for boys and girls, the authors of the mission's report strategically deployed the rhetoric of separate spheres in a rather confusing attempt to persuade their readers of the desirability of the democratic structure they proposed. For example, by way of explaining the need for both sexes to participate in the democratic process, the report states:

> Democratic citizens should be willing to pool their efforts, and this requires not only knowledge of the constitution and of high ideals but also a willingness to participate in practical politics. Women must see that to be "good" wives, they must be *good*; and to be "wise" mothers, they must be *wise*. Goodness does not spring from narrowness, and wisdom is not a hothouse plant. It grows from wide social experience and from political practice.[81]

By this phrasing, the mission representatives evidently wanted to emphasize that uninformed citizens cannot participate effectively in the democratic process and that therefore all citizens, male and female, required the benefit of a comprehensive education. However, by invoking the language of good wife, wise mother that had been historically used to justify gender-specific education for both sexes, the report's authors perhaps unwittingly reinforced the impression that sex-specific education was not incompatible with equality of educational opportunity.

Furthermore, the report's recommendations explicitly allowed for the possibility of some separation of the sexes during the educational process: "Segregation within the school for such activities as sports and physical education and, when desired, for certain manual activities, presents few difficulties, once it has become standard practice."[82] This last category of "manual activities" might be understood to include courses in home economics, which as we have already noted formed the core of the prewar system of Japanese education for girls. In other words, rather than challenge the presumption that girls should be prepared for very different future roles in society than boys, the language of the mission's report may actually have facilitated this outcome by providing discursive justification for an educational system that was discriminatory, in fact if not in law.

On the subject of coeducation per se, the Stoddard report is also equivocal in its recommendations. Although it expresses firm support for coeducation at the primary school level, its commitment to this cause seems to waver a bit at the lower and upper secondary levels, perhaps in deference to Japanese sensitivities on this point. Consider the phrasing employed in each section. The report clearly states: "We recommend that the primary school be conducted on a coeducational basis."[83] Since during the prewar period girls and boys were often educated together for at least the first few years of primary school, this likely would not have struck many Japanese as particularly objectionable. However, regarding lower secondary school education, the report seems to hedge its wording a bit, stating that such schools "should become coeducational, as rapidly as conditions warrant, the principle involved being as applicable at this level as in the primary schools."[84] When it comes to the problem of upper secondary education, the authors' support for coeducation seems even more tenuous:

> Beyond the "lower secondary schools," we recommend the establishment of a three year "upper secondary school," free from tuition fees and open to all who desire to attend. Here again, coeducation would make possible many financial savings and would help to establish equality between the sexes. However, separate schools might be used at the level during the transition stage, provided equal educational opportunity could be guaranteed.[85]

Note that the report carefully avoids "recommending" coeducation at this level, presenting the idea as a cost-cutting solution and relegating the "establish[ment of] equality between the sexes" to the status of an auxiliary benefit. The wording of the final sentence furthermore provides cover, perhaps unwittingly, to those who would argue that it is possible to provide "equal educational opportunity" through a sex-segregated system of education.

It is clear that the authors of the U.S. Education Mission report were aware of Japanese sensitivities regarding social mixing of the sexes during adolescence and that its phrasing was to some degree calculated in anticipation of possibly strenuous objections by MOE bureaucrats or the Japanese public more generally speaking. Mark T. Orr acknowledges this desire of the Americans not to impose too drastic an agenda for change on the Japanese:

> At the time the [U.S. Education Mission] Report was released to the Japanese public, the Supreme Commander announced that it was not to be considered as official policy but that it would serve as a source of inspiration and valuable suggestions as the program of educational reform developed. There were three principal reasons for this view. First the Report contained many specific reform proposals. Second, a few of the proposals were of a highly controversial character. Third, the Supreme Commander did not wish to impose a detailed blueprint for reform upon the Japanese.[86]

Nevertheless, Orr goes on to acknowledge the "authoritative" impact the document had on the subsequent course of Japanese education reform, describing it as the "most influential document in the field of education produced during the course of the occupation."[87] It profoundly impacted the drafting of the FLE of 1947, which is perhaps not surprising given that many of the same members of the JEC who contributed to the production of the U.S. Education Mission report were also entrusted with negotiating the final wording of the law.

Although the U.S. Education Mission report was clearly influential in guiding the process of subsequent educational reform, it was not the final arbiter of change. The report merely listed recommendations, and the Japanese were themselves entrusted with debating them, deciding policy, and then writing it into law. Certain members of the JERC and their allies in the Occupation bureaucracy advocated for many of the mission's recommendations to improve education for women. However, this required extensive negotiation with MOE bureaucrats, who drafted the initial text of the law and took a markedly more conservative stance, specifically objecting to the recommendation of coeducation in junior and senior high schools.[88] At this stage, the influence of a few female CI&E staffers, in collaboration with Japanese female allies and members of the JERC, proved decisive in carrying language on coeducation into the final draft of the law. On the other hand, resistance by MOE bureaucrats to the concept resulted in a rather tepid "recognition" of coeducation that gave individual school districts wide latitude in deciding whether to actually implement it beyond the compulsory level of middle school.

Negotiations over the wording of the FLE began on September 20, 1946, and ended with the finalization of the wording the following March. At the eighth meeting of the JERC, the chairman of the subcommittee on lower-level education, Toda Teizō, gave an interim report on the findings of the committee, which included recommendations to fix the length of middle school education at three years and to make such institutions compulsory, full-time, and coeducational. By way of explanation of this last item, Toda remarked that "at the very least, we have no intention of obstructing coeducation for students up to this age. We do not expect moral problems or other issues. Furthermore, in terms of the actual benefits of coeducation, it would be easier to cultivate virtuous behavior in [students'] social lives through co-education than by educating them separately."[89] Thus, by this point there seems to have been little objection to the idea of coeducation through the nine years of compulsory schooling that ended with graduation from middle school, at least among members of the JERC.

On the other hand, the prospect of coeducation at the high school level was met with a great degree of consternation. At the eleventh meeting of the JERC on November 15, 1946, the same committee proposed a three-year high school system that could be either full-time or part-time and "not necessarily co-educational." The explanation for this was as follows: "It is acceptable for such schools to be co-educational, but it is also acceptable for them to be all-female or all-male. We will leave the question of how to administer these schools up to the school administrators."[90] This wording was evidently the result of a compromise between members of the committee who supported coeducation at this level and those members who voiced concerns about the moral implications of teaching boys and girls between the ages of fifteen and eighteen together in the same class.[91]

Planning documents drafted by the MOE during this period of negotiation reveal that it strenuously resisted inclusion of the term "coeducation" in the letter of the law. "Matters Requiring Consideration Regarding the Establishment of the Fundamental Law of Education," drafted by a deliberative council of the MOE and dated September 25, 1946, listed three problems for consideration under the heading "Education for Girls" (Joshi Kyōiku)—the number of years of compulsory education that should be required of girls, the problem of "equalizing" the curriculum for middle schools and girls' higher schools, and the question of how to ensure equality of educational opportunity.[92] Though the objectives listed here certainly conform to Occupation goals concerning sexual equality, they are phrased within the framework of the existing sex-segregated system of education (particularly at the high school level). This indicates that at this stage the MOE still envisioned making adjustments to the current structure rather than the wholesale restructuring advocated by the U.S. Education Mission (at the behest of key members of their Japanese advisory board). Further resistance to inclusion of the term "coeducation" is evident once drafting of the legislation began. The earliest drafts of the FLE retained the phrasing "Education for Girls" employed in the planning documents mentioned above, such that the draft of the law's preamble that was presented at the November 15, 1946, meeting of the JERC read:

*Part IV: Education for Girls*

Because men and women must respect and cooperate with one another, they must receive equal treatment as a basic rule of education.[93]

Not only does the phrasing of this portion of the draft avoid the term "coeducation," but discussion of this section during the meeting also reveals a clear aversion to use of the word on the part of some members of the committee.

However, discussion of the preamble during the November 29 meeting of the JERC, just two weeks later, indicates that this stance had mysteriously begun to soften. While the wording of the draft had not changed, retaining a focus on "education for girls" rather than coeducation, the subcommittee chair remarked by way of explanation that while the section appears "under the name of 'education for girls,' we request that you read this as 'coeducation' (*danjo kyōgaku*)."[94] By the December 29 meeting of the JERC, the draft language presented by the MOE had changed significantly:

*Part IV: Education for Girls*

Men and women must respect and cooperate with one another. Therefore, coeducation must be recognized (*danjo no kyōgaku wa mitomerarenakareba naranai koto*).[95]

This was the first time that the term "coeducation" had appeared in the process of drafting the FLE.

This rather abrupt turnabout in attitude was evidently the result of intense pressure by CI&E staff behind the scenes to include references to coeducation in the wording of the law. During discussion at the JERC meeting on December 20, Vice Minister of Education Yamazaki Kyōsuke revealed that his office had been pressured by General Headquarters (GHQ) to accept coeducation at the high school level, in addition to lower levels of education.[96] Adachi Kenji, who served in the division of the MOE responsible for deliberating the language of the draft law, later recalled: "The people at GHQ demanded that we include the word 'coeducation' (*danjo kyōgaku*). At the time the thinking [at the MOE] was that we wouldn't go so far as using the term 'coeducation'; we were told we should use 'equal opportunity of education for men and women,' but we had no thought of going so far as 'coeducation.'"[97] Sekiguchi Takakatsu corroborates this assertion; he recalls being verbally "beaten down" (*sanzan yattsukerareta*) by three unnamed "older ladies" (*obasan*) from CI&E who demanded that the ministry use the term "coeducation" in the final language of the law. As a compromise solution, Sekiguchi and his team settled on the wording "coeducation must be recognized" to avoid directly imposing it as a uniform requirement.[98]

By January 15, 1947, this new wording was incorporated into the draft of Article 9 of the law itself. The Cabinet Legislation Bureau then examined the draft and suggested revisions to clarify the meaning and structure of the passage, including changing the heading of the section from "Education for Girls" to "Coeducation."[99] Over the next two months, minor changes were made to the wording as a result of discussions within the JERC, and finally the Privy Council also made some suggestions for revision. Upon incorporating all these suggestions, the text was moved from Article 9 to Article 5, and the final draft version read as follows:

*Article V (Coeducation)*

Men and women must respect and cooperate with one another, so in the realm of education, coeducation must be recognized (*danjo no kyōgaku wa mitomerarenakareba naranai*).[100]

This draft was approved at the Ninety-Second Diet session, and the wording of the FLE was thus finalized.

That MOE bureaucrats felt little resistance to the phrase "equal opportunity of education for men and women" but balked at an explicit reference to "coeducation" is particularly interesting and suggests a preference for nonspecific language that could be interpreted liberally to suit the preferences of the ministry. One might argue that "equal opportunity," interpreted broadly, could be ensured through a separate but equal structure of education that would essentially replicate the prewar sex-segregated structure. But faced with SCAP's insistence on inclusion of the term "coeducation," MOE bureaucrats apparently decided to cut their losses with the noun and to renegotiate the verb instead, opting to "recognize" coeducation but leaving it unclear what exactly that might entail beyond the level of compulsory education. As we will see in subsequent chapters, this weak endorsement of coeducation, along with the persistent logic of separate spheres for men and women that motivated it, would produce an educational system riven with contradictions that embraced coeducation on the surface but attempted to structure it so as to produce gender-specific outcomes for boys and girls.

## CONCLUSION

The modern Japanese educational system was created in 1872 amid an ebullient atmosphere of radical experimentation, resulting in an extraordinarily ambitious and thoroughly impractical plan for a vast network of schools that were initially envisioned as coeducational. For this brief period of time, the nation flirted with a model of equality of educational opportunity that allowed for girls to receive the same type and degree of schooling as boys. This first draft of the education law thus opened a window of opportunity for some girls to receive an unprecedented level of formal education alongside their male peers.

But this window soon closed. As early as 1879, the government began to walk back these promises of equality-as-sameness, and subsequent revisions to education law increasingly shaped (and were shaped by) a separate but equal logic that emphasized gender-specific training to prepare girls and boys for very different roles in society. By the end of the nineteenth century, education for girls had been restructured to produce good wives and wise mothers. While there was some prewar exploration of coeducation and other progressive pedagogical techniques among liberal-minded educators, these limited experiments were insufficient to debunk the notion of separate spheres for women that dominated the mainstream educational system.

The logic of *ryōsai kenbo* proved remarkably resilient over the following decades, adapting itself to a succession of historical, cultural, and economic shifts with an amoeba-like capacity to absorb all obstacles in its path. It initially focused more on the good wife aspect of the dyad, with the objective of elevating women's intellectual faculties to enable them to better support and understand their husbands' public sphere activities. Over time, it came to lean more heavily on the "wise mother" side of the term, emphasizing a stronger role for women in rearing and educating their children. Both iterations of the discourse were used to justify progressively higher levels of education for women that nevertheless channeled their energies into the domestic sphere. And yet when women's labor outside the home, and later women's patriotic service to the nation, came to be seen as necessary to the success of the empire, these activities too were recoded in feminine terms and incorporated within the *ryōsai kenbo* paradigm.

The primacy of this model of femininity produced an understanding of equality that valued women (at least in theory) as equally human and useful to society, while expecting them to contribute to the nation in a very different way than their menfolk. So long as women did not intrude upon "male territory"—itself a slippery concept that perpetually morphed in response to historical context—they were allowed a variety of opportunities for self-expression and activity in the public sphere. The prewar *ie* system thus acted as a floodgate that served to contain this feminine energy within appropriate bounds. Women were still legally subordinated to the male head of the household, who was empowered to decide many aspects of their lives (domicile, marriage partner, level of education, employment, etc.) and was expected to keep them in line.

The Occupation threatened to upend this separate but equal system of gender roles because it promoted a model of equality that presumed men and women should have the same basic rights and responsibilities. This vision of equality was an ideological construct that bore little resemblance to the actual situation of women in American society at this time, but no matter—the Occupiers were riding high on a wave of confidence that convinced them of the moral superiority of their own ideals to the "feudalistic" tendencies of the Japanese. This idealized vision of "American" equality thus produced a new Japanese constitution—and documents based off of it, such as the FLE—that went much further than its parent document in declarations of "gender equality." By granting women the power to vote and run for office, to receive the same type and degree of education as men, and to make autonomous decisions about their lives, the legal reforms proposed by the Occupiers opened all manner of formerly male territory to the potential encroachment of women. Coeducation provided girls with a powerful opportunity to do all of these things, and as a result the debates over its implementation were fraught with claims by conservatives that it posed a grave danger to the integrity of the national body and the "beautiful customs" of Japan.

As we will see in subsequent chapters, legal recognition of coeducation in the FLE did not settle these debates. The document itself was riven with mixed messages regarding the nature or extent of equality promoted by Occupation staffers. For their part, Japanese government representatives tended to interpret constitutional guarantees of "gender equality" in flexible terms that conformed to their own presumption of the separate but equal status of Japanese women. Thus, negotiations over the text of the FLE failed to clearly define what was meant by equality of educational opportunity, adding to the confusion when educational authorities began to implement coeducation and intensifying the debates that ensued in Japanese society over its purpose and likely outcome.

Occupation-led plans to implement the new system of education were thus met with staunch opposition from conservative sectors. Some claimed that coeducation was doomed to failure either because women were inherently intellectually inferior to men or (more often) because the prewar system of sex-segregated education had left girls irrevocably behind boys in terms of preparation for a coeducational curriculum. Others raised the specter of moral problems—ostensibly meaning adolescent sexual experimentation but also encompassing transgression of gender norms—that would surely ensue if boys and girls were educated in close physical proximity to one another. While adults argued vociferously about the merits and demerits of coeducation, the young people who were its object were left to sort out for themselves how to adapt to this new ethos of equality. In the chapters that follow, we will explore how these debates over coeducation played out in the press in various types of media—regional newspapers, comics, student-authored school newsletters, and roundtable discussions in popular magazines—during the Occupation period. We will then explore the postwar backlash against coeducation that ensued in these media once the Japanese were left to their own devices to decide whether to retain, restructure, or scrap entirely the Occupation-era reforms.

# CHAPTER 2

## *Coeducation in the News*

## From Hokkaidō to Kyūshū

"COEDUCATION WILL NOT BE MANDATORY," screamed the February 6, 1947, headline of the *Kahoku shimpō,* as if channeling the collective relief of its entire Miyagi prefecture readership.[1] One year later, a newspaper serving readers in Ōita prefecture issued a dismal "report card on coeducation one month in," declaring "All the Girls Fail."[2] Not long after that, readers in Sasebo were alarmed (and perhaps titillated) to hear of "pink incidents"[3]—a euphemism for adolescent sexual experimentation—that their local newspaper attributed to the recent introduction of coeducation. The following year, Hiroshima-area residents were put on notice of an anticipated "September crisis" (*ku-gatsu kiki*), suggesting the "moral problems" (*fūki mondai*) that were thought certain to occur once students returned to class after the first summer vacation of the newly coeducational school system.[4]

As these headlines illustrate, when coeducation was introduced in the late 1940s, it created a great deal of controversy that was fanned in part by sensationalistic coverage in local news outlets. At the same time, local newspapers served as vital sources of information about Occupation reforms, particularly for readers outside the Tokyo metropole. In this sense, we may view these news sources as both reflecting and producing anxieties about coeducation among the readerships they served. Newspapers actively covered this issue from the first hint that coeducation might be among the proposed educational reforms, through the process of deliberation of its advantages and disadvantages, and finally to its implementation on the local level in elementary, middle, and (some) high schools across the archipelago.

In this chapter, we will analyze how coeducation was discussed in regional newspapers from 1946 to 1949, paying particular attention to the way

arguments expressed for and against the practice revealed societal values regarding gender and sexual norms at this moment of transition between the
prewar and postwar educational systems. After a brief overview of major
trends in coverage of coeducation nationwide, we will focus on three concerns that were typically raised in discussions of the merits and demerits of
coeducation: (1) the academic gap between boys and girls that resulted from
differential educational systems in the prewar period; (2) the possibility that
coeducation might facilitate premarital sexual experimentation, particularly among adolescents; and (3) the potential for the transgression of gender
roles and norms of behavior as a result of "mutual influence" between the
sexes. We will see that while arguments for and against coeducation were
made on the basis of all of these areas of concern, anxieties about moral
problems engendered the most urgent and lasting resistance. Furthermore,
while on the surface these moral problems were expressed in terms of a heterosexual panic that erroneously assumed coeducation would produce
widespread adolescent sexual experimentation, these anxieties about sexual
licentiousness among youth in fact masked a deeper concern about the potential of coeducation to facilitate the transgression of gender norms.

## CHARTING THE COURSE OF COEDUCATION: 1946–49

Coeducation was a major topic of interest to Japanese readers from 1946 to
1949, and newspapers from Hokkaidō in the far north to Kyūshū in the south
sated readers' desires for information about how this "new system" of education would be implemented. A keyword search of the Prange Collection archives revealed 146 separate newspaper articles on the topic of "coeducation" (*danjo kyōgaku*) published between October 10, 1946, and October 10,
1949. The analysis in this chapter is based on a comprehensive quantitative
analysis of these articles and a selective qualitative analysis of articles that
appeared in newspapers that published ten or more articles on this topic
during the period of study.[5]

   Some of these articles were standard-issue wire service reports covering
major announcements of national policy by MOE or Occupation staffers regarding the course of educational reform. However, the majority were profoundly local in their scope of concern, ranging from announcements by
prefectural officials attempting to translate national policy into local practice to firsthand reportage of experiences of coeducation at neighborhood

schools. Opinion pieces also proliferated. Some of these were drafted by professional reporters or education experts, but the opinions of average citizens were also published in regular columns that featured readers' voices. The experiences and opinions of schoolchildren were also anxiously sought and were published particularly in the form of survey data and anecdotal examples. While some articles played upon readers' fears of social upheaval, presenting coeducation as a somewhat scandalous and disruptive practice with dangerous moral consequences, others accepted it as a fact of life going forward and seriously addressed questions of best practices in implementation and measurement of student success.

Practical considerations and local circumstances played an important role in the degree to which coeducation was adopted in provincial high schools. The structure of the new system of education put new pressure on already strapped school districts to educate all students through the middle school level; this in turn increased the number willing and able to continue on to high school. Several articles in the *Hokkaidō shinbun*, a major newspaper serving the northernmost prefecture of Japan, indicated that these pressures motivated prefectural school board authorities there to embrace coeducation with a remarkable degree of enthusiasm. They frequently cited the difficulty of meeting the increased demand for high school education as motivation for quickly expanding coeducation to as many school districts as possible.[6] Furthermore, in many areas, the devastation of wartime seriously compromised the ability of local school districts to meet the demand for education at any level. In addition to the fact that many buildings were completely or partially destroyed during the final stages of the war, the remains of such structures were frequently looted. This was the case in the Chūgoku region of Japan, where the local newspaper reported that even those buildings that did survive often lacked enough desks and chairs for students, forcing many to stand during class.[7] In some cases this material deprivation made coeducation desirable, allowing districts to consolidate two schools into one and thereby pool their resources.

In other cases, coeducation was considered desirable because it reduced the amount of time students had to spend in commuting to class—a significant concern particularly in provincial and more sparsely populated areas of the country. For example, in Miyagi prefecture, in the rural north of the main island of Honshū, coeducation at the high school level was included among a host of reforms designed to improve the "efficiency" of the school system. This was explicitly intended to make school commutes easier for all students since they could simply attend the closer of two schools rather than have to travel to a single-sex institution that might be farther away from home.[8] These considerations affected students at all stages of the educational system, not just high school. For example, one mother of a male student at the Niigata No. 1 Normal School (Niigata Dai-ichi Shihan Gakkō), also in northern Honshū, wrote an impassioned letter to the editor of the prefectural newspaper in favor of a recent proposal to make the local teacher training school coeducational, imploring, "You don't know how much it would help us financially if he could commute to school from home." The writer suggests that her family would enjoy enormous financial savings if her son were able to commute to the nearby Nagaoka campus—at the time used as a branch campus for female students only—rather than pay to live in a dormitory at the all-male main campus in Niigata city, over sixty kilometers away.[9] Less than two months later, the paper followed up with another article announcing the approval of this proposal to make both campuses coeducational and explicitly mentioned ease of commuting for students as a major reason for this decision.[10]

However, in other cases the lack of gender-specific facilities posed a barrier to coeducation. Most schools naturally lacked bathrooms for both sexes, given the long history of sex segregation in Japanese schools. Furthermore, historically all-male schools lacked rooms and equipment for instruction in home economics, which in spite of the push for coeducation was still considered a crucial subject for girls. Conversely, girls' schools typically lacked sports grounds and equipment for athletic club activities and physical education classes, which were considered requisite for boys. These problems were cited as barriers to coeducation by some of the twenty principals polled by the *Ōita gōdō shinbun*, a major newspaper servicing part of the southern island of Kyūshū, even when the principals themselves hoped to implement it.[11]

But even in those areas that considered themselves to be practicing coeducation, the degree to which girls and boys were actually taught side by side in the same classroom with the same teachers and curricula was sometimes questionable and varied widely according to local circumstance. Particularly in rural areas with less dense populations and fewer resources to construct specialized schools, it was common for coeducational high schools to nevertheless maintain separate tracks for vocational versus academic training, and many of these tracks had gendered implications. For example, it is likely that tracks identified as devoted to instruction in "home economics" (*kateika*) or "sewing" enrolled few if any male students. It is also likely that academic tracks at historically prestigious college prep institutions enrolled few female students, even when they were technically classed as coeducational, due to the inferior academic preparation girls had received under the "old system" and the competitiveness of the requirements for entry. For example, when the No. 1 Ōita High School (Ōita Dai-ichi Kōtō Gakkō) in Kyūshū was constructed on the basis of the former Ōita Middle School (Ōita Chūgakko)—a regionally prestigious all-male academy—it admitted 140 female students from the two highest-ranking prefectural girls' higher schools. However, this only amounted to 7 or 8 female students out of approximately 40 students per class.[12]

In some areas, the "consolidation" of one or more schools may have occurred largely on paper, without any actual rearrangement of students, teachers, school facilities, or curricula. This seems to have been the case in Tsurusaki, Ōita prefecture (Kyūshū), where Tsurusaki High School (Tsurusaki kōtō gakkō) was ostensibly formed through the fusion of the historically male middle school (*chūgakkō*) with the local girls' (*jogakkō*) and vocational (*kōgyō*) schools. But although the three institutions held a common opening ceremony, each of the component institutions seems to have retained its basic form, with the addition of other subjects. The middle school added agricultural and business departments to become the "No. 1 section" (Dai-ichi bu), the vocational school planned at the time of publication to add agricultural and carpentry divisions to become the "No. 2 section," and the girls' school planned to continue on in its current facilities in the short term but to later become the home economics track for the other two schools. So depending on local circumstances, the adoption of coeducation might have meant dramatic change for the students and teachers transitioning to the new system, or it might have meant not much change at all.

Coverage of coeducation in regional newspapers tended to spike at key moments when major announcements or initiatives were introduced—for example, on October 10, 1946, the day the government announced it would change the implementation policies of the Elementary School Law (Kokumin gakkō rei) to officially permit coeducation,[13] and on October 25, when it revealed its intention to make education through middle school compulsory and coeducational.[14] There was another spike in publication activity in February 1947, when the outlines of the new system of education were made clearer to the public. Many of these articles appeared on the heels of a press conference held on February 5 by SCAP education officers to explain how the plan for education reform would be phased in with the onset of the new academic year (beginning in April) in middle schools as well as elementary schools, with exceptions made for localities that experienced destruction severe enough to prohibit immediate implementation of the new system. A similar announcement in mid-February 1947 regarding implementation of coeducation at the high school level prompted a new flurry of media attention in certain areas. While most high schools delayed the start of the new system until 1948 or later, nine prestigious prefectural and national high schools voluntarily integrated their campuses in the spring of 1947.[15]

It was the widespread implementation of coeducation at the high school level that generated the most attention in the pages of regional newspapers. Fully half of the total number of newspaper articles published on the topic of coeducation appeared during the second year of the new system (April 1948–April 1949), when coeducation was phased in for many high schools. The intense interest in coeducation at the high school level among the general public was partly related to the fact that academically oriented schools were expected to prepare young people for university entrance exams. Many parents expressed fears that the inferior academic preparation of the girls in coed classrooms would hold back the progress of the class as a whole, thus hampering their sons' readiness for competition for university placements. But it also reflects prevalent cultural anxieties about the moral problems that were thought likely to occur if adolescents in the throes of puberty were taught in close physical proximity to one another. While anxieties about moral problems were most commonly acknowledged in terms of fears of premarital sexual experimentation, as we will see below, the way these concerns were phrased also indicates a significant degree of anxiety about the possibility of the transgression of gender roles and norms of behavior, frequently described as "androgyny." In the next three sections, we will examine how each of these concerns was expressed in regional newspapers.

MIND THE (ACADEMIC) GAP

Newspaper coverage of coeducation as it was first implemented in Japanese schools, particularly at the high school level, leaves no doubt that female students entered the coeducational classroom at a distinct academic disadvantage when compared with their male counterparts. This is amply documented both by statistical information and by anecdotal accounts. For example, in a roundtable discussion from Niigata prefecture between female high school students experiencing their first year of coeducation and female university students in their second year of an integrated medical school, both groups complain of struggling to keep up with their male classmates.[16] The high school students note the very real difference in preparation in English and math between the male students, who had attended more rigorous all-boys middle schools, and the former girls' school students, particularly in terms of fundamentals such as English grammar.

However, they place the blame for this differential squarely on the insufficient preparation they received in girls' school rather than on any innate difference in ability between the sexes. One adds, "In the future, if discrimination in the academic level of middle schools and girls' schools disappears, this problem will probably resolve itself." The university students concur. One reports that she transferred from the home economics department (*kaseika*) of Japan Women's University (Nihon Joshidai) to the Niigata Medical School (Niigata Idaigakubu) and thus lacked the basic scientific knowledge to compete with her male classmates, adding ruefully that the current group of female high school students is "lucky" to be able to attend school with males.

The differential in academic preparation seems to have been the greatest for high school girls who entered formerly all-male elite college prep academies, of the kind described by Donald Roden in his study of the "number schools," which prepared boys for eventual entrance into the imperial universities.[17] For example, in the aforementioned article bearing the rather lurid title "All the Girls Fail: A Report Card on Coeducation One Month In,"[18] we learn that after the first reporting period of the first year of coeducation, girls' scores at the prestigious Ōita No. 1 High School were no more than half the total points earned by boys in all academic subjects. As the article's title indicates, none of the girls managed to exceed the fifty-point threshold necessary for a passing grade.

To their credit, the writer(s) of the unsigned article also seem to attribute this dismal result to the fact that girls and boys had historically "been educated separately and in different ways" rather than to any inherent intellectual inferiority on the part of the girls. It seems that this understanding was generally shared by parents, teachers, and school administrators as well, because the article further indicates that parents willingly donated 200,000 yen of their own money to fund special enrichment classes after hours for struggling students. Proactive efforts to help girls catch up to their male classmates academically seem to have been effective in other parts of the country as well. A report from Honbetsu High School (Honbetsu Kōkō) in Hokkaidō credits the creation of a special supplementary class for girls for helping them catch up to the boys, so that by October of the first year of the new system girls and boys performed more or less the same on exams.[19] So it also seems clear that girls worked hard to overcome this academic gap and in many cases were able to do so remarkably quickly.

However, this does not mean that this strong performance on the part of female students fully convinced the public that concerns about innate intellectual differences between the sexes were unwarranted. For example, we see evidence of this presumption of feminine intellectual inferiority in a lengthy two-part series of articles in the *Sasebo jiji shinbun* (Kyūshū). These articles report on a public presentation of research on the academic impact of coeducation by a teacher named Amasaki Yoshio at the local Yamanobori Middle School. One and a half years into the new system, Amasaki found that girls scored higher in every subject at every level than the boys did. However, he also argued that boys tended to score above average on measures of intelligence, whereas girls tended to score below average.[20] While he did not provide any information as to how "intelligence" was measured, he did characterize the boys' test results as having measured an "innate" (*sententeki*) form of intelligence, as opposed to the "acquired intelligence" (*kōtenteki na chinō*) demonstrated by the girls in their classroom performance.

On the basis of these findings, Amasaki argued that girls tend to get relatively better grades for their level of intelligence than boys do. He notes that even among those with an inferior level of intelligence, a few girls get excellent grades but no boys do. He interprets this finding as indicating that girls are hardworking but "lack future potential," suggesting that the innate intelligence demonstrated by the boys was somehow superior to the acquired intelligence of the girls. Throughout he seems to assume that innate intelligence is a natural and immutable characteristic that is somehow impervious to context or environment. In a two-part editorial that followed this coverage, Amasaki affirmed the value of coeducation as a measure to ensure "equal educational opportunity," while stressing the need for caution in implementing this measure:

> It goes without saying that when human beings enter puberty their sexual differentiation becomes most obvious, and comes on suddenly. At that point for these few years of crisis, they separate themselves voluntarily and develop

separate lives. This is a natural tendency and the correct path, so we must properly respect this law of sexual differentiation. . . .[21]

Thus it becomes an important matter for us to give ample consideration to sexual difference in implementing equal opportunity of education for boys and girls [*danjo byōdō kikai kintō*], which is a main principle of democracy. Accordingly, it is necessary to give some consideration to sex in [determining] subject matter and educational principles, because if we implement coeducation passively as a categorical imperative of the new system of high school consolidation then we cannot avoid creating confusion, since students have not been trained this way from youth and teachers and parents also have no experience with it.[22]

While he may not have felt empowered to attack the merits of coeducation in such a public venue at a time when it was championed so forcefully by the Occupation, he seems to want to imply the logic of separate spheres for men and women by suggesting that boys are "naturally" intellectually superior to girls without stating so outright. That he was given such a public forum in which to expound on these ideas, first through a public presentation and then through extensive coverage in the local newspaper (spanning four issues, no less), also suggests that the editors of the *Sasebo jiji shinbun* found his arguments compelling and presumed their readers would as well.

In summary, while some members of the public—and particularly the younger generations—seem to have been convinced that the academic gap between girls and boys was the product of a history of unequal access to education and could therefore be overcome, this presumption was clearly not shared by all. Even some of those tasked with implementing coeducation still seem to have taken a jaundiced eye toward the ability of girls to measure up to boys intellectually. Evidently the logic of separate spheres that had underwritten the prewar sex-segregated system of education still framed the thinking of many, in spite of the introduction of coeducation. (We will see further evidence of this in chap. 4.)

## MORAL PROBLEMS AS HETEROSEXUAL PANIC

The fear that coeducation might facilitate premarital sexual experimentation, especially among high school students, was the most urgent concern cited by opponents of the practice in advance of the implementation of the new system of education, and such worries particularly plagued parents of girls. Once coeducation was actually implemented, most reports found few actual examples of the kind of moral problems feared by parents, though this did not seem to stop people from worrying about this possibility. We can see the persistence of these anxieties in an October 10, 1949, article published in the *Ōita gōdō shinbun* that documents the sports day activities held at the Ōita No. 1 High School (discussed above as the school where "all the girls fail[ed]").[23] The article notes that "the sight of male and female students playing freely together and putting on their exhibits relieved the hearts [*kokoro o hogusu*] of their parents and elders." The language expressing this "relief" is particularly interesting. The verb *hogusu* (解す) is rendered with a Chinese character that implies disentangling something (in this case, the "hearts of their parents and elders") that had been tied up in knots. This seems to be a clear reference to the anxiety felt by many parents and teachers that coeducation would invite widespread social disruption. Since this article was printed nearly a year and a half *after* the school became coeducational, it should have been clear by this point that the dreaded moral problems thought to accompany coeducation had failed to materialize. Yet coeducation is still portrayed in this paper as a profoundly anxiety-producing measure. As we will see in this section, although some educational authorities and members of the public spoke out in favor of coeducation, in some cases even arguing that it would help to prevent the very moral problems most feared by parents, this seems to have done little to quell these sorts of fears in the general public.

While newspapers dutifully reported on the absence of moral problems of this kind, they also eagerly sought out evidence of such problems wherever they could find it and prominently featured this news, thus fanning the flames of societal concern about coeducation. For example, in the Kyūshū-based *Sasebo jiji shinbun*, we see a large number of total articles devoted to coverage of coeducation.[24] This newspaper also featured one of the very few articles in this sample that attempted to provide documentation of the moral problems thought to be associated with the practice. According to this article, published on September 9, 1948, the compulsory levels of education (through middle school) were made coeducational in the spring of 1947. High schools were not scheduled to become coeducational until the spring of 1949. The article reports with alarm on what it perceives as an epidemic of "*momoiro jiken*"—or "pink incidents," with "pink" connoting eroticism. The

incidents in question involved nearly fifty young people of both sexes between the ages of sixteen and nineteen who were found to be "indulging in
carnal play" (*nikutai no yūgi ni fukette iru*), producing a sense of a "grave social
problem" and "attracting the concern of citizens." The guilty parties were
said to hail from the ranks of middle and high school graduates and current
students at schools throughout the area. Reportedly there were no schools
unaffected by this problem. Parents were therefore said to be apprehensive
about the approaching unification of high schools under the new system of
coeducation the following spring. The article identifies several possible reasons for this "rash" of immoral incidents among young people, including
unsupervised attendance at movie theaters, trouble at home, failure of parents and teachers to guide students properly, and the "low intellectual level
of society." It concludes by emphasizing the need to "plant awareness of [the
importance of] chastity firmly in [the minds of] pubescent students."[25]

While it is clear from this article that coeducation aroused pervasive
fears of moral licentiousness, it is unclear that there was any direct connection between coeducation and the grave social problem of sexual experimentation suggested here. First of all, the incidents in question took place
in advance of, not subsequent to, the integration of area high schools.
While middle school students were also implicated and coeducation was
ongoing at this level, it is unclear that the number of students involved was
significant enough to constitute an epidemic, as the article suggests. Other
articles in the same newspaper certainly do not bear this out. For example,
a survey of middle school students at the aforementioned Yamanobori
Middle School indicated the usual childish complaints by boys and girls
regarding the opposite sex—boys were too "rowdy" and uncouth in their
behavior, girls giggled too much and tattled on classmates—but otherwise
seemed to indicate a relatively successful transition to the new system.[26] In
fact, a far larger number of articles in this sample indicate that while concerned adults anticipated such moral problems with dread prior to the implementation of coeducation, in its aftermath most news outlets reported—
with a mixture of surprise and chagrin—that no such problems could be
documented.[27]

Another article covering a debate among middle school students hints
that these concerned adults might actually have been projecting their own licentious assumptions onto the behavior of young people. When asked to debate the merits of coeducation, the youthful speakers at this meeting were
generally positive about the system in spite of the usual complaints about the

opposite sex, and they conversely took adults to task for their own "low morals," suggesting that they served as poor role models for children.[28] Toward understanding the context for these remarks, one cannot underestimate the importance of local circumstances in fanning the flames of moral panic. Sasebo was home to an Allied naval base that no doubt attracted its share of moral problems due to the prevalence of prostitution in such areas. It is likely that the resentment and discomfort that accompanied the everyday sight of native women for hire in the arms of foreign soldiers played a large role in reflexive fears of the impact of such licentiousness on young people.[29]

We see a similar trend in the *Chūgoku shinbun*, published in Hiroshima, which was likewise situated near an Allied military base (Iwakuni, thirty-three kilometers away). According to a roundtable discussion among reporters from the newspaper, the local police had begun referring to an anticipated September crisis, a reference to prevalent concerns regarding the moral problems that were anticipated as students returned to class after the first summer vacation of the newly coeducational school system.[30] Yet just ten days later an article in the same paper noted that such fears had been found to be completely groundless. Subtitled "Nearly All Sing the Praises of Coeducation,"[31] it reported the results of a survey conducted by students at Miyahara High School (in nearby Kure) of their peers. It found that with the exception of a few of the usual complaints—for example, that girls' academic preparation for the new system lagged behind that of the boys, who wanted more rigorous coursework—there were no reported moral problems and both sexes cited the benefits of learning to understand one another better thanks to coeducation.

Some educators did write in favor of coeducation, and a few even argued that it might help avoid the kind of moral problems feared by parents by giving students concrete skills and practice at interacting productively with the opposite sex in a supervised environment. One example of this may be found in an article in the *Niigata nippō* reporting on a recent rash of "elopements" by young women who were "seduced" by "fake students" (*nise gakusei*) and ran off with them. Unlike the aforementioned article in the *Sasebo jiji shinbun* covering an epidemic of "pink incidents," which placed responsibility for this menace squarely at the door of coeducation, this article presents coeducation as a *solution* to the problem of premature sexual experimentation among youth, as is evident from its title: "What Mass Elopements Teach Us: Facts about Warped Youth—Enlightenment through Coeducation."[32] While a text box at the top sets the stage by describing the nature of the problem as a "tragedy of youth," the bulk of the article consists of ideas solicited from members of the community as to how to handle this "problem."

The first such contribution, penned by a female principal of a local elementary school, reads:

> I think this is a sad sacrifice that has been borne by the social conditions of the new era. Because they have so suddenly been liberated from feudalism, children are confused and don't understand what relationships between men and women should be, and this is probably why they were seduced. Along with reflecting on the fact that young women these days are grappling with concepts like "liberty" [*jiyū*] and "equal rights" [*danjo dōken*] without knowing how to interpret them, it is also important to train them to deal properly with the opposite sex.

She then proposes a number of "concrete measures" in this regard, including "implement[ation of] coeducation from the preschool level on" and creation of new youth organizations (*seinendan*) to foster "cheerful social interactions between men and women appropriate to the new age." She also notes the need to "fundamentally change the thinking of parents" so that they do not "look askance" at the idea of boys and girls socializing together and argues that this will allow them to educate their children about how to do this properly. While other contributors do not link these incidents to coeducation either positively or negatively, they echo the sentiment that young people are woefully unequipped to deal with the brave new world of social mixing between the sexes and require guidance rather than censure.

However, such arguments do not seem to have satisfied many members of the public, perhaps because newspaper articles covering coeducation persistently returned to the issue of moral problems even when they reported on the success of the new system generally speaking. For example, a Hokkaidō prefectural newspaper ebulliently reported on the smooth transition to coeducation there as follows:

> "It's too soon, it's not good for morals" . . . in the midst of such opposition from some parents, coeducation is flourishing. This April the prefectural board of education decided on a plan to make high schools coeducational as well. It's been half a year since approximately 30% of regular high schools (31) and 70% of irregular high schools (87) began implementing coeducation. Students who felt awkward at first from shyness and the unusualness of the

situation have now grown to the point that they join hands in square danc-
ing. One might say that even though there are some remaining problems,
generally speaking coeducation has been successful.[33]

But while the article describes the adage that boys and girls should not sit
together after the age of seven as "old thinking," it also reports that there was
stiff opposition by local parents to the implementation of coeducation and
that the policy was ultimately adopted over and in spite of these objections,
requiring schools to go to great lengths to "enlighten" parents about its merits. While the language here indicates a generally positive attitude toward
coeducation, at times portraying parents' resistance as wrongheaded and
the product of outmoded thinking, it simultaneously panders to their fears
by raising the specter of moral problems even though none had so far been
discovered:

> However, after three or four months [students'] initial caution disappeared,
> and their awareness of one another as members of the opposite sex grew
> faint. [As a result,] the appearance of some of the boys became more dishev-
> eled and they became careless in cleaning the classroom. As for the girls,
> some became masculinized [*danseika shi*] in their actions and speech, com-
> fortably using words like "kimi" and "boku" [rough forms of personal pro-
> nouns]. Also, a few boys and girls were seen associating with one another
> outside of school, raising fears among high school principals of moral prob-
> lems. This prompted the prefectural board of education's guidance office to
> plan a program of guidance for correct relations between men and women to
> encourage students to make correct distinctions [between right and wrong]
> even in this [atmosphere of] freedom. Although no such problems have yet
> surfaced, every school finds this to be the most pressing issue for coeducation
> going forward.

So despite that the article itself clearly states that no evidence of moral problems had been found, it nevertheless ends on a cautionary note, as if to im-
press upon its readers the need for constant vigilance. It also seems important here to underscore the low bar set by school administrators for such
sexual transgressions. Evidently, the mere prospect of "a few boys and
girls . . . seen associating with one another outside of school" was enough to
"rais[e] fears among high school principals of moral problems."
    While the moral problems referenced here primarily refer to premarital

sexual experimentation, as we will see in the next section (and in the quotes above), they were also intimately associated with concerns about androgynous behavior. We see this referenced above in the concern about girls using rough forms of address ("kimi") and first-person masculine pronouns ("boku") rather than the more refined speech expected of young ladies at this time. In fact, we see a kind of slippage between these two sets of concerns, indicating a close conceptual relationship in the minds of contemporary readers between transgression of sexual mores and transgression of gender roles and norms.

## MORAL PROBLEMS AS GENDER TROUBLE

Although the troubling possibility of moral problems got a lot of attention in the Japanese news around the time coeducation was first implemented, this term seems to have signified more than a fear of premarital sexual experimentation to many concerned parents, teachers, and members of society. As noted above, anxieties about sexual transgressions were often raised together with the equally disturbing prospect of transgression of gender roles and norms, and in accounts of these fears we frequently see one category of concern morph unexpectedly into the other. While both sexes were at times figured as the object of these concerns, most of this discourse seems to have been focused on androgyny as it related to girls straying beyond the boundaries of acceptably feminine behavior. Put differently, the potential for "mutual influence" between boys and girls disproportionately aroused desires to police girls' (rather than boys') behavior so as to reinforce normative femininity and thus guard against the opportunities presented by coeducation for girls to "trespass" on historically male territory and prerogatives.

For example, in a public debate titled "Coeducation: Pro or Con?" that took place in Kure (Hiroshima prefecture) and was covered by the *Chūgoku shinbun*,[34] the representative of the "con" camp objected to coeducation in part on the grounds that it eroded gender differences:

> There may be good things about coeducation, but there are also very negative things about it too. If we suddenly make [schools] coeducational we can't avoid a decline in academic ability [among students]. Just as both men and women have equal rights [*dōtō no kenri*], there are also responsibilities that go along with that. From the perspective of such responsibilities, it's equal

[*byōdō*] to say that men must be masculine and women must be feminine. It's concerning that there might not be sufficient distinction between men and women.

In a rather ingenious rhetorical move, this speaker seems to categorize gender conformity as one of the "responsibilities" that accompany acquisition of equal rights. He implicitly ranks obedience to masculine and feminine norms of behavior as of equal importance as exercising newly acquired democratic freedoms (unstated here, but perhaps he was thinking of women's recent acquisition of the right to vote?). Given that the person voicing these views is credited as a "professor of medicine," his audience may well have found his remarks persuasive on the grounds that his profession gave him considerable social capital. At any rate, it seems clear from the tenor of his remarks that he saw the prevailing discourses of equality as a dangerous challenge to conventional gender norms and objected to coeducation specifically on the grounds that it facilitated transgression of these distinctions between the sexes.

Conversely, we see criticism of persistent gender stereotypes echoed in the aforementioned *Niigata nippō* roundtable discussion between female high school students and female medical school students, where participants assail critics of coeducation as attempting to enforce outmoded notions of gender roles for girls in particular. The participants in this discussion note the prevalence of societal concerns about improper relationships between men and women, women losing their "femininity," and women becoming "uppity" (*namaiki*) because of higher education. However, they insist that these fears are all groundless and show a lack of understanding of the actual situation (*jitsujō*) of coeducation. They are in agreement that societal conditions that require young women to give up their studies in favor of "kitchen work" need to change and argue that society as a whole must progress by embracing the kind of mutual understanding and respect between the sexes that coeducation can help cultivate. They conclude that the gates of coeducation should be opened widely so that more women can attend high school and university with men.[35] That these ambitious young women all seem to have shared the experience of having their femininity questioned because of their academic skill underscores both the rigidity of these gender distinctions and the widespread societal concern about women transgressing these boundaries.

On the other hand, it is also clear that many students themselves had internalized notions of the "naturalness" of these gender distinctions and struggled to balance these conventions against postwar democratic discourses of equality between the sexes. In some cases this seems to have resulted in young people policing the behavior of their classmates so as to reinforce gender norms—even as they sometimes complained about the stark differences in behavior and communication styles that resulted from this strict gender differentiation. These mixed messages are expressed in the very first article published on the topic of coeducation in the *Ōita gōdō shinbun*—a survey of 150 fifth-year students at the prefectural No. 1 Higher Girls' School (Dai-ichi kōtō jogakkō) about their feelings about coeducation and the new "6-3-3" system. It was published on January 24, 1947, after it had become clear that coeducation at the compulsory levels of education would be mandatory, but prior to its actual implementation.

The students generally expressed positive feelings about the potential of the new system to make higher levels of education available to all on a more equitable basis. However, they also expressed concerns about the suddenness of the transition, particularly given that young people their age had so little experience interacting with the opposite sex. The conservatism of the views expressed here by a group of young women who were best positioned to benefit from these new opportunities is particularly interesting. Many stressed the need for girls to work hard to develop a self-awareness of "correct woman[hood]" (*tadashii onna*) to rectify their ignorance of the opposite sex and form "correct relationships" (*tadashii kōsai*) with boys. Some also criticized "girls in uniform" (no doubt meaning other schoolgirls) who are too eager to "ride the wave of the times" and who need to reflect on what is proper and what is not through "self-criticism" (*jiko hihan*). The above remarks suggest that these students, like their elders, harbored concerns about moral problems and felt a consequent need for self-restraint to counteract the new liberalism of the era.

These girls also fretted about the possible blurring of gender lines and hoped that coeducation would make boys "essentially" (*honshitsu*) more masculine and girls more feminine rather than result in the "androgynization" (*chūseika*) of both groups.[36] Somewhat paradoxically, the use of language here implies that gender is an innate quality—thus making androgyny unnatural and disturbing—that is also highly vulnerable to disruption by social forces. Fortunately for these ladies, a follow-up article reported with satisfaction that girls from this area continued to conduct themselves in properly feminine fashion even after entering the newly integrated Ōita No.

1 High School (Ōita Dai-ichi kōtō gakkō). When asked to comment on the results of coeducation at this school, the vice principal noted less tardiness and cleaner classrooms, adding that the girls had entirely taken over the responsibility for cleaning and decorating the rooms with floral arrangements and would not allow the boys to help.[37]

Other students expressed conflicting sentiments regarding the desirability of preserving gender differences. While some confessed fears of androgyny (*danjo no chūseika*) and expressed the expectation that members of the opposite sex conform to gender norms, there were just as many complaints about behaviors that *did* conform to societal expectations. For example, boys criticized girls for being too reticent, and girls complained that boys should pay more attention to their clothing and physical appearance. But these behaviors were consistent with prevalent ideologies of gender that rewarded women for docility and self-restraint, while dissuading men from exhibiting concern with their physical appearance by construing this as a "feminine" preoccupation.[38] In other words, boys and girls were somewhat confusingly exhorted to preserve some aspects of conventional gender norms, while shedding other ostensibly gender-typical qualities that were perceived to be unattractive or unproductive. These mixed messages serve as eloquent testimony to the transitional moment that the Occupation period represented in discursive constructions of gender. It is clear from these narratives that children carried the lessons of the prewar sex-segregated system of education into their experience of the new postwar system of coeducation and were then forced to negotiate the gap between the two systems on an individual level. Under the circumstances, it is hardly surprising that their expectations of the opposite sex—and of themselves—appear to have been self-contradictory.

CONCLUSION

As we have seen above, the intellectual gap between boys and girls that was created by the sex-segregated educational system prior to 1945 posed a very real problem for the implementation of coeducation, though this problem was also swiftly resolved as girls caught up to boys academically. On the other hand, concerns about moral problems continued to haunt Japanese society well after coeducation had been implemented. In fact, the kind of premarital sexual experimentation feared by parents and teachers turned out to be a rather rare occurrence—though this did not stop the mass media from fanning the flames of moral panic. Beneath these concerns of sexual misbehavior lurked fears of transgression of gender roles and norms, and these worries proved even harder for advocates of coeducation to eradicate.

This did not really produce an epidemic of androgyny, to use the term favored by the popular press of the time, in the sense of obviously "masculinized" women or "feminized" men who might today be understood as transgender. Rather, the term androgyny seems to have been used at this time to connote not an individualized performance of nonnormative gender *identity* but the adoption of a position or *role* in society that was thought "natural" for the opposite gender. Coverage of coeducation in the early postwar period featured many complaints about girls using language considered too rough for their gender, but no reports of cross-dressing or other practices more commonly associated with androgyny. Furthermore, girls seem to have disproportionately aroused such fears of androgynous gender bending. Parents and teachers might have fretted about girls' use of masculine pronouns or their tendency to assert themselves and their rights, but what they really seem to have been afraid of was the possibility that these shifts in behavior might translate into a greater willingness to stake out "masculine" positions in society, thereby eroding historically male privileges and prerogatives and threatening the structure of male dominance.

This framing of the problem of androgyny contrasts in some interesting ways with Donald Roden's discussion of what he terms "gender ambivalence" during the Taishō period (1912–26).[39] Roden's concept of gender ambivalence is capacious and seemingly includes all manner of transgression of norms of gender and sexuality, such as cross-dressing, hermaphrodism, homosexuality, sexual "inversion," and sexual "pathologies" of all types. With the exception of concerns about girls being "masculinized" by adopting rough behavior or speech, we do not see the kind of dramatic displays of gender or sexual transgression documented by Roden in Occupation-era discussions of androgyny. What we do see is a heightened concern about the possibility of girls and women "intruding" upon male territory or prerogatives—as suggested by Koyama Shizuko in her discussion of "good wife, wise mother" ideology (see chap. 1)—and a corresponding effort to police gender distinctions so as to discourage such transgressions.

This variance in understanding of the term "androgyny" is likely a direct result of the very different social and historical backdrop encountered by Japanese under Occupation rule, vis-à-vis the Taishō-era landscape depicted by Roden. Roden argues that this era was characterized by transgression of gender and sexual norms in the realm of cultural expression "in conscious reaction" to the way gender roles were bifurcated and reified by social institutions such as the educational system and the military during the previous Meiji-era push toward rapid modernization:

> Meiji [1868–1912] educators drew elaborate distinctions between the character-building missions of young men and women, especially in the secondary schools. "Liberals" and "conservatives" agreed that the "duties of womanhood" (*onna no honbun*) destined the "weaker sex" to devote themselves to the home, as "good wives and wise mothers" (*ryōsai kenbo*), while the "duties of manhood" (*otoko no honbun*) demanded that young stalwarts seek their fortunes in the outside world of politics and commerce. Accordingly, just as the spokesmen for women's secondary education stressed the virtues of chastity, modesty, submissiveness, and good taste, the headmasters of the all-male middle and higher schools trumpeted the countervailing values of performance, unyielding determination, and fortitude.[40]

Roden argues that precisely because gender roles were policed by a vast network of societal institutions that conspired to produce "masculine" men and "feminine" women, Taishō-era Japanese who found this situation to be oppressive retreated to the realm of culture to express resistance to these ideologies through obvious and dramatic forms of gender bending.

However, concerns about androgyny expressed in the pages of the Occupation-era newspapers discussed above were voiced at a time when the institutions that had policed such gender distinctions had been officially dismantled by postwar reforms. The educational system in particular, which had been a primary means of instilling gender conformity in the prewar period, was now in the process of being reconstructed so as to effectively facilitate the transgression of these prewar ideologies of gender. Rather than preparing boys and girls for very different roles in society, as the prewar system had done, the introduction of coeducation during the Occupation era allowed girls to aspire to many of the same roles in society that had previously been the exclusive privilege of their brothers.

In other words, coeducation opened up a space for women to encroach upon "territory" that had historically been coded as masculine. From the perspective of Occupation-era Japanese, whose understanding of appropriate gender roles had been shaped by the prewar institutions described by

Roden above, this rendered girls androgynous merely for aspiring to historically masculine goals. As we will see in chapter 6, the number of women taking university placements and jobs "away" from men in the early postwar
period remained quite small. However, the psychological threat that this
posed to the integrity of the idealized gendered division of labor motivated a
societal backlash that increasingly became figured as fears of "coeds ruining
the nation" in the journalistic press of the 1950s and 1960s and as social and
sexual anarchy in "sun-tribe" fiction and film. Before exploring that backlash, though, we will see in the next three chapters that these anxieties manifested in a wide variety of other Occupation-period media too, including
comic strips, student-authored newsletters, and roundtable discussions published in mass-circulation journals and magazines.

# CHAPTER 3

## Female Bodies in Male Spaces

### Coeducation as Portrayed in Occupation-Era Comics

The immediate postwar period was one of hunger and black markets, of orphans and limbless veterans. More than anything else, people wanted to rebuild their lives. In the daily newspapers, serialized four-panel strips for the family were humorous, reassuring, and immensely popular. Favorite themes were average families making the best of hard times, and lovable little children. Most of the strips were subdued, endearing, and notable for their similarity of style.[1]

SO WRITES FREDERIK L. SCHODT in his classic guide to the Japanese cartoon industry, *Manga! Manga!* But as Peter Duus notes, Japanese "comics" (*manga*) could be serious business indeed.[2] More than merely "endearing" forms of escapism, manga offered Japanese artists a potent weapon for social satire, effectively inviting readers to laugh at otherwise disturbing forms of societal upheaval. The subversive potential of manga is clear from the keen interest displayed by both the Japanese authorities during wartime and the Allied Occupiers afterward in monitoring and censoring their contents. From the beginning of the modern period, irreverent humor magazines like the *Marumaru chinbun* (first issued in 1877) had published political cartoons that riled the Japanese censors and sometimes resulted in the imprisonment of their editors.[3] The Japanese cartoon industry blossomed in the 1920s along with the expansion of literacy rates and print journalism, and cartoonists like Kitazawa Rakuten (1876–1955) and Okamoto Ippei (1886–1948) revolutionized the Japanese political cartoon through adoption of American-style techniques.[4] Though social and political satire was heavily censored during the war years, and many cartoonists collaborated with the war effort,[5] "the comic strip got back on its feet after the war. Satirical newspapers reappeared, as did weekly cartoons"[6] such as the much-beloved *Sazae-san* by Hasegawa Machiko.[7] "From the end of the Second World War, the numbers of manga reviews for the young, satirical magazines, and humorous comic strips swelled ceaselessly."[8]

While Occupation censors banned outright popular genres of manga that they believed encouraged "feudalistic" tendencies—for example, those depicting "combat sports" such as judo, karate, and kendo and pretty much anything featuring samurai[9]—early postwar Japanese artists seem to have had free rein to lampoon coeducation in the pages of newspapers and comic magazines.[10] In an era when it might have been permissible, but was probably not comfortable, to directly criticize the Occupation regime's promotion of coeducation as a democratic good, comics offered one way of venting these anxieties obliquely and working through the contradictions they produced in the lives of average men and women.

A keyword search of the Prange Collection archives using the term *danjo kyōgaku* (coeducation) revealed twelve cartoons on the subject of coeducation. Of these, five portray university-age students, four feature high school or middle school students, and three depict elementary school students. Drawn from a variety of publication types ranging from mass to "small media," and authored mostly by adults purporting to depict the experiences of young people, these cartoons portray coeducation as a failed pedagogical tool and a source of moral corruption. They thus implicitly refute Occupation claims that coeducation would benefit society by promoting equality and harmony between the sexes. Even as Japanese artists such as Hasegawa Machiko took inspiration from comics like *Blondie*[11] that portrayed American middle-class life in aspirational terms, others harnessed this medium to refute the vision of "progress" promoted by the Occupiers through reforms like coeducation.

In this chapter, we will see that these comic portrayals of coeducation reveal a remarkably persistent concern with the impact of this reform on male students, providing an intriguing counterpoint to the concerns about the "masculinization" of girls discussed in chapter 2. Specifically, these cartoons convey a pervasive sense of the danger of male students becoming so preoccupied with the attractions of the opposite sex that they are distracted from their primary goal as students. These concerns also draw upon anxieties regarding erosion of the strictly gendered division of labor discussed at the end of the last chapter but shift the object of focus from girls to boys. In doing so, they highlight not just the danger that girls might transgress upon previously male territory and prerogatives but also the fear that boys themselves might fail to live up to the expectations placed upon them by society.

These anxieties were predicated upon the prewar construction of the elite (male) student as the raw material upon which industrialization and empire had been built. In this sense, the prewar male student ideal represented an implicitly moral construct that emphasized single-minded devotion to scholarship as the path to advancement in society and eventual leadership of the country. According to this logic, education was not an individual but rather a national concern, in the sense that Japan invested enormous resources into educating these talented young men so that they could benefit the nation, not pursue their own interests. While Occupation efforts to reform the Japanese school system attempted to change the conversation from education in the interest of the state to education in the interest of the free and autonomous individual, we can see from these cartoons that that logic had not yet taken root. (In fact, we will see in chapter 6 that this prewar ideology regarding the purpose of education continued to hold sway into the 1950s and 1960s.)

This version of idealized masculinity as single-minded devotion to study eschewed heterosexual interaction not merely as a harmful distraction from male students' basic purpose but as a potential threat to the health and integrity of the body politic itself. As Sabine Frühstück has demonstrated, prior to 1945 "the quality of boys' bodies became especially crucial for the strength of the nation," given the increasing importance of military service to masculine subjectivity. Premarital sexual activity was thought to risk all manner of physical and mental ailments, from venereal disease to neurasthenia.[12] In his study of the prewar "number schools," or elite higher schools for boys, Donald Roden illustrates how this concern for instilling properly disciplined forms of masculinity contributed to the construction of an aggressively homosocial space that denigrated women and discouraged young men from expressing any interest whatsoever in the opposite sex: "Students continuously admonished each other on the importance of maintaining an aggressive and unkempt appearance so as not to entice the opposite sex. According to one Ichikō student in 1900, young men who attracted young women by washing their faces and cutting their hair were, in a spiritual sense, 'too dirty to write about.'"[13]

As we will see, the notion of sexual contact between unmarried young men and women as threatening to the integrity of the nation persisted into the postwar period, as Japan relied upon the public sphere efforts of its young men to rebuild the country. In this context, the figure of the female student lurked in the Japanese political unconscious as an impediment to fulfillment of these national goals. In the cartoons examined in this chapter, we insistently see the furor over "moral problems" reflected in looking-glass fashion to reveal its obverse. As we saw in chapter 2, when concerned adults described their reservations about coeducation, they frequently focused on girls as objects of concern—because they were unprepared for the intellectual rigors of the new system, because they supposedly had the most to lose from premarital sexual experimentation, or because the social construction of "femininity" required constant vigilance over one's speech and behavior so as not to be seen as "masculinized."

But the cartoons analyzed in this chapter belie this rhetoric of protection of the feminine, casting male students as victims of their own baser urges and female students as (perhaps unwitting) accomplices in this erosion of vital national human resources. Coeds in these pages are portrayed not as aggressively threatening to usurp male prerogatives but rather as subtly dangerous because their womanly attractions may convince young men to abdicate their scholarly responsibilities in favor of basking in the individualistic pleasures of romance. These young women "ruin the nation" not because of what they do but because of what they are—female bodies in "male" spaces that threaten the moral integrity of those spaces. Consequently, the coeducational classroom is uniformly portrayed in these comics as an eroticized space where the mere proximity of male student bodies to female ones was sufficient to invite moral hazard. Furthermore, these concerns seem to have been remarkably consistent regardless of the age of the young people in question; we see a similar set of anxieties expressed in depictions of elementary school, middle school, high school, and university students.


CONTRIBUTING TO THE DELINQUENCY OF A MINOR

Fears that coeducation would facilitate precocious sexual experimentation were so pervasive that even elementary school students were understood to be vulnerable to the "moral dangers" posed by this system. For example, in a single-panel cartoon by Okada Jun run in the *Yomimono chūgoku*, a regional monthly published in Hiroshima, we see young children preoccupied with the charms of the opposite sex (fig. 1).[14] The panel depicts rows of elemen-

Figure 1. Okada Jun, "Opposed to Coeducation" (Danjo kyōgaku hantai), *Yomimono chūgoku*, October 1949. Courtesy of the Gordon W. Prange Collection, University of Maryland Libraries.

tary school children seated at desks in the foreground of the frame. In the background a teacher stands atop an instructor's platform to the right of the lectern. He is facing the blackboard and has written on it in chalk: "Coeducation: Pro or Con?"[15] There is no caption, but the title of the cartoon—"Opposed to Coeducation"—presumably represents the view of a stout little boy standing at the very back of the room, raising his hand to vote in response to the teacher's question. The children in front of him sit in pairs, one boy and one girl per desk, and are smiling merrily. The boy raising his hand to vote "no" on coeducation is the only one without a partner.

In addition to the obvious joke about coeducation fanning the flames of romance among students, this cartoon seems to parody the common practice of debate as a pedagogical tool in the early postwar classroom. Schools were instructed to employ more "democratic" methods of education that developed children's abilities to think for themselves and express

Figure 2. Shioda Eijirō, "A Model of Coeducation" (Danjo kyōgaku no han), *Hōpu*, August 1946. Courtesy of the Gordon W. Prange Collection, University of Maryland Libraries.

their opinions, and debate was one way teachers complied with that directive. Coeducation too was promoted as a technique for fostering democratic behavior and amicable relations between the sexes. What the cartoon seems to suggest is that such practices lacked substance; rather than learning high-minded democratic values, this boy seems preoccupied primarily with the unfairness of being excluded from the opportunity to flirt with a female classmate.

Another single-panel cartoon in the general-interest magazine *Hōpu*, titled "A Model of Coeducation," offers a twist on this theme of coeducation as a potentially corruptive influence on young children (fig. 2).[16] A young man and woman embrace on a park bench; the man leans in for a kiss. At that moment, a proper-looking matron clad in a tastefully somber kimono passes by with two small children in tow, a little boy and a little girl. The boy points at the couple and says, "Oh, mother, that's our teacher!" Here we have another example of the dangers of exposing children to the immorality that was thought to accompany coeducation, but the cartoon clearly turns this anxiety on its head by suggesting that teachers themselves might serve as a poor influence on their charges. This portrayal also simultaneously undermines the authority and dignity of members of the educational profession. This was typical of the times, given that after defeat in World War II teachers were held responsible for instilling their male

Figure 3. Kogane Haruo, "Amateur Manga Entry: Coeducation" (Honshi ōbō shinjin manga: Danjo kyōgaku), *Shin sekai*, February 1947. Courtesy of the Gordon W. Prange Collection, University of Maryland Libraries.

students with patriotic fervor and motivation to go off to war and fight for the empire. Clearly this author felt that the "model of coeducation" offered by teachers carried little moral authority.

It is interesting that in both cases the child envisioned as most in need of protection from moral corruption is male. In the first instance this dangerous distraction is figured rather innocently as a desire not to be left out of the opportunity to socialize with girls, and in the second it is depicted more ominously as premature exposure to adult sexual hijinks. While the notion that students of this age might themselves engage in such behavior strains credulity, these portrayals are nevertheless revealing of adult fears of moral corruption projected onto the younger generation. In an era when children engaged in role-playing games such as "black market" and "prostitute and client" in imitation of the adult world they observed every day on the streets,[17] parents understandably feared the impact that observing these social dislocations might have on their children. Thus, coeducation became a convenient scapegoat for what they felt was wrong with their nation, so recently brought low by defeat and forcibly "reformed" by a foreign occupying power.

## COEDUCATION IN THE THROES OF PUBERTY

At the middle school and high school levels too we see coeducation portrayed in manga as a dangerous distraction with the potential to threaten the morals of impressionable young men. For example, the Osaka-area publication *Shin Sekai* featured a single-panel cartoon that purported to expose the devious measures boys might employ to capture the attention of the opposite sex (fig. 3).[18] The frame depicts the interior of a typical classroom; the students appear to be of either middle school or high school age, given their clothing and appearance. The reader is positioned from the teacher's point of view; we see him from behind, standing atop the teacher's platform, with a large question mark above his head, observing the students with confusion. Some students are sitting close together in mixed pairs, chatting animatedly and sharing a book; other students sit singly and look on with interest. The caption reads: "Lately there seem to be a lot of boys forgetting their textbooks!"[19] The implication here is that male students are purposely forgetting their books so that they can share with the girls, thus creating the opportunity to get on friendly terms with them. While humorously portrayed, this cartoon nevertheless connotes a degree of anxiety that students' preoccupation with the opposite sex may interfere with attention to their studies.

We see a rather ingenious example of this kind of distraction in the general-interest magazine *Toppu*, where coeducation is parodied as one in a series of "contemporary scenes" (fig. 4).[20] The "scene" here is of a classroom interior, with boys and girls sitting individually at desks arranged in neat rows. No teacher is visible; perhaps this is meant to take place during a break between classes, but the absence of the teacher raises the troubling possibility of boys and girls associating without adult supervision. The reader's perspective is situated toward the back corner of the room, offering a view of the students seated from behind in three-quarter angle. The panel's focus is on a young girl and boy; the girl is sitting in the fourth seat from the front of the room, and the boy occupies the seat in front of her. Taking advantage of the teacher's momentary absence, he lifts up the jacket of his school uniform in full view of the girl. She sits bolt upright, her mouth agape. The caption describes her thoughts: "'He's fidgeting. Oh dear, perhaps he has lice?' Just as her nerves were starting to get to her . . . Ah! Actually, there was writing on his back in clear, bold brushstrokes that said: 'I love you.'"[21]

This cartoon obviously capitalizes on the comedic potential of misun-

現代風景 1

男女共學

植木　敏

もぞもぞしてゐるので、あら、シラミがゐるのぢ
やないかしら？
と、いささか彼女は神經を疲らせてゐましたが、
あゝ、その實體は、
ぼっこんあざやかに
――あなたを愛してゐます――

Figure 4. Ueki Bin, "Contemporary Scene 1: Coeducation" (Gendai fūkei 1: Danjokyōgaku), *Toppu* 1, no. 2 (July 1946). Courtesy of the Gordon W. Prange Collection, University of Maryland Libraries.

derstandings between the sexes. It is revealing that she first thinks his strange behavior is due to lice. This casts a humorous light on the pitiful conditions under which Japanese lived in the early postwar period, but it also may suggest that the girl harbors few romantic ideals toward the opposite sex. In fact, many adults at the time expressed the anxiety that coeducation might make romance impossible by rendering men and women familiar enough with the opposite sex that they no longer cherished romanticized ideals about one another. The girl's attitude is in dramatic contrast to the boy's determination to communicate his feelings to the girl, going so far as to have someone inscribe a love note on his back in beautiful calligraphy.

Here too we see boys as objects of concern, but in contrast to the depictions of elementary school students discussed above, cartoons featuring middle school and high school students portray boys as active agents willing to resort to devious measures to win the attention of their sweethearts. In the first case, the boys conveniently "forgot" their textbooks to create the opportunity to socialize with a member of the opposite sex, allowing baser urges to overcome their passion for academics. In the second case, we see an even more dire spectacle of a young man putting the moves on a female classmate away from the watchful eyes of a responsible adult. Though played here for laughs, both cartoons reveal intense concerns about the possibility of sexual impropriety if adolescent boys and girls were educated together in the same classroom.

## "FORGET SCHOOL—COEDUCATIONAL UNIVERSITIES ARE ALL THE RAGE"

University students too found their way into the pages of manga that poked fun at coeducation. In fact, in the sample of manga consulted for this chapter, the largest number of cartoons depicted coeducation at the university level, as opposed to the elementary, middle, or high school level. This is particularly interesting, given that coeducation at the university level was said to be relatively unproblematic in comparison to the coeducation of adolescents (see chap. 1). However, judging by the fact that all levels of education were represented in this sample of manga, it would seem that coeducation under any circumstances had the potential to create anxiety.

Two cartoons suggest that university students demonstrated a troubling level of enthusiasm for coeducation that was grounded in the desire for heterosexual romance, and here too anxieties about its potential to distract male students from the path of academic excellence take center stage. A single-panel cartoon that appeared in the small independently published collection *Shin manga* illustrates the attitude of university students "Post-Coeducation" (fig. 5).[22] The frame depicts the interior of a family home. An older matronly woman sits on a cushion on the floor, with a young man who

Figure 5. Kobayashi Genzaburō, "Post-Coeducation" (Danjo kyōgaku igo), *Shin manga*, June 1946. Courtesy of the Gordon W. Prange Collection, University of Maryland Libraries.

男女共學
「作近頃熱心
に學校に行く
やうになつたワイ」

若月三郎

Figure 6. Wakatsuki Saburō, "Coeducation" (Danjo kyōgaku), *Sakura*, May 1947. Courtesy of the Gordon W. Prange Collection, University of Maryland Libraries.

is presumably her son sitting opposite her. He is clearly a university student,[23] judging both by his clothing (he wears a school uniform) and by the distinctive student cap and school pennant hanging on the wall next to him. In the background between the two figures we can see what looks like a small desk and lamp, presumably for studying. Above the mother's head is a thought bubble containing another male figure. The caption, "You certainly look more stylish than you used to,"[24] suggests this is a memory of the young man in earlier days. Compared to the student sitting next to her, who is clean-shaven with neatly coiffed wavy hair, the one in her memory does seem a bit scruffy, with what looks like a crew cut and stubble on his face. The implication is clearly that the young man has begun taking more care with his appearance since his school became coeducational, ostensibly for the benefit of his female classmates.

Another single-panel cartoon in the general-interest magazine *Sakura* features a typical neighborhood street scene, with a young man striding toward the foreground of the frame (fig. 6).[25] He wears a student uniform, cap, and glasses and carries a book bag. His body language is dynamic, walking in a long stride with arms akimbo, indicating enthusiasm and perhaps haste.

His face bears a broad grin. He is clearly leaving home for school in the morning and is just rounding the corner of a wooden fence. Standing against the fence on the other side, invisible to his family home but clearly visible to the reader in the foreground of the frame, is a young woman wearing a mortarboard and gown and also carrying a book bag. She smiles broadly at the young man, and her posture indicates pleasure and anticipation at his arrival. Judging by their clothing and accessories, the two figures in the frame are likely university students. The cartoon caption reads: "My son has recently been enthusiastic about going to school."[26] This line is evidently voiced by the young man's father, who watches his son leave, apparently oblivious to the fact that his progeny might have reasons other than passion for academics for going off to school with "enthusiasm." In addition to the aforementioned anxieties about premarital sexual experimentation and dereliction of scholarly duties, this cartoon adds an element of secrecy to the relationship between the two young people. In other words, it illustrates not only the perils of young people besotted with one another to the point of distraction from their schoolwork but also parental fears that their children may be indulging in such liaisons without their knowledge or approval.

It is also significant that these words are expressed by the father of the young man, given that Japan had only recently—and at the insistence of Occupation authorities—invalidated the logic of the patriarchal *ie* system. The Meiji Civil Code of 1898 had given family patriarchs exclusive control and authority over the members of their households, including the power to decide whom children of both sexes would marry.[27] This custom ruled family life in Japan until the new postwar constitution legally abolished the *ie* system and gave both men and women the right to make such decisions for themselves. This new constitution went into effect in May 1947—the very same month that this cartoon was published. It is therefore easy to see this as a veiled critique of both the "new system" of education and the legal structure of democracy and individual rights that underwrote coeducation, both of which are portrayed here as reforms that have effectively undermined the authority of parents (and particularly fathers) in determining the future of their children.

Other cartoons address the "moral problems" that were presumed to accompany coeducation more directly, depicting love affairs between university students as dangerous not merely for their potential to distract from academic work but also because of the threat they posed to the chastity of young people. For example, a single-panel cartoon in the "new family magazine"

Figure 7. Kakimoto Hachirō, "Strange Tales of Coeducation" (Danjo kyōgaku ibun), *Baton*, November 1947. Courtesy of the Gordon W. Prange Collection, University of Maryland Libraries.

*Baton*, titled "Strange Tales of Coeducation" (fig. 7), imagines a student accidentally turning in a love letter in place of a class assignment, implying that the mere fact of young women and men sitting and studying together carried undertones of sexual impropriety.[28]

Another such cartoon that appeared in the general-interest magazine *Repōto* depicts a young man and woman who are already dating, sitting together outside on the grass (fig. 8).[29] Their clothing marks them as students—

Figure 8. Katō Yoshirō, "Coeducation" (Danjo kyōgaku), *Repōto* 3, no. 7 (July 1948). Permission to reproduce this image graciously granted by Jiji Press. Image courtesy of the Gordon W. Prange Collection, University of Maryland Libraries.

particularly the young man, who wears a standard school uniform with cap and glasses, a bundle of textbooks to his side. He has his arm around the young woman, and they gaze adoringly into each other's eyes. They are reading together, each holding one side of a book that bears the English title "Love" in romanized lettering. In the distance is a large structure with a ziggurat-shaped roof that suggests the National Diet building. Two other young couples embracing on the lawn fill in the background in between. The cartoon's caption reads: "Forget school—coeducational universities are all the rage."[30]

In addition to playing on fears of premarital sexual experimentation among youth, this comic also suggests the frequently expressed anxiety that young people educated in coeducational environments will become so preoccupied with relationships with the opposite sex that they will "forget" about their studies. This is reinforced by the pile of textbooks lying disregarded on the grass, with the formerly studious young man—his eyes presumably ruined by years of academic diligence, hence the glasses—now turning his attention in the other direction to focus exclusively on the young woman. The vague evocation of the Diet building in the background suggests dire implications not merely for the morality of the young people involved but also for the nation itself, if its young men are permitted to indulge themselves in excessive preoccupation with romance at the expense of preparation for future leadership of the country. The English-language title of the book they hold leaves no doubt as to the foreign origins of this pernicious influence.

In a similar vein, a four-panel comic strip in *Yomimono kurabu* pokes fun at the brave new world of postwar morality that encourages free socialization between members of the opposite sex. Bearing the title "Coeducational Bridal School" (fig. 9),[31] its panels are labeled from top to bottom as A, B, C, and D. Panel A depicts a classroom scene, with male and female students seated in mixed pairs in the foreground. In the background of the frame, the teacher stands before the chalkboard with his hands planted firmly on the lectern. His eyes boggle, and he wears what looks like a stern expression; he is staring at a young couple embracing and kissing in the front row.

Panel B portrays the teacher escorting the couple down the hallway toward the principal's office. That the young people are taller than the teacher and wear street clothes rather than the school uniforms common to middle school or high school pupils indicates that they are likely university-age students. Panel C shows the teacher whispering into the ear of the principal to report the students' behavior; the principal stands cross-eyed with the palm of one hand flat on the top of the desk, as if he's just slapped it in anger. The young couple stands to the right of the frame with downcast eyes, frowning as if they are ashamed of themselves. In the final panel, D, we see the principal grinning broadly and presenting the couple, who now appear pleased with themselves, with a certificate of achievement that reads: "Graduation with honors."[32] The teacher smiles approvingly in the upper-right corner of the frame.

The humorous conclusion of the strip helps to explain its title. The term "bridal school" (*hanayome gakkō*) refers loosely to the prewar practice of sending young unmarried women to schools or private tutors for instruction in feminine arts such as sewing, etiquette, tea ceremony, flower arranging, and other skills considered necessary preparation for marriage. As Takie Sugiyama Lebra notes, outside of specific skills such as dressmaking, "the general goal was not so much to learn the specific technique of an art as to internalize proper manners and comportment *through* the art."[33] In other words,

Figure 9. Yokoyama Yasuzō, "Co-educational Bridal School" (Danjo kyōgaku no hanayome gakkō), *Yomimono kurabu* 1, no. 1 (July 10, 1946). Courtesy of the Gordon W. Prange Collection, University of Maryland Libraries.

such "training" was as much about reproducing middle-class norms of femininity as it was about instilling mastery of specific domestic skills.

Thus, whereas the term "bridal school" evokes an old-fashioned model of feminine propriety, with intimations of modesty and chastity, the joke here turns on pairing this concept with the new atmosphere of social mixing between the sexes that was encouraged by coeducation. The juxtaposition of the two terms "bridal school" and "coeducation" strikes the reader as jarring—"funny" in the sense of being both humorous and strange—because, at the time, coeducation was widely characterized as a space for transgression of these norms of gender and sexual propriety. Educating both sexes in close physical proximity to one another was presumed to evoke sexual arousal and potentially facilitate premarital sexual experimentation. That this experimentation is seen in the first panel as taking place in full view of one's teacher and classmates only adds to the joke, which invites readers to laugh in spite (or because) of discomfort and anxiety at the way postwar social changes have undermined these prewar norms. In fact, the strip counts on these mixed emotions for its humorous impact. Until the final panel, we are invited to assume that the young couple will be punished for their transgression; only in the last frame is this tension relieved by the smiles and congratulations of the parties involved. In the end, coeducation rewards what had only recently been seen as anathema to good sense and proper morals, infusing this strip with a not-so-subtle undertone of social criticism.

## AND NOW FOR SOMETHING COMPLETELY DIFFERENT

Because the manga discussed above were penned mostly by professional illustrators, it may be assumed that most of these contributors were adults and therefore that these comics reflect the anxieties with which older generations met their children's transition to coeducation.[34] However, one rare example of a student-authored comic hints that young people themselves may have understood these social changes very differently. In contrast to the comics analyzed above, which uniformly depict the coeducational classroom as a state-sanctioned safe space for sexual hijinks thinly disguised as "democratic" education, a single-panel cartoon contributed by a student at the No. 8 Tokyo High School to its night school newsletter suggests that students experienced an entirely different set of anxieties with respect to coeducation.

Figure 10. "Student N.S." (N.S.-sei), "Coeducation Blues" (Danjo kyōgaku no urei), *Tomoshibi*, no. 1 (December 1948). Courtesy of the Gordon W. Prange Collection, University of Maryland Libraries.

Titled "Coeducation Blues" (fig. 10),[35] it depicts a frontal view of two students sitting side by side at a classroom table. The one on the left is female, in typical sailor-suit-style school uniform, with her hair tied back in a ponytail. She is eagerly raising her hand to speak in class. The boy sitting next to her is cringing in shame. This is indicated by the motion lines surrounding his upper body and the fact that he is shrinking down into his seat, his arms covering his head. Because there is no caption, the cartoon invites the reader to decide the cause of the boy's embarrassment. Is it because the teacher has asked a question that the girl can answer but he cannot, or because he finds it embarrassing to sit next to a girl in the first place? Or perhaps he is at a loss as to how to respond to this newly empowered model of postwar femininity,

embodied in the figure of an attractive young girl with the confidence to express herself openly in public.

This cartoon provides an ironic counterpoint to the adult anxieties about
coeducation illustrated above. While these cartoons also depicted male students as objects of concern, these males were nevertheless envisioned as active sexual subjects whose libidos, while dangerous, were understood within
conventional structures of masculinity that envisioned them as aggressive
and dominant. This cartoon, in contrast, subverts that structure of masculinity in several ways. It seems to mock the presumptions of girls as intellectually disadvantaged vis-à-vis boys with this image of active and confident
female class participation, highlighting male students' fears of being shown
up in class by the girls in spite of prevalent stereotypes of masculine intellectual superiority. Furthermore, the figure of the girl physically dominates
that of the boy, whose shrunken posture conveys vulnerability, in dramatic
contrast to the womanizing Lotharios who populate the cartoons authored
by adults above.

What this comic seems to imply more than anything is a sense of masculinity in crisis, in diametric opposition to the fears of aggressive masculine
sexuality represented above, thus suggesting a generation gap in perceptions
of the risks of coeducation. (We will see further evidence of this generation
gap in the next two chapters.) In other words, whereas adults seem to have
been inordinately preoccupied with the possibility of student distraction
and the potential of coeducation to facilitate precocious sexual experimentation, this student-produced cartoon hints not only that many male students may have lacked the confidence to pursue such liaisons but also that
coeducation—at least in its early stages—had the potential to destabilize
conventional structures of masculinity.

CONCLUSION

Rather than fears of the threat posed by coeducation to female chastity, one
gets the impression from these cartoons that their adult authors were primarily concerned with protecting boys from their own potential for distraction by sexual impulses. The figure of the male student appears everywhere
in these depictions, with strikingly consistent iconography—always wearing
the black button-down military-style uniform and cap typical of prewar elite

higher school students and nearly always wearing eyeglasses as emblems of academic diligence. But despite that girls too historically wore school uniforms (not to mention glasses), there seems to be no agreed-upon visual iconography to depict the girl student in these pages. Perhaps this was because her physical presence in such "male spaces" was seen as anomalous, or even threatening, and adopting a stereotyped portrayal of female studenthood would have the unwelcome effect of normalizing that presence. Or perhaps this was because adults were simply more preoccupied with the figure of the male student, upon whose shoulders the fate of the nation was thought to rest. As we will see in chapter 6, these concerns would become even more pronounced once female university students became more of a demographic force in the following decades, when mass and "small media" alike were rife with claims of "coeds ruining the nation" by taking coveted placements at elite universities away from prospective male students.

Though the ostensible purpose of manga is to entertain, in this chapter we have seen that cartoons may also have helped to "*media*te" the anxieties provoked by coeducation. On one level, these visual narratives of coeducation likely provided a safe space for adults in particular to process their anxieties through laughter, thus mitigating the threat to the established order that coeducation was feared to represent. But on another level, they may also have allowed the public to indirectly criticize the Occupation government's promotion of coeducation as a means of instilling values of democracy and equality of the sexes. While there appears to have been little effort by Occupation censors to prevent criticism of coeducation from being published, we cannot discount the impact of self-censorship in shaping the form and content of expressions of such concerns. By portraying coeducation as a dangerous distraction, rather than a useful pedagogical tool, these cartoonists seem to have channeled a complex mix of emotional responses to Occupation reforms that they may have hesitated to express in a more direct fashion in public discourse.

At the same time, the contrast between cartoon depictions of coeducation by adults and the student perspective discussed above hints at a generation gap in the understanding of the possibilities and pitfalls of coeducation. In the next chapter, we will see this illustrated dramatically in essays penned by student authors and published in newsletters created by and for a student audience. While these student authors discuss many of the same areas of concern as their elders—the academic gap between boys and girls, "moral problems," and "androgyny"—they often voice very different opinions about their significance for the brave new world of postwar coeducation. In these student testimonies, we see the beginnings of an attempt to reconcile the mixed messages given to young people about norms of gender and sexuality toward a new postwar order that combined prewar ideals of gender difference with Occupation-era values of "equality of opportunity."

# CHAPTER 4

## *"Separate but Equal"*

### Negotiating the Meaning of "Equality" within Gender Difference

*Coeducation*

We take our seats amiably
The charm of coeducation: one another's strong and weak points
"I'll mend your torn sleeve."
Math for me, vocational education for you
My mother thinks coeducation is dangerous
"Soft words win hard hearts." Learning together,
The boys are persuaded to give up their side dishes
Even the teacher is amazed at how well we get along[1]
"Senryūshi Tōrō," March 1948

THIS BRIEF ODE to coeducation, penned by a male middle school student toward the end of his first year of experience with it, encapsulates much of the emotional complexity surrounding these first encounters between boys and girls who had previously been sheltered from one another in single-sex environments. Though coeducation is portrayed here in a somewhat romanticized light, the fifth line of the poem hints at the "moral problems" that many adults feared might accompany this new system. Parents in particular fretted about the possibility of precocious sexual experimentation. Indeed, the poem depicts adolescent boys as responsive enough to the charms of the opposite sex to give up a portion of their own lunches—a remarkable gesture at a time of horrific privation when many Japanese struggled to feed themselves.

There are intimations of other problems as well in this short poem. Prior to coeducation, girls had been relegated to a less intellectually rigorous and highly gender-specific form of education that stressed mastery of domestic skills. Thus, they were at a distinct disadvantage once the two groups were mainstreamed into the same classroom and taught according to a curriculum that played to the superior academic preparation of the boys. The poem alludes to this gender-specific training in the third line, where "I" is rendered with a pronoun that is distinctively feminine (*atai*), suggesting a young lady who paid careful attention in sewing class and has internalized the expected behavioral traits and accomplishments of her sex. It is hard not to detect a note of approval—even relief—on the part of the author when faced with this display of appropriately feminine deportment, especially given prevalent fears that coeducation would promote transgression of gender norms. Instead, we are presented here with a rather idealized and harmonious vision of gender complementarity wherein boys and girls can appreciate one another's "strong and weak points" and supply those qualities that are lacking in the opposite sex.

This poem appeared in the first issue of "School Friends" (*Kōyū*), a publication of the "friendship society" (*kōyūkai*) of Kitaadachi-gun middle school in Fukiage, Saitama prefecture, just north of the Tokyo metropolitan area. In the early postwar years, as the Occupation regime reorganized the Japanese school system and promoted coeducation as a means of instilling democratic ideals in young people, there was an explosion of "small media"[2]—newsletters, magazines, and journals published by amateur writers. Schools seem to have embraced this trend enthusiastically; even middle schools and high schools in tiny rural hamlets often put out the occasional newsletter written by and for students, just as students today in the United States join journalism clubs to produce a school newspaper or yearbook.

This chapter is devoted to a close reading of first-person student accounts of coeducation that were published in these student-produced school and youth association newsletters. Specifically, I am interested in what these accounts reveal about underlying gender and sexual norms at the moment when prewar assumptions of "correctly" gendered behavior collided with the postwar rhetoric of democracy and equality of the sexes. This generation of students encountered these social transformations at a sensitive age, when their social and sexual personas were still under construction, so they were both shaped by the prewar system of sex segregation and yet still adaptable to postwar changes. They thus embody all the promises and pitfalls of the

Occupation effort to remake Japanese society in the immediate postwar period. In this sense, the coeducational classroom may be seen as a microcosm of early postwar Japan, pulsating with relief at the end of the war, excitement and optimism at the new opportunities that lie ahead, and a heady dose of anxiety at the social changes being imposed from on high.

As noted in chapter 1, prior to the modern period women had been thought to be intellectually inferior to men, thus "naturally" justifying separate spheres for men and women in premodern Confucian hierarchies. This way of thinking was mitigated, but not eradicated, by efforts in the late 1800s to construct a place in a newly modernized Japanese society for "good wives and wise mothers," whose contributions to the private sphere were (in theory) of equal value to the contributions of men in public space. However, women were still presumed incompetent to manage their own affairs, and women's subordination to men was reinforced through laws such as the Meiji Civil Code (discussed in chap. 3) and Article 5 of the Public Peace Police Law of 1900, which excluded women from political activities. Thus, there was an inherent tension prior to 1945 within discourses of gender that sought to value women's social roles while restricting their activities to the domestic sphere, or at the very least rationalizing their activities outside the home through their roles as nurturing wives and mothers.

The Occupation attempted to alter this way of thinking by promoting a type of equality that was predicated on a logic of the same—granting women the same political rights as men (dōken) based on the understanding that they had the same level of innate ability to make judicious decisions. This conflicted with the prewar presumption of separate spheres for men and women, even given the expanded roles for women outside the home permitted by the gradual reformulations of good wife, wise mother discourse discussed in chapter 1. Young people were better able to navigate this conflict than their elders, and in the first-person student narratives that follow, we see them trying to reconcile these two discourses through incorporation into a newly reformulated logic of gender complementarity that differed in important ways from its prewar predecessor. This new understanding of gender role distinctions accepted the prewar ethos of separate spheres for men and women but sought to fuse it with the recent recognition of coeducation as a means to ensure "equality of opportunity," which was now defined as an important goal of postwar democracy.

However, defending coeducation required young people to grapple with the commonplace objections their elders often cited as reasons why the practice was impossible or unwise. As noted in chapter 2, adults who expressed reservations about coeducation almost invariably cited one of three concerns: the difficulty of implementing it, given the inferior academic abilities of girls; the potential for moral problems (a euphemism for precocious sexual experimentation) if girls and boys were placed side by side in the same classroom; and concern that it might provide a space for transgression of gender norms. Frequently expressed with the shorthand term "androgyny," this last concern implied that girls might become "masculinized" and boys "feminized" by spending too much time in the company of the opposite sex.

Student supporters of coeducation thus had to confront these objections through rebuttal, whereas the minority of students who opposed coeducation tended to raise the same objections as their elders. However, what is most interesting about these student narratives is that regardless of the position students took on coeducation—pro or con—they tended to articulate their views according to the same basic logic. Like the older generation, many of these students took it for granted that there were innate differences between the sexes, regardless of their position on coeducation. However, unlike their elders, they were more likely to understand these differences in terms of men's and women's social roles rather than inherent intellectual abilities. Thus, most young people tended to see men and women as equally capable in intellectual terms, but they also agreed with the older generation that these talents could and should be channeled into gender-specific contributions to society that showcased the unique qualities of each sex.

Most young people also disagreed with parents and teachers who fretted that implementing coeducation would open the door to moral problems, meaning transgression of gender and sexual norms. The younger generation tended either to deny this was the case or to emphasize the benefits of coeducation in promoting harmonious cooperation between the sexes rather than its pernicious social consequences. This resulted in an understanding of equality based on complementarity between the sexes, according to a "separate but equal" logic that supported coeducation but incorporated many of the philosophical presumptions that underlined the prewar sex-segregated educational system.

In this chapter, we will first review how students engaged with these discourses through a close reading of arguments presented both for and against coeducation by students. Specifically, we will look at the reasons they offered for the academic gap between boys and girls and the degree to which they acknowledged the presence of moral problems or androgyny in the coeducational classroom, along with their understanding of the causes and consequences of such problems. We will then see how these arguments formed the basis of students' understanding of equality between men and women, ultimately yielding the kind of separate but equal discourse that sought to suture the gap between past and present.

## A NOTE ON THE PRIMARY SOURCES

Though not all students took as rosy a view of coeducation as our poet quoted in the epigraph above, and a few actively resented the change, most young people seem to have met the introduction of coeducation with relative equanimity. The files analyzed for this chapter were located through a subject search of all Prange Collection materials using the keyword *danjo kyōgaku* (coeducation). Of the 406 entries that resulted, 37 of these were single-author essays penned by students and published in student newsletters from across the Japanese archipelago. Out of these 37 accounts, just 7 writers clearly objected to coeducation, whereas 23 were clearly in favor of it and 7 others were ambivalent or did not express a preference. The majority of these authors were high school students, the age parents and teachers considered to be most problematic for coeducation.[3] While boys were more likely to express opposition to coeducation—6 out of the 7 writers who were opposed were male writers, along with 4 of the 7 who expressed ambivalence—they also were more likely to express their opinions in the first place and to sign their names to the articles they contributed for publication.[4] This imbalance is not terribly surprising, given that prewar girls' education stressed inculcation of "traditional" virtues such as docility, chastity, and modesty—repertoires of femininity that would have precluded public speech and frequently even private expression of one's true feelings or opinions.

The path to coeducation was not uniformly smooth. In fact, even its staunchest student advocates noted problems that accompanied the transition. These included cultural clashes between gender-specific modes of communication and behavior and a general sense of awkwardness—particularly in the first few weeks or months, when the mere fact of sitting side by side in class conjured up feelings of intense embarrassment and chagrin. Yet it is striking how often these narratives concluded on a note of affirmation of the value of coeducation, frequently accompanied by an exhortation to one's fellow students to work harder to overcome their differences.

It is not uncommon to see these sentiments articulated through the new and still relatively unfamiliar postwar buzzwords—"democracy" (*minshushugi*), "equal rights for men and women" (*danjo dōken*), and "equality of the sexes" (*danjo byōdō*)—that adults too struggled to understand in the early days of the postwar constitution. It is difficult not to see the imprint of Occupation rhetoric upon these narratives, many of which excoriate the various sources of Japanese "tradition"—Confucianism and Buddhism especially—in favor of a more enlightened and "natural" set of democratic values that were insistently promoted by SCAP personnel at this time. The school system was certainly one important vehicle for disseminating these values, and it is certain that these students were exposed to Occupation propaganda. However, it would be a mistake to assume they were merely brainwashed by the new orthodoxy into touting these values themselves. This would imply that there was no room for disagreement with the new system of coeducation, but in fact, as we will see below, there was often criticism of the practice as well. Archival evidence indicates that Occupation censors tolerated most criticism of coeducation, in mass and small media, in the name of promoting the right to free speech.[5]

These student newsletters therefore provide an invaluable window into what students were thinking about coeducation at the moment of its introduction. Many of these publications were written and illustrated by hand and reproduced through mimeograph or some other rudimentary duplication technology in small press runs on low-quality paper. In the pages of these early postwar newsletters, some of which are now crumbling with age, we witness a remarkably frank and diverse array of viewpoints on the pros and cons of coeducation, the difficulties that attended its adoption, and the personal transformations experienced by students who were its object. We also see heartfelt and often touching declarations of discovery—of the mysteries of the opposite sex, of the writer's own understanding of his or her place in the world, and of the personal responsibility many of these young writers felt for shaping the contours of a newly peaceful and democratic Japan.

OVERCOMING THE ACADEMIC GAP

Given the obvious and intentional difference in rigor between the educational experiences of girls and boys under the prewar school system, few doubted that girls were less well prepared than boys for the academic challenges of the new system of postwar education. But according to opinion pieces published by students themselves as coeducation was implemented in the late 1940s, most also understood these differences to have been products of this history of gender-specific training rather than any innate differences in intellectual ability between the sexes. There were some differences of opinion regarding what should be done about this legacy of sexual discrimination. While a few student commentators found the academic gap between boys and girls to be so crippling as to make coeducation impossible or inadvisable, echoing the concerns of their elders, most took the opposite tack, arguing that it was a problem that could and should be overcome as part of Japan's democratic transformation.

Criticisms of coeducation highlighted this academic gap between boys and girls as a fatal flaw that would make the practice unworkable, given Japan's prewar history of sex-segregated education. One young man from Mie prefecture (southeast of Kyoto), who was in his third year of normal school at the time of writing, highlighted the problems instructors would likely face in managing classrooms where boys and girls had very different levels of academic knowledge. While he acknowledged that this was the fault of the prewar educational system rather than the result of innate differences between men and women, he nevertheless suggested that equality might be more easily fostered within a sex-segregated educational structure.[6] A few of these commentators also hinted that innate differences between the sexes might play a role in girls' inferior performance in the classroom. A young man from Iwate prefecture, in northeastern Japan, opposed coeducation for "reasons related to psychology and to differences in academic ability [*gakuryoku*]" between the sexes.[7] Like the normal school student referenced above, he likewise noted the problems that teachers would likely experience in pitching lessons to mixed-sex classes, given that the girls were at least a semester behind the boys in subjects like science and foreign languages. A third young man from Hiroshima prefecture, in southwestern Japan, seemed to deny the notion of equality of the sexes altogether, in flagrant opposition to Occupation propaganda: "I think that women's ability to think is inferior to that of men and they lack the ability to assert themselves; in other words, they're vague. So even if you attempt to implement coeducation and equal rights, it's meaningless."[8]

However, most students seem to have approved of the practice, even as they acknowledged the problems that accompanied its implementation. An essay by a first-year female student at Kurogi High School in Fukuoka prefecture, on the southwestern island of Kyūshū, provides a fascinating glimpse into students' attempts to reconcile the practical problems with coeducation against the new postwar rhetoric of democracy and equal educational opportunity.[9] This school had just been converted from a vocational institution for girls to a prefectural coeducational high school seven months prior to the time of writing. The essay demonstrates the rapidity with which young people adjusted to the new coeducational atmosphere, going from awkward silence to active debate over democratic principles in just a little over six months:

> With the fragrant breezes of spring, our Kurogi Girls' High School made a fresh start as one of two prefectural coeducational high schools. When school first started, we weren't used to it so the classroom was filled with a heavy atmosphere that just wouldn't go away. But with the passage of time, that disagreeable atmosphere too naturally dissipated. At first the boys always seemed [self-]conscious about talking to girls, but now it doesn't seem that way anymore.
>
> Also, during class, in contrast to the lively class atmosphere that I had been expecting beforehand, everyone seemed to be holding themselves back, and there were few students who spoke out or asked questions. But now there isn't the slightest indication of this. Since school has become coeducational, everyone studies hard and there's a more spirited tone to our studies than when we were just a girls' school. Social studies is the most interesting. Recently we discussed democracy. The girls' and boys' opinions about this conflicted.
>
> Until now girls' intelligence has been low and their abilities have been inferior to those of boys in many ways, so society has treated girls in an extremely discriminatory fashion. However, I don't think girls are naturally inferior to boys. Therefore, through many such discussions we can express our own opinions honestly and see girls' intelligence level rise. In this sense I think coeducation is beneficial.
>
> My biggest worry about coeducation was that until now there has been an enormous difference in the contents of education for boys and girls, so I wondered what would happen. However, now that we've become coeducational, there isn't much difference. In matters like math and common knowledge, the boys are progressing a bit faster. [But] in terms of self-government activities, those who were conservative during their years at girls' school have become more lively.[10]

From this essay, it is clear that girls had to work harder to surmount the handicap placed upon them by the prewar educational system—particularly in math and science, as evidenced by the description of boys progressing faster in these subject areas. However, it is striking how quickly girls were able to adapt to the postwar expectation that they too should not only have opinions regarding current events but also be prepared to defend those opinions, even if it meant arguing with the boys. The essay conveys a clear sense of optimism that although girls may have started the new system a few steps behind, they were nevertheless equal in terms of innate potential and could overcome their deficiencies with time, effort, and practice.

Another essay in the same vein by a girl from Saga prefecture (Kyūshū), in her third year of middle school, suggests that the mixed-sex environment of the coeducational classroom may itself have been instrumental in helping the girls catch up to the boys academically. In a critique that was evidently penned after completion of a mixed-sex group research project, she writes:

Coeducation is a fundamental characteristic of democracy, to the point that it was the first thing intoned when we began the new system of education. In our country, the belief that "boys and girls should not sit together after the age of seven" has been handed down since olden times. Just sitting together would be one thing, but the restriction even went so far as to forbid [boys from] speaking to girls.

. . . In our country today, according to conventional custom, the course of study in girls' schools was of a lower level than that of middle schools [for boys], and third-year students who until last year had been [educated separately] in middle schools and girls' schools now are suddenly together, so you can't say there's no difference in academic ability. But on the whole, mentally, and particularly in terms of general ability to study, there is no difference. It's a fact that in social life men and women must respect and cooperate with one another. Lately mixed groups of boys and girls studying together have flourished.

Reflecting on these experiences, the following are good points [of studying together]:

1. One person was able to explain something difficult to the group using pictures so that we could understand well, which was wonderful.
2. We cooperated well in groups and completed a number of research

surveys, and all six of us became able to explain [the results] well, which was lovely.

3. Mixed together with the boys, we girls always worked diligently, which is the true form of coeducation.
4. Boys and girls became able to exchange opinions and cooperate together to do research.[11]

She begins by placing blame for the academic gap between boys and girls squarely on the prewar educational system and, like the high school girl quoted above, emphasizes that this difference is a product of nurture rather than nature. She then credits the coeducational class structure not only for promoting cooperation and frank communication between the sexes but for motivating the girls to work harder and learn from the superior academic preparation of the boys. She subsequently includes a list of "bad points" of this group project, including the potential for quarrelsome or irresponsible behavior, inattentiveness or interruptions during individual presentations of research findings, and confusing or disorganized presentation styles. However, what is most interesting about this list is that none of these complaints seem directly related to the experience of coeducation per se. Rather, they are more likely attributable to the immaturity of the participants themselves or to the kind of individual personality quirks that might equally plague single-sex work groups at this age. On the other hand, many of the "good points" listed above appear to derive directly from the mixed-sex educational experience itself, indicating academic as well as social benefits of coeducation.

There were also many boys of middle school and high school age who wrote approvingly of coeducation, citing the need to bring the educational level of women up to that of men as an important step toward the development of a democratic society. Here too coeducation is seen as a solution to the problem of gender inequality, with the boys making many of the same arguments for the practice as those in narratives penned by female students. For example, a male student from a prestigious high school in Beppu, Ōita prefecture (Kyūshū), writes:

Since the end of the war, the vigorous tide of American liberalism [jiyūshugi] has washed against this country, completely wiping out Japanese feudalism, planting the flag of equal rights for the sexes [danjo dōken], and becoming a raging wave that presses upon us from the other side of the Pacific, attempting to return our country to the natural state of equality between men and women [*danjo byōdō*]. These days it seems all too natural that at our school too, [formerly] a tightly locked moss-covered ivory tower, the bell of liberty peals loudly and the signal fires of coeducation blaze high into the air. Because of the influence of Confucian thought, our country has continued the extreme practice of sex-segregated education [*bunri kyōiku*] that says "Boys and girls should not sit together after the age of seven." This way of thinking is completely passive and conservative, and this enervated and unrealistic system of education truly deserves the name "evil custom."

. . . After the war women were given the right to vote. This is truly a fortunate occurrence. But why is it that not a few members of the intelligentsia opposed it, saying it was "too soon"? It was because they said that "the intellectual level of women is so inferior." Through coeducation, women will have the same academic opportunities as men. Women must put forth extraordinary effort to earn true equality with men. Also, conservative men must refuse to think of women pursuing academics as heretical and abhorrent.[12]

In this essay, equality between the sexes is envisioned as a "natural state" and a place of "return" rather than a foreign value that is imposed upon Japan by outside forces. The old Confucian adage forbidding girls and boys from sitting together after the age of seven is quoted to refute its logic as antiquated and "extreme," an "evil custom" that must be abolished. Coeducation here is described as a solution to the problem of gender inequality in general, as well as the more specific problem of women's inferior intellectual preparation when compared with men. Importantly, he emphasizes that both sexes bear responsibility for the transformations that lie ahead, noting that while women must work hard to live up to the expectations placed upon them by democracy, men must also change their way of thinking to accept and appreciate the contributions of the women.

Another young man, writing in the same publication, echoes this view, criticizing the structure of prewar Japanese society for artificially suppressing the intellectual abilities and "self-awareness" of women:

From ancient times, in every country men have performed work outside of the home and women have performed work inside; that is, domestic labor. Consequently, the sexes were equal [*dōtō*] in terms of the value of their work, and therefore they should have been equal [*byōdō*] in the sense of having equal rights [*dōken*]. So why is it that male chauvinism [*danson johi*] was born?

This is the result of the legacy of Buddhist thought, whereby women were gradually oppressed by men, so that in the end men became the active parties and women became passive. Then, in terms of ability, women were thought of as ignorant, incapable, and powerless, dependent upon men and required to obey them absolutely. Furthermore, men demanded that women do as they wished, and obedience and chastity became the highest virtues for women. However, was this chastity and obedience truly the product of self-awareness on the part of the women of our country? Wasn't their chastity and obedience simply mechanical, like that of a doll? Thus, we must make men and women equal [*danjo dōtō ni*] in all things by making women self-aware. In order to do that, we must first raise women's educational level to that of men. The current educational system is inadequate to that purpose. We must have men and women study together, bringing women's intellectual level close to that of men, giving them the same kind of [*dōyō*] intellectual ability and life skills as men so that they achieve the same status in society as men."[13]

Here too "tradition" is taken to task for enforcing an artificial separation between the sexes that is understood as debilitating both to the individual and to society, rendering women "mechanical dolls" who are incapable of contributing productively to society on par with men. This is described as aberrant and disruptive to the "natural" workings of democratic principles that date back to the agrarian roots of "ancient times," when men and women are presumed to have been equal "in terms of the value of their work." Once again, coeducation is envisioned as a positive step toward "bringing women's intellectual level close to that of men."

We have seen in this section that most students wrote approvingly of coeducation, even as they acknowledged potential problems with the practice—in particular, the gap in academic preparation between men and women that resulted from the prewar sex-segregated system of education. While a few students disagreed with the desirability of coeducation and echoed the concerns of their elders as discussed in chapter 2, these dissentions only seem to illustrate that in spite of Occupation-era censorship, students were relatively free to express those views. In the next section, we will see what students had to say regarding another common concern about coeducation during its early years of implementation—the potential for moral problems so feared by their elders. Here too we will see that students were generally both less concerned about the severity of this problem and more positive than their parents' generation about the potential of coeducation to overcome any such problems.

## THE MYTH OF MORAL PROBLEMS

Adults, accustomed to a tradition of sex-segregated education, were particularly concerned about the potential for moral problems if coeducation were implemented. To this older generation, the coeducational classroom seemed an eroticized and perilous space of certain moral turpitude. But while student narratives also mention the issue of moral problems, more often than not it is with the purpose of refuting their parents' concerns on this point.[14] Almost without exception, students either denied the existence of these problems in the first place or else suggested that any such problems were more likely the result of the chaotic postwar situation than a response to coeducation. While they did agree that boys and girls needed to be better educated about the opposite sex, they were more likely to see coeducation as providing a safe opportunity to attain this knowledge in a supervised context.

Several students directly challenged the presumption of their elders that coeducation would lead to moral problems. For example, in an essay emphatically titled "This Female Student Is Strongly in Favor of Coeducation!" one young woman from Hiroshima prefecture rather pointedly refuted the notion that the practice would invite moral corruption:

> With regard to moral problems, so long as men behave responsibly there shouldn't be any. Isn't it true that the more they sense their own level of responsibility, the more prudently they would have to behave? At any rate, it seems that arguments against coeducation are based on nothing more than needless suspicion that resembles defeatism. Not just with regard to coeducation, but in general when something new is introduced it is certain that people will raise arguments against it that it's too soon. Then there will be no progress. The real question is how the pluses compare to the minuses. If the pluses outweigh the minuses, we should bravely implement it. This is my view. Parents, please consider it![15]

The exhortation to men to behave responsibly here suggests that young women felt more entitled by the postwar emphasis on democracy and equality to challenge male treatment of women as sexual objects. It also presages the rise of the "purity education" movement, which advocated chastity for both sexes until marriage (see chap. 6). This young woman also seems to implicitly chastise her elders for resisting "progress" simply out of fear of the unknown, concluding with a remarkably direct exhortation to parents in particular to change their outmoded way of thinking about relations between the sexes.

Other students countered their elders' fears with arguments that coeducation would actually help prevent moral problems by promoting better understanding of and communication with the opposite sex, thus helping students to develop positive patterns of interaction that stressed friendship over romantic encounters. While protesting the tendency of the older generation to embarrass their children by treating coeducation as scandalous fodder for gossip, one female high school student from Yamaguchi prefecture (in southwestern Japan) emphasized the benefits of the practice in fostering good relationships between the sexes. She noted that coeducation was difficult for students at first too, but although "at first it felt awkward, as though oil were mixed with water," now they have "become able to display the true value of coeducation":

> Isolated from one another, we found [the opposite sex] to be mysterious and as a result had the tendency to overestimate or underestimate one another, and could not understand one another however much we wanted to. But it goes without saying that once those barriers were removed this tendency gradually lessened. While learning together and enjoying sports activities, the clear consciousness that we've had of one another as members of the opposite sex has correspondingly decreased.[16]

This student does not deny the difficulties students experienced in adjusting to the coeducational classroom. However, she portrays these problems as a minor and temporary inconvenience that pales in comparison to the benefits, primarily measured in terms of better communication and understanding between the sexes, that accrue to students who persevere in "display[ing] the true value of coeducation."

This benefit of coeducation was also echoed by a third-year male high school student from Hiroshima prefecture:

> Young people, who are [by nature] very sensitive, learn just as much from their fellow students as they do from their teachers. I think that the most important element of academic life is the friendship that grows among students in the

course of study and informal conversation. I think it is premature to decide that friendship among members of the opposite sex is the first step toward love.

Generally speaking, under coeducation it is natural to have friends of the opposite sex; in fact it would be meaningless not to have such friendships. It would be unfeeling and crude to think that friendship for the opposite sex necessarily leads to love. I would like to think that there is depth and breadth in friendships appropriate to students of the new age, and that likewise there are heights and depths in love. I would also like for us to advance the ethics of love along with the age.[17]

This author hints at a profound generational gap in values and philosophy between adults and children that arose from Occupation-era reforms. Raised in a strictly sex-segregated society where any interaction between unrelated members of the opposite sex was likely to promote gossip, parents of children who first experienced the postwar coeducational system evidently found the notion of strictly platonic friendship between boys and girls to be incomprehensible and highly suspect. Their children, on the other hand, were increasingly inclined to build relationships based on equality of the sexes that were not primarily driven by erotic impulses. Though it was unclear to many what this might actually mean in practice, the goal was evidently widely (though not universally) shared among members of this younger generation.

Another male high school student from Kyūshū takes this logic even further, emphasizing the moral problems implicit in the prewar sex-segregated method of educating young people:

Can one really prevent the dangers thought to accompany relations between young men and women by simply taking a firm stance against any kind of interaction between them and segregating and isolating them from one another? Let's say that you throw young people with no prior knowledge of one another and no sex education into the real world of freedom between the sexes beyond the halls of campus. In such a case, can you really expect correct relationships between members of the opposite sex who have suddenly been confronted with one another? It's doubtful. Therefore, there should be sex education from an early age and young people should be endowed with enough understanding of one another. Grave mistakes are unlikely when they understand one another completely.[18]

According to this logic, coeducation is understood as the solution to, rather than the cause of, the moral problems feared by parents and educators.

The persuasiveness of this logic was apparently evident even to some of the few students who opposed coeducation in principle. For example, one male high school student from Nagasaki, in the course of substantiating his argument against the practice, nevertheless located the source of the moral problems currently experienced by Japanese society in the debased postwar landscape rather than in the coeducational classroom:

> The town is overflowing with street urchins, foul and unscrupulous things occur in society, and these surging waves of defeat have even encroached upon our school grounds—some run wild with dissipation, some indulge themselves in luxuries and pleasure, while others' eyes grow bloodshot in the attempt to provide for their livelihoods each day and they quit school broken by the struggle for survival, or become twisted and desperate from the war. The current conditions of society present us with many problems; people's hearts are greatly preoccupied with the struggle for food, clothing, and shelter, and rent by confusion, they increasingly become disorderly and commit evil deeds. Thus we break with the ancient customs of our country and have even developed to the point where we have combined our local middle school, commercial school, and girls' school into one and made it coeducational.[19]

Here the student alludes to the spirit of "decadence" that was widely believed to plague the landscape of postwar Japan, suddenly released from the vise-like grip of wartime authoritarianism and adrift amid prevailing social problems of widespread hunger, unemployment, and crime. Having cast off the social controls of prewar Japan and uncertain how to put the brave new postwar ideal of democracy into practice, he sees his native land as "rent by confusion" and prone to the commission of "evil deeds." Because he blames these larger social ills for the "dissipation" of his fellow youth, he seems to suggest that coeducation is an unfortunate result of these moral problems rather than its cause—the inevitable result of "break[ing] with the ancient customs of our country." In other words, that society has pursued this unfortunate course of breaking with the past to integrate high school classrooms is (for him) but one of many symptoms of the moral degradation of postwar Japanese society, which is ultimately caused not by coeducation but by the societal chaos brought about by Japan's defeat. Many supporters of coeducation also cited postwar social disruptions, rather than coeducation, as a cause of prevalent moral problems.

As we have seen in this section, young people had a very different appreciation of the nature and causes of postwar moral problems than their elders did. Furthermore, many students seem to have resented the prurient interest taken by the older generation in the sexual politics of coeducation, and some even directly challenged the notion of the coeducational classroom as an eroticized space that preoccupied the minds of their parents and teachers. Thus, the furor over moral problems in the coeducational classroom— understood as parents' concerns that coeducation would facilitate premarital sexual experimentation among adolescents—illustrates a clear generation gap in perception between parents and their children. On the other hand, we will see in the following section that students and parents were generally united in expressing concerns that androgyny might result from coeducation, illustrating a desire to shore up "innate" differences between the sexes even in the minds of the younger generation.

## "ANDROGYNY IS NOT DESIRABLE EVEN IN HELL"

As students sought to reconcile discourses of equality with expectations of different life courses for men and women, they also expressed a substantial preoccupation with the preservation of what they saw as fundamental and innate differences between the sexes. Both supporters and opponents of coeducation were often acutely interested in maintaining societally sanctioned and normative expressions of gender through everyday behavioral repertoires. Opponents of coeducation invariably sought to discredit it by claiming that it promoted androgyny—that is, the erasure or mitigation of normative performances of gender—whereas proponents of coeducation typically denied that it had this effect.

While opponents of coeducation were decidedly in the minority among the young writers examined here, we find members of both sexes in this camp. For example, one male high school student from Nagasaki opposed coeducation on the grounds that it "feminized" male students:

Coeducation should make boys more masculine through contact with girls but the result of it is that they become more like girls. . . . [As a result of this influence] we students become extravagant [in our behavior], and our forthright and stalwart character as students with passion for learning is compromised, our spirits become animated, and we cast aside the studies that are our primary duty as students in order to live frivolously. Can the present conditions be good for any [man] who would perfect his studies?[20]

It is important to note here that education is described as an implicitly masculine pursuit. The "we students" of the second sentence are clearly young men like the speaker who are distracted from the "stalwart" pursuit of academic excellence by the corrosive influence of "frivolous" female classmates. This remark evokes the fears implicit in caricatures of coeducation drawn by adults (see chap. 3). But while adults tended to portray boys as distracted by the pursuit of romance, this young man seems to view masculinity as vulnerable to destabilization by coeducation, suggesting that femininity is a sort of contagion that robs his fellows of the desire to study. This sense of masculinity in crisis echoes the perspective of the student cartoonist discussed at the end of chapter 3.

A female student from Tokyo, in her second year of middle school, makes similar claims that members of her own sex have been unfortunately influenced through close contact with male students:

Since the war the equality of men and women has been proclaimed, and as part of that we began to practice coeducation. When that happened, the first thing I experienced was the violence of boys. Even when we try to get along with the boys, they immediately try to avoid us. They also deliberately oppose even our good ideas. Perhaps this is a sign that the militarism of the past still remains in some form. For the girls, there have been no good results of coeducation. In general girls have lost their femininity in the face of the boys' violence. It's deplorable.[21]

It is difficult to know what the speaker is referencing here with the word "violence" (*bōryoku*). While girls during the early years of coeducation commonly leveled such accusations at boys, this term seems to have covered a wide range of speech and behavior, from blunt or rude language all the way up to actual physical violence such as hitting and kicking one another (see chap. 5). Such remarks were often accompanied by complaints of girls being "influenced" by such male behavior—meaning anything from lashing out physically to merely failing to use the polite and deferential speech expected of girls (but not boys) at this time. But at the very least, it is clear that the speaker feels that coeducation has resulted in a dangerous form of mutual influence between the sexes.

However, most student pioneers of coeducation seem to have embraced the opposite perspective, arguing that coeducation promotes harmony and mutual understanding among boys and girls and therefore promises to contribute productively to the development of a democratic Japanese society. This is the case for a male high school student from Kyūshū, who argues that coeducation actually reinforces "correct" displays of gendered behavior that contribute to a harmonious complementarity of the sexes:

> The advantage of coeducation is that it impedes the extreme expression of the special characteristics of each sex and allows for the perfection of true manhood and womanhood. Conventional masculinity was generally understood to mean valor and this was apt to result in a perverted course of development whereby barbarous and violent behavior was seen as heroic. For women, too, gentleness and chastity were said to be good, but this developed into hesitation and vacillation and this has impeded our ability to develop societal and public interests. Without a doubt, men and women can help one another to polish these special qualities so that they develop correctly and so that both sexes can mature smoothly. Stanley Hall's[22] fear that "coeducation promotes a decline in masculine men and feminine women" is extremely pessimistic. It is being amid members of the opposite sex that awakens one to one's own gender/sex [sei] and makes one feel responsible for it, so I think his fears are unfounded.[23]

In contrast to the concern expressed above that "mutual influence" might have pernicious consequences, this commentator actually argues the opposite—that boys and girls will encourage one another to "perfect" and "polish" their expression of appropriately gendered identities. It is as if gender is envisioned as a kind of *kata*, or form, that can and must be mastered through continual practice and reinforcement, in contrast with its natural opposite. This mastery of repertoires of gender seems critical to this student's understanding of "smooth" maturation into adulthood, which is facilitated rather than disrupted by coeducation.

But even some students who fundamentally supported coeducation registered concerns about its potential to provide a space for transgression of normatively gendered behaviors. For example, a male high school student from Hiroshima prefecture provided this opinion on how coeducation might be made most effective:

> The first step for the sexes to understand one another through coeducation is to understand that members of the opposite sex also have a different disposition. For example, even faced with the same problem, men and women look at it differently on the basis of different . . . customs, ways of thinking, and life experiences. Though there may be an infinite variety of ways of thinking about life, there are also commonalities among members of the same sex.
>
> We must give up the bad habit of judging the opposite sex to be superior or inferior to us based on the degree to which they are or are not similar to us. We must take seriously the notion that each sex can contribute something to society on the basis of their own standpoint.
>
> There are qualities that men and women possess [even] under coeducation. The spirit of scholarship is the same; at the end of the day, men are men and women are women. Can there be any women who would give their respect to a man who is not manly [otokorashiku nai]? . . . Society is based on the fact that men are men and women are women. Particularly under coeducation, I'd like men to be masculine and women to be feminine. I've heard that androgyny [chūsei] is not desirable even in hell. I believe that true coeducation brings us step by step closer to human perfection [kanzen naru ningen] by regulating and encouraging one another to adopt the good points and discard the bad points [of our sex] in this way.[24]

Based on this essay, it is clear that even for this supporter of coeducation, the "human perfection" envisioned here is decidedly of two types—feminine and masculine. Furthermore, though this view is implicitly described as natural and innate, it is also presumed to be highly contingent upon circumstance. Otherwise, it would not be prone to disruption through displays of androgyny.

A male middle school student from Hokkaidō echoes this point by acknowledging that androgyny is a potential consequence of coeducation but arguing that this demerit is outweighed by the considerable benefits of this system:

Basic human rights are respected in the new constitution, to the point of equality between the sexes [*danjo dōken*]. However, even if men and women are the same in terms of basic human rights, they are different in terms of ability and character, so how coeducation is implemented is an extremely important matter that requires prudence.

. . . In order for coeducation to be effective, it is most important for men and women to understand and help one another. There are differences between men and women in terms of their way of looking at things, their tastes, and their level of understanding, so it is extremely important for schools to plan well and give careful consideration to these things in conducting classes.

Reflecting back on the experiences of my own class so far, I can offer two or three reasons why coeducation has yielded good results:

1. Boys and girls have begun to compete with one another in terms of academics [*kyōsōteki ni benkyō suru*].
2. Boys and girls can each do their chores effectively by relying on their own strengths.
3. The school grounds have become cleaner.

Also, the bad points are as follows:

1. Girls have become coarse like the boys.
2. Boys and girls both have become ill-mannered and lacking in a spirit of respect.

Based on the above points one might think that it's extremely difficult for boys and girls to study the same thing in the same place with the same teacher in the same way, but the harm this causes is probably extremely slight in comparison with the effective aspects of coeducation, and if we give increased reflection and consideration to its implementation in the future, coeducation will probably yield even better results.[25]

As in many of the testimonies above, here too the notion of gender complementarity through cooperation between boys and girls who "rely on their own strengths" is categorized as a definite benefit of coeducation, whereas the kind of "mutual influence" that results in androgynous behavior is high-lighted as an unfortunate result. So it seems that there was remarkable agree-ment on the "fact" of innate differences between the sexes, though a great deal of disagreement as to the significance of that, with commentators on either side harnessing this information in support of their arguments for or against coeducation. In the following section, we will see that this desire to preserve normative gender distinctions informed the way young people un-derstood the concept of equality between the sexes that was said to under-write the future of democracy in Japan.

## RECONCILING MIXED MESSAGES

The first cohort of young people to experience coeducation faced profoundly mixed messages regarding the nature of equality and the naturalness of pre-war gender roles and norms. While their parents' generation tended to advo-cate prewar ideologies of sex segregation, the new postwar gospel of equality of educational opportunity preached by the Occupation regime assumed a logic of sameness—the same rights and opportunities for men and women to be ensured by receipt of the same academic preparation through coeduca-tion. This left the younger generation to reconcile for themselves two very different visions of postwar society.

As noted above, Japanese children had internalized and were comfort-able with the idea that men and women might be very different from one another, in ways that were considered to be natural and inevitable. Interest-ingly, most of these children did not perceive this idea to conflict with the notion of equality between the sexes. Rather, most attempted to reconcile the two by envisioning equality as a state of harmonious gender comple-mentarity, as illustrated in the poetic tribute to coeducation that serves as the epigraph to this chapter. According to this logic, both men and women had the capacity to contribute productively to society in ways that were equally important yet gender specific. This is effectively the same logic that underwrote the prewar sex-segregated educational system, yet here coeduca-tion, rather than sex segregation, was envisioned as the best way to instill mutual respect and cooperation between the sexes.

There were some students who argued against coeducation on the under-standing that equality is incompatible with difference, but they appear to have been in the minority.[26] The most vocal member of this group, a male high school student from the regionally prestigious Beppu No. 1 High School, argued as follows:

> As society advances and civilization develops, it is more and more necessary for men and women to be segregated from one another and separated into groups. This is because progress toward a perfect society requires, from an ethical perspective, that we approach an awareness of the opposite sex in a healthy way, making clear physical distinctions between men and women and seeking spiritual fulfillment and satisfaction in those relationships. As the famous social philosopher Stanley Hall says, what modern society needs is masculine men and feminine women. Of course, because of democratic liberation women have been placed in a status equal [kintō] to men and have embarked on a new life journey to build a New Japan. However, women and men have innate [sententeki] characteristics by virtue of their sex. I am certainly not advocating that we die for our beliefs, but Japan must have its own unique beautiful virtues. Blindly eliminating and destroying those would be a regrettable thing from the perspective of national development. We must clearly resolve the meaning of this "new life." The necessity of separate education arises from the need to develop these special characteristics for the sake of national development and the progress toward an ideal society.

> . . . It goes without saying that men and women are completely different, physically and emotionally. If women engage in occupations like men it will be difficult for them to avoid exhaustion and injury. Also, there are people who say that because of these emotional differences between the sexes, men and women can benefit from coeducation by improving and complementing one another, but these differences will ultimately create the opposite effect of coeducation and so from the perspective of individualism sex-segregated education is the natural choice. Whatever people may say about equal political, economic, and social rights [danjo dōken], due to physical and emotional differences between men and women, inarguably they should naturally have separate employment. Therefore it is clear that educators should also differ according to sex and their methods should also be different.[27]

Here, the existence of innate qualities that are specific to each sex is cited as justification for separate spheres for men and women in Japanese society and therefore for a sex-segregated system of education that can nurture these qualities in ways that allow each sex to contribute to society in their own way. While nodding to recent historical developments that have enshrined the notion of equality in the service of democracy, the language he uses here suggests more of a separate but equal arrangement than a logic of equality that is defined by sameness. The first word he employs to articulate this concept, *kintō* (均等), connotes two ideas or objects that are on an "even level" with one another but not necessarily the same. The second time he mentions this idea of equality, he employs the term most commonly used at this time to denote the kind of equality promoted by the Occupation regime—equal (meaning "same") rights for both sexes, *danjo dōken* (男女同権). But here he cites the term only to refute it by arguing that "whatever people may say," men and women are fundamentally different. He therefore strongly suggests that the model of equality promoted by Occupation staffers is fundamentally and logically flawed, at least when applied to Japanese culture, which has "its own unique beautiful virtues."

While this was a common argument made by adults who were critical of coeducation, it was far less common in young people's accounts of the practice. Most young writers actually argued the opposite—that while there may be qualities that are innate and "natural" for each sex, these are fully compatible with the concept of equality, understood as cooperation between the sexes based on a mutual complementarity of strengths and weaknesses with highly gendered implications.[28] Figured in this way, the kind of equality embraced by supporters of coeducation may be seen as remarkably similar to the concession to separate but equal status (*kintō*) made by its opponent above, but employed to support coeducation rather than to critique it.

For example, one supporter of coeducation, who had herself benefited from the opportunity to enroll in a pharmacy course that had previously been closed to women, nevertheless struggled to reconcile the goal of equality with the societal expectation of different gender roles for men and women. We see this student, just like the one above who argued against coeducation, employ language that endorses the "fact" of women's difference from men, understood in both biological and ideological terms:

> Having at last taken the great step forward of implementing coeducation as part of the proclamation of democracy and women's liberation, we women have attained the long-desired dream of being able to study freely at university just as men do. Today, when this dream has been attained with astonishing speed, I honestly wonder if we've acquired the bravery and readiness for it. Of course we must not forget the many pioneers of women's liberation in our country who devoted their lives to that cause, but the desirability of edu-

cation has been accepted as a self-evident truth with little space for thorough investigation, and I think it's a shame that there has been little criticism or opinions expressed on this topic from the perspectives of educational and cultural philosophy. So, in an attempt to provide principled inquiry into the problem of coeducation, we find that women's right to equality [*byōdōken*] must mean complete acceptance of their value and special characteristics. The right to equality means the right for women to rise to the same heights of cultivation as men, and this must mean not leveling [the differences between] men and women [水平化, *suiheika suru*], but rather responding to the differences between men and women that are imposed on both sexes by nature. Or rather, it must mean liberating women from the educational methods of men.

Although when you search for the fundamental and general differences between men and women you find that they are equal and comparable in terms of individual ability, women have different core personalities from men and different attitudes toward life. You can say that the most important element of our character is motherhood, but it's difficult to correspondingly grasp the essence of men's character as fatherhood. This difference in essence produces a kind of psychological tension that must be clarified.[29]

While clearly appreciative of the opportunity to study at the university level, she nevertheless seems to have struggled with the fact that women enrolling in historically male professional courses of training were held to gender-specific educational standards that were not responsive to the realities of women's lives. Women were still expected to privilege motherhood over all other forms of "contribution" to society. She astutely notes the gender imbalance upon which this expectation is predicated; men's gender roles are simply not reducible to the expectation of parenthood in the same way that women's are. Furthermore, she hints at (but does not explore in detail) the inherent contradiction between allowing women access to such professional training and nevertheless expecting them to fulfill their "destiny" as future mothers.

Interestingly, she does not seem to question the assumption that this role is a product of nature rather than nurture; rather, she seems to take the naturalness of women's maternal destiny for granted while acknowledging that this has not been adequately theorized by those who have lobbied for women's greater access to university-level education. She seems not so much to question the goal of women's "cultivation" itself as to argue for the necessity to make pursuit of this goal compatible with women's different life

course. The vocabulary she uses to draw this distinction is particularly interesting. She explicitly argues for a vision of equality that allows women to
"rise to the same heights of cultivation as men" but without a "leveling out"
of gender difference. Here she employs a term commonly used in chemistry—
the "leveling effect"—to describe the suppression of differences between
otherwise distinct entities. In chemistry this would involve the use of chemical solutions to mitigate the expression of extreme chemical properties (for
example, in acids or bases), but here she applies the same logic to the dissolu-
tion of gender difference, specifically figured in terms of societal roles and
expected life course. So rather than arguing for a vision of equality that "dis-
solves" gender differences to treat men and women as effectively the same,
she advocates a model of equality that simultaneously accepts and accounts
for what she sees as fundamental differences between the sexes, in striking
similarity to the opponent of coeducation quoted above.

CONCLUSION

Both parents and children during the Occupation period seem generally to
have been in agreement that the sexes were inherently different from one
another and thus had distinct but complementary social roles and obligations. As noted in the introduction and further explored in chapter 1, this
presumption of gender complementarity was neither "traditional" nor ahistorical. Rather, it was predicated on a relatively recent formulation of good
wife, wise mother ideology based on a "mythologized" ideal of motherhood
developed in the 1930s,[30] as women's personal destinies were discursively interwoven with national narratives of modernization and empire. Women
were offered a privileged place as good wives and wise mothers within this
ideology of national identity and belonging in exchange for subordinating
their individual desires and ambitions to service to the family-state. Though
this model of femininity was a relatively recent "invention" in historical
terms, it was nevertheless firmly instilled in the minds of Japanese subjects
by 1945 and retained a persuasive hold on the imaginations of many
thereafter—even those like the young female pharmacy student above who
stood to benefit most from the postwar reforms.

   These testimonies of coeducation by the first cohort of students to experience it also suggest that while this notion of gender complementarity was
understood as natural and inevitable, it was also somewhat paradoxically

understood to be vulnerable to disruption and therefore had to be carefully policed through social institutions (such as schools) that took on a disciplinary function. In plain language, this meant that educational institutions should teach boys to be boys and girls to be girls. The prewar sex-segregated system of education was designed around this basic goal, and when the Occupation began to promote democracy through coeducation, Japanese children sought to harmonize the two goals of democratization and sex-specific training.

They did this by defining equality of the sexes through a separate but equal logic that understood the coeducational classroom as a training ground for boys and girls to learn to cooperate and work together, while honing their "naturally" endowed and gender-specific talents to contribute to society in sex-specific ways. Ideally, this was expected to result in a harmonious complementarity of the sexes that would enact the democratic ideals promoted by the Occupation regime without threatening the prewar presumption of separate spheres for men and women in society. As we will see in chapter 6, rather than resolve the contradictions between prewar and postwar ideologies of gender, this logic enabled postwar conservatives to preserve the appearance of coeducation while increasingly undermining its ideal of equality of educational opportunity. This was ultimately achieved by channeling most women into separate educational tracks that emphasized preparation for careers as latter-day good wives and wise mothers, thus preserving the prewar gendered division of labor well into the postwar period. In the next chapter, we will see how "mediation" of student testimonies about coeducation, which were edited and packaged by mass-market periodicals so as to highlight the disruptive potential of the new system of education and incite moral panic, helped to forward these conservative goals.

# CHAPTER 5

# *Mixed Messages*

## Mediating Coeducation through Student Roundtables

The plot of the 1949 feature film *Blue Mountains* (*Aoi sanmyaku*) turns on a seemingly innocuous encounter between two young people that sets an entire town aflame with gossip. A high school girl walks into a family-owned housewares shop selling eggs. The young man behind the counter offers to buy some if she will prepare them for him—his parents are out of town, and he has not had a hot meal in some time. She agrees and sets to work in what might appear a flawless performance of conventional femininity (save for her declaration that she does not really enjoy cooking). They banter a bit over the simple meal she prepares, and the two evidently become friendly, because a subsequent scene depicts them visiting a fortune-teller together, blissfully unaware of the havoc that will ensue when word gets around her all-girls school that she was seen "associating" with a boy. A pack of mean girls circulates rumors of our poor heroine's "unchaste" conduct that steadily grow more and more salacious—first she is merely seen with the boy, then the two are reported to have asked the fortune-teller about their compatibility for marriage, and so forth—until the teachers begin to take sides, and ultimately a parent-teacher conference must be convened to sort out the mess. The intensity of the debates that unfold in the course of this meeting serves as powerful testimony to the mixed messages young women encountered in the early postwar era, as the new values of democracy and equality of the sexes collided with prewar ideologies of femininity and social propriety.

We see the very same controversies regarding association between young men and women play out in the Japanese print media of the late 1940s. Nowhere was this more evident than in the form of the roundtable discussion, that quintessential staple of postwar magazines that brought members of all walks of life together in small groups to debate the promises and problems of a nation in transition. Typically, in preparation for such articles, the editors of a magazine would convene a small group of discussants—sometimes as few as three people, possibly as many as six to eight—to gather around a conference table and comment on a prearranged set of topics or questions. A moderator—usually someone employed by the magazine but occasionally an academic, public intellectual, or other noted authority—would guide the discussion by asking questions, calling on participants to respond to the comments of others, adding their own opinions, or transitioning to new topics or questions. A stenographer (invisible, at least in the written record of the conversation) would be present to record the proceedings, which would then be edited and condensed, sometimes extensively, to fit the space allocated to the article by the publication in question.

Roundtables were not new to the postwar era, but they found renewed relevance in postwar Japanese print media as the country attempted to put the principles of democracy into practice, providing an ostensibly egalitarian forum for debate and discussion of prevalent social trends. The merits and demerits of coeducation was a favorite subject, and roundtables on this topic involving students, teachers, educational experts, and ordinary citizens may be found in all manner of magazines published during the Occupation period, from the small-circulation student publications discussed in the previous chapter to mass-circulation popular magazines targeted to the "general reader" on a national scale. While these roundtables purported to present a transparent record of the discussion, they were prone to sometimes heavy-handed editorial intervention, not merely through the principles of omission or restructuring at the editing stage but also through the guidance and commentary of the moderator as the discussion was taking place. Editorial staff were also known to use subtler techniques of textual reframing through juxtaposition with captions or illustrations that colored the substance of panelists' utterances, sometimes in ways that radically reshaped the apparent intent of the commentary. As a result, such columns should not be understood as providing a "faithful" recounting of the discussions that transpired in this venue. On the other hand, taken on their own terms as a *reproduction* of a conversation that was "mediated"—that is, shaped through the dynamics of group interaction, guided by an authoritative intellect (the moderator) motivated by a specific set of interests, and filtered through the often unspoken editorial policies of the publication in question—these roundtable discussions provide rich textual evidence of the ideological collisions between prewar and postwar norms of gender and sexuality during the Occupation era.

Of the fourteen articles in the Prange Collection database clearly identifiable as roundtable discussions on coeducation featuring student participants, all but one were published in magazines targeted at audiences of women, children, and general readers—that is, the objects of the "new system" of coeducation (young people) or their parents (especially mothers).[1] We will see that while students themselves were mostly positive on the topic of coeducation—though they complained about some of the short-term drawbacks of the practice, such as clashes in communication patterns between boys and girls—these discussions were often reframed through editorial techniques that emphasized the disruptive potential of the practice. This produced an impression of coeducation as a moral hazard that was out of proportion with the concerns expressed by the students themselves. This exaggerated portrayal of the "moral problems" raised by coeducation was not limited to concerns about premature sexual experimentation but expanded to encompass transgression of gender norms as well. These portrayals of coeducation suggest deep-seated anxieties about the potential for "androgynous" behavior that clashed in confusing ways with the messages of democracy and equal opportunity that underwrote the new system of education. Students themselves were influenced by the constitutive contradictions of the new age, and these mixed messages about the relationship between gender and education that originated during the Occupation would ultimately set the stage for the debates over "coeds ruining the nation" that would rage in Japanese print media of the subsequent two decades.

## GENERATIONAL PERSPECTIVES ON KŌSAI

In Occupation-era roundtables on the topic of coeducation, few themes seem to have been as absorbing as that of *kōsai*, or association between boys and girls.[2] Underlying this often prurient interest in mixed-sex socializing was a fundamental contradiction between the expressed intent of the postwar educational reforms—to promote "cooperation" between men and women by training them to interact productively with one another through coeducation—and the prewar structure of morality that viewed unsupervised interaction between unrelated members of the opposite sex as a threat to the social order. Because of these presumptions, coeducation was frequently portrayed in the mass media of the late 1940s as a moral hazard that brought the bodies of adolescent boys and girls into unacceptably close proximity and invited premarital sexual experimentation. Because the introduction of coeducation facilitated such association between boys and girls beyond the protective and watchful eyes of their elders, this seemingly innocuous word became invested with all manner of anxieties regarding the potential for coeducation to undermine family discipline and invite moral turpitude. In the early postwar years, when the logic of the prewar sex-segregated system still held sway and a new ethics of democratic and egalitarian relationships between the sexes had yet to be invented, merely striking up a conversation with a member of the opposite sex represented a challenge to the status quo with profoundly political implications for these young people.

That said, students who came to these roundtable discussions having had some experience with coeducation[3] tended to speak positively about the practice, even as they freely discussed the difficulties they experienced in adjusting to the new system. While young people acknowledged feeling an initial sense of awkwardness and uncertainty, they were more likely than their elders to describe coeducation as having a positive impact on society and to balance complaints about the practice with optimistic assertions that these problems could be overcome. They were also frequently critical of adults' tendency to portray coeducation as an invitation to degeneracy, noting with chagrin that this made it harder for them to interact naturally and unaffectedly with classmates of the opposite sex for fear of incurring the censure of parents and teachers (or classmates, as we see depicted in *Blue Mountains*). We will first examine a rare example of a relatively "unmediated" roundtable discussion by students about the coeducational experience to understand how their experiences of *kōsai* contradicted adult anxieties about the practice. In subsequent sections, we will see examples of the way similar conversations were reproduced in the mass media to highlight the problems thought to be associated with coeducation. Such publications presented images of coeducation mediated through adult anxieties about the practice to validate fears by parents, teachers, and the general public that coeducation posed a moral hazard to Japanese society.

Students frequently complained that adults' fears regarding coeducation were baseless and overblown, and we see ample evidence of this in a roundtable discussion published in the regional magazine *Hana no kyōshitsu* in September 1948.[4] Unlike the many general-interest magazines with large circulation figures that tended to portray coeducation in a scandalous light, this publication advertised itself as a "culture magazine created by female students of Nagano prefecture"[5] and presents a relatively unmediated impression of student views by giving the participants wide latitude to structure the discussion themselves. It is not a student newsletter of the type analyzed in the previous chapter; for one thing, its contributors and readership were not limited to the student body of one school, and its appearance suggests better production values than many of the student newsletters discussed in the previous chapter. It is professionally typeset rather than handwritten and mimeographed, and the cover art (fig. 11) employs an attractive portrait of a young girl framed against a background of dwarf pine executed in watercolor or colored pencil (it is unclear which from the reproduction), as opposed to the simple line drawings that typically adorned the covers of amateur student magazines.

On the other hand, its editorial policies suggest a family resemblance to the student newsletters analyzed in chapter 4, in the sense that the magazine addresses itself to a geographically limited audience and invites that audience to view themselves as part of a community of readers who are simultaneously interpellated as producers of its content. This is suggested from the very first page, which presents the table of contents along with a short preface, penned by a student at a Nagano prefectural women's college, that is thoroughly immersed in the rhythms of school life. The essay, titled "Looking Ahead to Autumn," reflects back on the forty-day summer vacation that is just concluding and looks forward to the impending start of the new semester. It makes brief mention of contemporary issues of specific interest to students—the changing times are described in terms of the recent spate of educational reforms, and there are several references to the resurgent student movement, as well as quintessentially student-like experiences such as part-time jobs. There is also a nod to the new ways that young Japanese women in particular are exhorted to participate in public life in the early postwar period. Recalling a recent walk in a field of sunflowers, the author muses: "I thought I'd like to become bright and strong just like those sunflowers. Certainly they are a symbol of something that is demanded of the modern woman."[6] In addition to the roundtable, contributions to the magazine include poetry, reportage, reflections, and reviews of art, literature, and film authored by female students at high schools and colleges from across the prefecture, thus cementing the impression of the publication as something written primarily by and for students from the perspective of female

Figure 11. Cover Art, *Hana no kyōshitsu* no. 2 (September 1948). Courtesy of the Gordon W. Prange Collection, University of Maryland Libraries.

students. While this does not necessarily preclude the possibility that these contributions may have been shaped by other hands, it does indicate that the publication attempted to appeal to its readers by presenting itself as a mouthpiece for their interests and concerns and that this impression of age-graded authenticity was achieved in large part by publishing work produced by their readership.

The roundtable of interest for this analysis, titled "On Coeducation,"[7] gathered female high school students from six high schools in Nagano, some of which had recently become coeducational at the time of discussion and some of which were still single-sex schools. It was moderated by two representatives from the magazine, one male and one female. While the moderators perform the usual tasks of introducing new topics of conversation, inviting representatives from each school to comment, and occasionally interjecting with a humorous aside, they are relatively unobtrusive in terms of shaping the discussion. For example, the opening remarks by the male moderator are brief and framed in neutral language, inviting the participants to speak up while avoiding leading questions: "Thank you for coming so far in spite of the rainy weather. Today I'd like for us to speak candidly about coeducation. First of all, let's hear from those at schools that are implementing coeducation. How are things at the commercial high school?"[8] More often than not these moderators respond to the trend of the discussion rather than attempting to impose their respective points of view upon the participants, and on a few occasions the participants seem to usurp their role—for example, when a student named Minemura completely changes the subject by posing a new question to her peers at coeducational schools.[9] So in comparison with the mass-market attempts to package coeducation in an alarming light that will be discussed below, this roundtable presents a relatively even-handed and unvarnished impression of the experiences of this particular group of female students at a moment of transition when coeducation was in the process of being implemented in some locations but was still a new phenomenon even for those who had experienced it.

As with many such roundtables featuring student perspectives, a common complaint was societal resistance to coeducation:

MARUYAMA: People say a lot of things, but I think you don't really
  know anything about coeducation until you've tried it. Also, I've begun to think rationally about social customs [*fūki*].

MINEMURA: I don't understand why most people are hesitant about coeducation.

MACHIDA: Isn't it because of the difference in [academic] ability levels
[between boys and girls]?

KAKIZAKI: Rather than the difference in levels, isn't it because of [con-
cerns about] moral problems [*fūki mondai*]?

SATŌ: Even when we asked for coeducation, we were refused because of
the lack of facilities.

. . .

MATSUZAKI: When we held a debate about coeducation, the [boys]
from the middle school and we girl students were all in favor of it, but
we were told that it wasn't necessary and we wound up going to high
school separately from one another.

. . .

TAKASAKA: When we debated it at our class meeting, [most felt that] if
we were put together with the boys they would raise the level of the
class and that there would be no need to worry about moral problems, so there would be a lot of advantages to it, but a few were worried about moral problems so that was the end of it.[10]

While practical considerations such as the lack of facilities for students of
both sexes were clearly a concern in some cases (see chap. 2), these students
generally seem in agreement that the main reason for resistance to the practice was fear of moral problems, particularly on the part of adults and other
authority figures. This much is clear from Matsuzaki's comment that student
arguments in favor of coeducation were overridden, presumably by school
authorities or parental opposition or both, as well as from Takasaka's[11] account, which illustrates that in spite of the overwhelming support for coeducation among students, the few who objected on the assumption of moral
problems were enough to put an end to the discussion.

Parental objections to coeducation are also mentioned in the course of
discussion about the choices that individuals and communities made between coeducational and single-sex schools. For example, students from Nagano Commercial High School describe their school as having become coeducational only by force of necessity. There was only one school of this type
in the entire city, so the decision was made to integrate rather than build a
similar institution for girls from scratch, over and beyond opposition from
the school itself.[12] Opposition to coeducation seems to have been particu-

larly strong at previously all-girls schools. For example, Tsuchiya suggests that such concerns may be responsible for the small number of boys at her school, in spite of its having recently become "coeducational." (Whether the school should actually be considered as such is in fact questionable, because according to her account, the boys who have enrolled are kept in a separate class, in spite of being taught the same curriculum as the girls.) She also notes that while students of both sexes are allowed to interact with one another while in school and under the supervision of their teachers, they are forbidden to associate freely with one another outside of school. She describes this policy as an attempt by school authorities to respond to parents' intense concerns regarding the moral hazards of coeducation.[13]

Likewise, two girls (out of a total of six) who recently entered a previously all-male school also report some degree of parental opposition to their enrollment at that school, despite that it represented an unprecedented academic opportunity for their daughters. Maruyama describes her parents as having been "not particularly in favor" of her choice, although not opposed enough to it to prevent her from attending. Machida explains that her father initially opposed her choice of school, although her mother was ultimately able to persuade him to change his mind after consulting with her principal.[14] His daughter's scholarly devotion may also have won him over; she concludes her anecdote with the comment, "Anyway, I'm going because I want to study, so I don't think he can object too much to that." When the moderator suggests that her new school would allow her to study in a more rigorous educational environment than an all-girls school, she agrees, lamenting the seven hours per week "wasted" in girls' schools on sewing instruction.[15]

Finally, when prompted to discuss the "good points and bad points" of coeducation, the biggest complaint seems to have been parental and societal hysteria about the transition to the new system rather than anything actually experienced as part of that system. While all seem generally in agreement that the girls are clearly behind the boys in terms of preparation for academic subjects, particularly in the sciences and foreign languages, and one girl notes that boys still seem to find it embarrassing when girls speak to them, most simply seem to wish that their parents would stop worrying and allow them to actually experience the full benefits of coeducation, including interacting socially with boys. For example, when invited to share their hopes for the future regarding coeducation, one girl laments, "I wish our parents and school authorities trusted us more." Another complains that her parents worry if she stays after school to participate in club activities.[16] Since extracurricular activities were often the only school-endorsed venue for social interaction between members of the opposite sex, such parental concerns may well have limited or compromised the quality of the coeducational experience for many girls. Finally, several students criticize Japanese society as a whole for taking a prurient interest in the issue of coeducation:

> SHIMIZU (MODERATOR): What about [the attitude of] regular people with regard to coeducation?
> NISHIKAWA: They're too curious about it.
> TSUCHIYA: They're too quick to bring up moral problems.
> NISHIKAWA: When boys and girls bow to one another on the street, there are people who make fun of them.[17]

Nishikawa's final comment about bowing underscores the newness of this situation for onlookers. Classmates and other acquaintances in Japan would naturally bow to one another if meeting unexpectedly on the street, yet just a year or two prior to this conversation it would have been unthinkable for members of the opposite sex to have been classmates in the first place, much less to publicly acknowledge such a relationship. That a simple and common form of greeting might meet with social censure is thus particularly revealing about the level of discomfort coeducation often provoked in Japanese society generally speaking. In contrast, many of the student participants in this conversation explicitly described coeducation as "natural" and the practice of separating young people until marriage as problematic, in contradistinction to prevailing prewar norms of societal "common sense." So, as noted in previous chapters, it is abundantly clear that there was a profound generational gap in the understanding of the societal implications of coeducation, with students more often than not welcoming the practice, while their elders fretted about the moral hazard posed by association between young men and women.

## REFRAMING *KŌSAI* AS MORAL HAZARD

This generational gap in perception of coeducation is evident in student roundtable discussions printed in mass-market magazines as well. But in these cases the guiding hand of adult editorial intervention is apparent in the way these testimonies are packaged and presented to highlight the moral dangers of coeducation. The most obvious way of mediating such narratives was through the intrusion of an activist moderator who guided discussion to focus attention on the negative aspects of the coeducational experience. We see one such example in a June 1949 roundtable discussion published in the general-interest magazine *Modern Times* (*Kindai*), which foregrounds the problem of *kōsai* in the very title of the article, "Atarashii danjo kōsai" (New social interactions between men and women).[18] While many of the students participating in this roundtable characterize adult fears of moral problems as overblown—for example, one complains that her parents have gone overboard in forbidding her to associate with boys before marriage, even though she has no "strange feelings" toward the opposite sex[19]—the moderator repeatedly returns the conversation to the various "problems" that coeducation poses for Japanese society, as if expecting the students to validate his concerns.

As if the title were not enough to cue the audience to expect salacious content, the article begins with prefatory remarks from the moderator that frame the discussion to follow as a conversation about a troubling social problem:

> The reason why we've had you assemble here today is to discuss the problem of relationships between boys and girls [*danjo kōsai*], what you or your families think about the morality of relationships between boys and girls, and what your teachers think about it. Depending on the school, there are some that have only female students, but at any rate, [generally speaking] coeducation has now been implemented. You high school students have traditionally been separated according to sex, but suddenly, at "that age" (as people say), you are studying, exercising, and playing together. For people in the old days, this would be an unprecedented event. Parents are uneasy that this will cause troublesome problems. . . . When associating with one another, I think you will have some sort of moral principles in mind. We've brought you together to speak frankly about these things. Please don't hold anything back.[20]

In contrast to the rather neutral approach to questioning practiced by the moderators discussed in the previous section, the language here frames *kōsai* as problematic in many ways. The word "problem" (*mondai*) itself is used twice, comforting "traditions" like sex segregation are contrasted with "unprecedented events" like coeducation, and the need for morality is invoked

in anticipation of its opposite, thus ostensibly justifying the parental concerns referenced by the moderator. The use of the euphemism "that age"
suggests young adolescents in the throes of hormonal frenzy and further invites participants (and readers) to view young people "studying, exercising,
and playing together" in a scandalous light. Not surprisingly, then, this elic-
its commentary that reflects the moderator's own presumptions back to
him, as one boy responds:

> It's fair to say that we boys and girls haven't had any chance to come into
> contact with one another so far, but with the end of the war, we've come to
> an age like the present, and interacting with one another will require a
> change in our way of thinking, but this will be extremely difficult, so we're all
> more or less suffering to some degree. I think that we'll have to associate
> [with the girls] with the same feeling as we do with boys, but this is a really
> difficult problem.[21]

Coeducation here is described not only as a "problem" but as a source of "suffering." Curiously, the only solution this student seems to be able to envision is to pretend not to see gender differences at all, treating students of the
opposite sex as if they are members of the same sex. Several other students
pick up this thread of discussion and run with it, and this notion of tran-
scending or ignoring the embodied-ness of their classmates in favor of see-
ing them in gender-neutral terms as generic "students" becomes a running
theme in the remainder of the discussion. Only one boy bothers to point out
the impossibility of this task,[22] an insight that is acknowledged and then inexplicably forgotten, as students continue to return to this fantasy of gender
neutrality—for example, when one girl declares, "I'd like to transcend the
male-female relationship and just socialize as if we're elementary school
children."[23]

 This strategy of framing questions continues throughout the discussion,
with a relatively intrusive moderator prefacing questions with lengthy pre-
ambles phrased in suggestive language to highlight the various ways that
coeducation is anticipated to disrupt Japanese traditions. For example:

> [MODERATOR]: In other countries, boys and girls are offered the chance
>     to associate with one another from the time they are small. . . . In Ja-
>     pan, this is limited to the children of relatives or neighbors. It's neces-

sary for boys and girls to be able to be aware of and associate more with one another from the time they're very young. However, in Japan there is no structure or opportunity for this, so naturally we've come to avoid such things. At any rate, on the surface it seems that boys and girls can get to know one another [by coming into contact with one another] in the same school, the same place, but socially we lack such institutions outside of schools. Adults are embarrassed because they don't know how boys and girls should behave when they come into contact with one another; they really need training on this point. Do you have any thoughts on how men and women should associate in the future?[24]

The implication underlying this question seems to be that while coeducation may work in other environments, it is woefully incompatible with Japanese tradition and something to be "avoided" for its potential to cause "embarrassment." He goes on to imply that while the "etiquette" for interacting in same-sex environments is already understood, it must be difficult in mixed-sex groups because students cannot be sure what sort of behavior or speech is permissible and what is not: "[For example,] it's fine to do this in a group of boys only, but you shouldn't do it in front of girls."

He obviously expects agreement with these pronouncements and seems surprised when one female student demurs: "At our school, when we first began coeducation, I felt terrified when faced with the boys, but now it's not an issue and we've become close, so boys and girls talk together without thinking anything of it."[25] Whereas the moderator portrayed the social awkwardness associated with coeducation as a potentially fatal flaw, this girl clearly disagrees, describing it as a temporary inconvenience that can be surmounted with time and practice. Undeterred, the moderator insists in his previous line of questioning, putting a finer point on the dangers associated with *kōsai*:

To put it bluntly, people are uneasy that boys and girls might make a mistake. There was a love suicide by a boy and girl student, so [the worry is] what would happen if love develops between young people. If a love affair were to develop, I think they would have to get married, but sometimes it doesn't go as far as marriage. This often happens in novels, but in society it can cause a lot of troublesome problems.[26]

He is finally able to gain a measure of agreement with this presumption only by calling on a student from an all-girls school, who simply responds that she has never experienced *kōsai* and can only think of those who desire such experiences as "delinquent" (*furyō*).[27] Throughout this discussion, the term *kōsai* is specifically invested with salacious intent; it is presumed by the moderator that association between boys and girls naturally leads beyond platonic social interaction to "mistakes" like premarital sexual experimentation. While the student he designates to respond to this comment evidently takes this assessment at face value, suggesting that one would have to be delinquent to desire such experiences, she also admits that she has no experience on which to draw in assessing the disruptive potential of such associations, so it is not surprising that she might simply echo the fears of adults on this point. But what is most interesting about this exchange is the activist stance taken by the moderator, not merely in guiding the tone and direction of discussion but also in using the conversation as a venue to attempt to impose his own attitudes about *kōsai* upon the student participants. Such intrusive moderators were quite common in roundtable discussions published in mass-market magazines[28] and may be seen as reflecting the anxieties of the adult readership of such publications, thus helping to fan the flames of controversy on the subject of coeducation by portraying it as a moral hazard.

## GENDER TROUBLE AS MORAL PROBLEM

Given that the participants in the discussion above were high school students, the age of greatest concern to many parents and teachers for its association with raging adolescent hormones, it is perhaps not surprising that the moral problems thought to accompany coeducation were assumed to involve premarital sexual experimentation. However, the desire to police expressions of gender roles and norms of behavior also lurked beneath these adult anxieties. On the one hand, the pervasive model of gender difference as innate and absolute (see chap. 4) led many adults to presume that the sexes were so incommensurably opposite to one another that conflict was bound to result from coeducation. On the other hand, the prospect of "mutual influence" between boys and girls that might serve to narrow this difference between the sexes filled parents with dread and raised the unwelcome specter of androgyny. These concerns also influenced editorial practices governing the framing and presentation of student accounts of coeducation, even in periodicals that were targeted at audiences of young children. For example, in the article "Good Things and Bad Things about Coeducation,"[29] published in the July 1948 issue of the children's magazine *Akatombo*, we see conversations between students on the subject of coeducation mediated through the use of captions and illustrations to invest the testimony of student participants with frequently unintended meaning. This packaging effectively shaped—and at times overwrote—what was said by the children to reflect and validate the fears of adults regarding the disruptive effects of coeducation.

The article reproduces a set of "pencil conversations" (*enpitsu taidan*)—so called because students were assigned to conduct their "conversations" in writing—among small groups of sixth-graders at a Tokyo-area elementary school. At this point these students had between one and two years of experience with the new system of coeducation.[30] Each "pencil conversation" is preceded by a caption and a thumbnail cartoon that purport to represent the main thread of the discussion. However, as we will see below, careful comparison between the text and its framing reveals an editorial attempt to heighten the sense of the disruptive effects of coeducation by exaggerating accounts of conflict between the sexes. This editorial strategy may be seen as simultaneously reflecting and producing adult fears of "gender blending" by exaggerating the degree to which boys and (especially) girls had begun to display behaviors considered transgressive of conventional gender norms.

Certainly the dialogues transcribed in this article reveal a litany of complaints by one sex against the other. Girls complain primarily about the roughness of boys' speech and behavior and their tendency to tease the girls and resort to mischief to get their attention. For their part, boys disliked the way that girls cried too much and excluded others socially, for example, by telling secrets. Of course, much of this behavior would not be out of place today on any elementary school playground, but what is remarkable about these testimonies is that in spite of these complaints, there is a clear desire to make friendships across gendered lines.

In fact, by far the most common complaint by both boys and girls is the way fellow classmates tease anyone who attempts to be friendly with a member of the opposite sex. While this seems to have resulted in a considerable degree of self-segregation, we can see even in the context of these dialogues that such gender divisions were not absolute, as is witnessed by the fact that several of these conversation groups contained both boys and girls. Although it is possible that conversation partners were assigned

rather than left up to the choice of the participants, the interactions between group members display a level of frank communication and famil-
iarity that belies the impression of a strict social division between students
along gendered lines.[31]

And yet in spite of obvious attempts to bridge the gender divide by these
students, many of these conversations are framed in such a way as to
heighten differences between the sexes and to emphasize the conflicts that
resulted from the new system that sought to educate them together. For example, in one conversation between two boys, Kawai and Imai, a rather
evenhanded and thoughtful discussion of the difficulty of bridging the gap
between genders is transformed in the illustration into a complaint about
girls being "crybabies."[32] To convey the emotional complexities of this conversation, it is translated in its entirety here:

I: During the school picnic, I had lunch with S-san (female). Who did
   you eat with? You'd probably laugh at me having lunch with S-san,
   right? I was a little embarrassed.

K: You had lunch with S-san? You're brave. I ate by myself. Eating lunch
   with a girl isn't really embarrassing, but people would probably make
   a big deal out of it. I think there are girls who are nice, and some that
   aren't nice too.

I: Yeah, my mom says that since school has become coeducational, the
   boys have gotten nicer. What do you think? Do you think everyone is
   getting along? Or that we aren't getting along? [At first] I thought it
   would be better if it were just boys, but now that we've become coeducational, I don't dislike it. What do you think?

K: Yeah, I thought so too. The boys have become kinder. But the girls
   now are throwing their weight around. Also, they're crybabies, and I
   really hate that. Any little thing and they cry, and I'm scared that the
   teacher will say something to me. If girls weren't such crybabies, coeducation would be fine. What do you think?

I: I think the girls cry because the boys bully them. But there are also
   girls who cry for other reasons.[33]

Taken in its entirety, this conversation is a quite poignant reminder of the
awkwardness felt by both sexes when the previously sex-segregated school
system was first integrated. In many places throughout this article, both girls
and boys complain of not knowing what to say to the opposite sex or how to

Figure 12. "Crybaby,"
*Akatombo*, July 1948.
Courtesy of the Gor-
don W. Prange Col-
lection, University of
Maryland Libraries.

behave in their presence. In this context, Kawai's remark that his friend is
"brave" for daring to have lunch with a girl at a school function is entirely
understandable. There also seems to be a willingness to reach out to the opposite sex or to see merit in interactions with them, as witnessed by remarks
that "some girls are nice" or that boys might learn social skills ("boys have
become kinder") through the influence of girls.

Furthermore, though Kawai complains about one stereotypical behavior that he finds annoying (girls are "crybabies"), Imai is quick to remind
him of the role that boys may well play in producing this behavior. And yet
this complaint alone is chosen to symbolically represent the tenor of the
entire conversation. The accompanying illustration depicts a young girl
wailing inconsolably, tears streaming down her face, with a boy looking at
her with a startled expression and moving away from her in consternation
(fig. 12). The caption within the illustration reads simply *"nakimusi"* (crybaby), as if it were necessary to further specify the problematic behavior. So
what proves to be a complex set of interactions in the dialogue is reduced to
a visual depiction that emphasizes stereotypically gendered behavior. The
implication is clearly that gender differences are so deeply ingrained that it
would be unrealistic to expect boys and girls to interact productively with
one another—in spite of the tone of most of the discussion, which indicates
that these children have learned much from one another in spite of their
differences.

In another conversation that is reminiscent of that between Kawai and

Imai, male student Ōnishi begins by lamenting the fact that when boys try to play with the girls they are teased mercilessly. In fact, he suggests that this is a bad quality that needs to be fixed and that Japan should become more like America with regard to ease of communication between the sexes.[34] However, he also complains that as a result of coeducation, girls have become more "rough" (ranbō na, lit. "violent") in their way of speaking. His friend Hayashi agrees: "Even with equal rights between men and women [danjo dōken], I think it's bad if girls don't use feminine language." However, he immediately returns to Ōnishi's point about the need for social change: "If you play with a girl the other boys will make fun of you. That's the problem with Japanese people. I'd like that problem to be fixed soon. We have to become a sensible and pleasant country like America."[35] Whatever the value of this cross-cultural comparison, it seems clear from this conversation that both boys are in agreement that the Japanese tendency to treat mixed-sex socializing as aberrant and of prurient interest is unfortunate and counterproductive.

Thus, the focus of the discussion is primarily on the social pressures faced by young people to segregate themselves into homosocial peer groups, in spite of recent democratic reforms promoting "equal rights" that coeducation was intended to bolster. The point about girls using "rough" language hints at the anxieties produced by these reforms and indicates that many students shared their parents' interest in maintaining clearly defined gender differences (see chap. 4). However, this issue is raised as a brief aside to the main thrust of the conversation, which is generally positive on the subject of cultivating harmonious relationships between the sexes. Nevertheless, the illustrator chose this comment about transgression of gender norms as representative of the entire exchange. The accompanying sketch depicts a young girl wildly kicking and punching a young boy, who has been knocked to the ground, with the caption "violent" (ranbō da) in the upper left-hand corner (fig. 13).[36] This is clearly not what was intended by the boys, who mentioned rough speech rather than rough behavior. So the illustration in effect completely rewrites the significance of the conversation in such a way as to dramatically inflate the threat posed by girls' increasing willingness to assert themselves as a result of coeducation.

We see exactly the same tactic employed in illustrating a conversation between two girls, Kamiyama and Usui. The conversation begins with Kamiyama noting that since coeducation, girls have become more articulate and boys kinder. Usui agrees conditionally, but counters that some boys still

Figure 13. "Violent,"
*Akatombo*, July 1948.
Courtesy of the Gordon W. Prange Collection, University of
Maryland Libraries.

seem to have been unaffected by the softening influence of the new system. Kamiyama acknowledges this but still thinks that on the whole boys are nicer now. She adds: "When I first came to this class, I really disliked talking with the boys. But lately I've become comfortable with it [*heiki ni natta*]."[37] The conversation continues in this vein, with a few complaints about bad behavior from specific boys. One of these problem children, "K-san," had evidently developed the unfortunate habit of intervening in the girls' playground games by snatching the ball away from them in mid-play. (Several other groups of girls complained about precisely the same behavior elsewhere in this article.)

However, Kamiyama and Usui generally agree that with a couple of exceptions, the boys in their class are on the whole better behaved than boys elsewhere, which makes the image chosen to illustrate this conversation seem bizarrely out of step with the thread of the discussion. Apparently inspired by the tale of playground malfeasance, the drawing depicts a girl holding a ball in her left hand and swinging her right fist angrily at a boy, who is running away with a mischievous grin (fig. 14). The caption above reads, "I've become comfortable with it" (*heiki ni natta*). So while this phrase was employed in the dialogue to express Kamiyama's increasing comfort level with engaging boys in conversation, when juxtaposed with the illustration it implies something much more disturbing—that girls have "become comfortable" engaging in physical violence directed toward boys. This is clearly

Figure 14. "I've Be-
come Comfortable
with It," *Akatombo*,
July 1948. Courtesy
of the Gordon W.
Prange Collection,
University of Mary-
land Libraries.

not what was intended by Kamiyama—in fact the references to bullying in this conversation were exclusively concerned with abuses that girls suffered at the hands of boys.

What is particularly interesting about these student conversations is that while the young people do speak of problems adjusting to coeducation, overall they seem quite positive on the topic. Most of the students recount initial feelings of trepidation at sitting in the same classroom with members of the opposite sex, but these reservations seem to have gradually evaporated, though this process of adjustment was clearly not without its problems. However, the complaints expressed by these students are intended to imply not so much that the objective of coeducation itself is flawed but rather that attempts to put it into practice had failed to live up to its lofty ideals. Some students even explicitly argued that they should redouble their own efforts to actualize the goals of democracy and equality underlying the new educational system.[38]

However, these generally positive impressions are overwritten by the way the conversations are framed and packaged to highlight examples of discord and social disturbance, even to the point of distorting the intention of the speakers themselves. These editorial decisions would seem to suggest that adults' perceptions of the corrosive effects of coeducation on Japanese society were out of step with the lived experience of their children and that attempts to rewrite children's experiences of coeducation were motivated by a deep-seated psychological need to justify adult anxieties about the new educational system. Furthermore, it is equally clear that these anxieties were founded on a host of constitutive contradictions that assumed gender differences to be inevitable and incommensurable yet also feared any narrowing of the gap that might result from young men and women learning to understand one another better. On the one hand, this seems to imply that gender difference is immutable—thus implying that coeducation is a futile attempt to mix oil and water, so to speak—whereas on the other hand, it has the opposite effect of suggesting that gender norms must be shored up precisely because they are so vulnerable to transgression. As we will see in the next section, these mixed messages also incorporated attempts to reinforce conventional gender roles in the face of Occupation-era discourses of equality of opportunity that sought to open up new avenues of personal and professional self-actualization for women through access to historically masculine spaces.

POLICING GENDER ROLES

As noted in chapter 1, Occupation personnel advocated for coeducation as part of the postwar educational reforms because they understood it to be a crucial mechanism for ensuring equality of educational opportunity for Japanese women. This vision of opportunity was underwritten by a presumption of equality as defined by sameness—in other words, an assumption that Japanese women could attain equality with men only through an educational system that offered them the same curriculum and educational standards as that afforded to Japanese men, at all levels of the educational system, from elementary school to university. As these reforms were implemented, they implicitly raised the question of the purpose of educating women "equally." Should young girls aspire to the same range of professional goals as their brothers, as the Occupation regime's vision of equality seemed to suggest? Or were women supposed to pursue education to become better wives and mothers, as was assumed during the first half of the twentieth century? Reluctant to be seen as mounting a wholesale attack on Japanese cultural values, the Occupation regime had sent its own mixed messages on this subject during the negotiations over the drafting of the postwar Fundamental Law of Education, touting equality of opportunity but also intimating that this might be routed through an updated version of the prewar good wife, wise mother ideology of womanhood.

These unresolved questions also haunted media coverage of coeducation as the new system of education was implemented in the late 1940s, presenting the public with a rather confused set of messages about its purpose and desired outcome, particularly for girls. We see these mixed messages reflected in published student roundtable discussions on coeducation, which simultaneously showcased the new roles to which girls could theoretically aspire and mediated these messages through highly conventional assumptions of normative femininity. As in the roundtables discussed above, this editorial intervention was evident both in the content of the conversations—where an intrusive moderator frequently reasserted such gender norms in response to participants who challenged them—and in the way such conversations were packaged visually for the consumption of readers.

For example, in February 1948 the general-interest magazine *Answers* (*Ansaazu*) featured a roundtable discussion between female college students titled "Roundtable of Contemporary Female Students: What Are They Thinking?"[39] in which an activist moderator pushed back against participants' expressed desire to pursue careers after graduation. Though the purpose of the discussion was ostensibly to explore the educational experiences of these young women, none of his questions actually address the academic aspects of university life; he seems entirely concerned with the way the new system facilitates social relationships between men and women as they near marriageable age. Questions range from decisions about career versus marriage to the degree of parental permissiveness in socializing with the opposite sex, the difficulty of distinguishing between friendship and romantic intentions, and the ever-popular topic "What Kind of Man Do You Like?"

The questions asked by this reporter are revealing of the intense pressures on women to embrace marriage and motherhood as the "natural" outcome of a woman's life, in spite of the new opportunities offered to them by the postwar educational reforms to aspire to professional careers. The very first question posed in this discussion is "Do today's intellectual [*interi*] women seek jobs after graduation, or do they think they will go straight into marriage?" Four out of five of the women assume they will pursue a career (the fifth is silent on this issue), which seems to disturb the interviewer, because he follows up with the rejoinder: "You can speak carelessly [now], but if you become an old maid [*ōrudo misu*] it's said that you'll have a tendency toward hysteria because the biological thing goes to your head, so you can't say that you don't think about this, right?" When he puts it this way, one student is pushed into admitting, "Of course that's true. So if a wonderful person were to appear, I can't say I wouldn't get married." However, the tone of her response is rather tepid in comparison with the aggressiveness of the interviewer's prompt, raising the possibility that the respondent is simply humoring her interlocutor. As if to soften his approach, the moderator then turns this into a joke—"So you're vigilantly waiting for a wonderful man to appear, then?"—to which she replies, "The biological thing hasn't gone to my head to the extent that I'm waiting yet."[40] While this female student is able to defuse the confrontation with humor, the moderator's persistence in pursuing this line of questioning leaves an indelible mark on the conversation by invoking the specter of the "old maid" whose rejection of marriage is so unnatural that it renders her "hysterical" and thus threatening to society on multiple levels.

In another example of sensationalistic participant baiting, the interviewer invites these young women to offer opinions on "those women at the forefront of the present era, the *pan-pan* girl [prostitute] and the female Diet member."[41] By juxtaposing these two iconic postwar "types," he seems to invite participants (and readers) to conceptually link female politicians with prostitutes, implying that both transgress conventionally feminine roles in ways that are unsavory. This section of the roundtable is entitled "Criticism of the *Pan-pan* Girl," as if to imply that opinions on this topic are unanimously negative, but this is not in fact the case. Three express criticism in various ways, but two are sympathetic to the plight of such women, suggesting that there are broader social considerations that need to be taken into account in understanding their choice to support themselves or their families in this way.

Interestingly, the *pan-pan* girl seems to garner more sympathetic treatment than the female Diet member. While only two of the participants express opinions on this topic, those who do speak out are overwhelmingly negative in their assessment of the role of female politicians in society. One student at a women's university argues, "I don't agree with the idea that we should have more of these women in the future. What we have now is plenty. Rather, I'd like those types of women to return to the home and fulfill their duties as women." While we might attribute such views to the fact that women's universities historically prided themselves on training good wives and wise mothers, the lone Tokyo University student expresses a similar view: "Of course those kinds of people are necessary, but just because a woman has received higher education, that doesn't mean that she has to become so serious [*shikatsumerashii*]. I think it would be most helpful [for society] if women of cultivation would [channel those talents into] making their homes splendid."[42]

It is difficult to reconcile these attacks on professional women politicians with the participants' remarks at the beginning of the conversation, where they express the desire for careers of their own. Challenged by the moderator for expressing these desires at the beginning of the roundtable, they may well have felt pressured to conform, or at least give lip service, to the more conventional vision of feminine roles that he clearly espoused. Furthermore, given the persistence of these conventional values in society as a whole, it seems likely that the moderator was not alone in feeling that these young women's ambitions were anomalous and potentially threatening to the established order. These female participants were surely keenly aware of these contradictions and likely sensitive about being associated with what society would consider overly assertive women. Particularly given the interviewer's crude suggestion that ambitious women are little better than prostitutes, it is hardly surprising that these young women may have felt the need to distance themselves from the specter of feminine transgression that these Diet women represented.

Likewise, in a roundtable discussion published in the April 1949 issue of the magazine *Sister* (*Shisutaa*),[43] targeted toward an audience of female high school students, an otherwise progressive attempt to introduce the new co-educated generation to possible career paths after graduation is somewhat confusingly riddled with paeans to the joys of conventional femininity. In addition to six high school students of both sexes from the Kyoto area, the roundtable participants include seven career women (*shokugyō fujin*) invited to advise the students and answer questions about their professions and three male journalists who share the job of moderating the conversation.[44]

The way the article is packaged for the visual consumption of the reader reveals mixed messages regarding women's roles in the new Japan. The lower right-hand margin of the first page contains a caption that underscores the transgressive potential of the new futures now imaginable for women in postwar Japan: "What occupation [*shokuiki*] will you choose after graduation?!"[45] That women are invited to consider an "occupation" at all—as opposed to the kind of part-time or temporary job that served as a prelude to marriage for their mothers' generation—seems thoroughly in keeping with the brave new world of postwar equality of opportunity promoted for women during the Occupation period. The addition of an exclamation point after

Figure 15. Untitled, *Shisutaa*, April 1949. Courtesy of the Gordon W. Prange Collection, University of Maryland Libraries.

the question particle "ka" at the end of the sentence simultaneously connotes girlish enthusiasm and the urgency of the question itself, as if failing to choose for oneself is no longer an option in this new postwar era of opportunity. Yet sandwiched between the title at the top and the caption at the bottom right side of the page is a hand-drawn illustration of a young girl holding a cat and gazing at the reader with a dreamy, pensive expression (fig. 15)—the kind of old-fashioned and stereotypically feminine portrait that would not have been out of place in any prewar girl's magazine. This rather jarring disjunction between the visual iconography and the stated intent of the article is echoed in its contents as well in eloquent testimony to the mixed messages that young girls received at this time regarding the degree to which they should venture beyond conventional gender roles.

While the older female participants are optimistic and outspoken in their promotion of new roles for women in the professional sphere, the male moderators frequently interject to reframe the conversation around discourses of normative femininity, as if to reassert the "naturalness" of women's destiny to become wives and mothers. For example, in one exchange, Futoda, a female employee of the Kyoto city government and the most outspoken of the "career women" in attendance, gives spirited encouragement to the female students as follows: "When you go out into society I'd like you to develop the confidence to exchange opinions on an even level [*dōtō no tachiba*] with men." In response to this, one female student demurs: "When men go out into society it's taken for granted that they'll go on to university, and they also somehow have that desire, but there are few who expect girls to go to university when they graduate from the new high schools, so don't they feel afraid to venture to do so?" While Futoda responds to this with further encouragement to prepare now for active participation in society after graduation, Tashiro, one of the male moderators, instead describes the value of scholarship for women as enabling them to "keep up" with their husbands intellectually.[46]

Likewise, when asked about discrimination against women in the workplace, Futoda indeed acknowledges that this is a problem. She then adds that she hopes the next generation does not suffer the way hers has and declares that "if the general level of women doesn't improve, society from now on won't develop in a good direction." To this overtly feminist pronouncement, Tashiro again responds with what sounds like a non sequitur: "It's a weak way of thinking to say that 'men will go on to university but we'll enter the home [so we don't have to study as hard].' It's important to feel that 'we should study even more than men precisely because we'll enter the home.'"[47] Once again, Tashiro reinscribes women's intellectual accomplishments within their obligations to home and family, as if trying to contain the transformative force of progressive reforms that allow women increasingly important roles outside the home.

While Tashiro is the most intrusive of the three moderators, these attempts at reframing are not exclusive to him. Elsewhere in the discussion, Usui, the male representative of the magazine responsible for publishing this article, affords the fairer sex the following rather backhanded compliment: "Men aren't blessed with the patience for the kind of things women do, like knitting. If I don't do something different every day, I can't stand it. I hate having to write the same letter three or four times." The implication here is that women have a high tolerance for repetitive tasks and a corresponding lack of creative intelligence, a claim that was frequently employed in the early decades of the twentieth century to argue against coeducation on the basis of women's inherent intellectual inferiority.[48] Futoda recognizes this implication immediately and shoots back, "But that's more a matter of individual difference than differences between men and women. Women also want to do creative things." To this, Usui responds, "Of course there are individual differences, but I think this has something to do with physical differences between men and women."[49] So while Futoda's insistence upon individual differences attempts to elevate the conversation beyond the realm of gender stereotypes, Usui repeatedly returns the discussion back to that point. It is as if he wants to reimpose the prewar model of gender difference as grounded in biology and thus innate and immutable, in opposition to an interlocutor who stubbornly attempts to transgress those conceptual boundaries.

CONCLUSION

As we have seen in the roundtables discussed in this chapter, the new postwar discourse of equality of opportunity for women raised anxieties among many Japanese about the possibility of changing gender roles, and particularly new roles for women in the public sphere. This discomfort is evident from the way editorial policies and framing of student discussions of coeducation attempted to counter these forces of change by muting their challenge to the status quo. In highlighting these strategies of reproduction or mediation of student discourses, it is evident that these roundtable discussions encapsulated the rather conflicted societal responses to the disruptive potential of coeducation. Specifically, these articles problematize coeducation's potential to foster troubling forms of association between young people of the opposite sex, to facilitate transgression of cherished distinctions between the sexes, and ultimately to erode conventional gender roles.

Occupation-era discussions of coeducation were thus permeated with a host of constitutive contradictions that reflected the collision of prewar and postwar value systems. Long-cherished assumptions that the sexes were fundamentally different from one another, and should therefore be educated separately, clashed with pronouncements of equality of educational opportunity by Occupation authorities who understood "equal" to mean "same."

Coeducation also provoked anxieties in many adults in part because of the fear of "moral problems," a term that is often understood to imply premarital sexual experimentation among adolescents but that I argue also encompassed an intense dread of the transgression of gender roles and norms of behavior as well. Attempts by mass-market publications to reframe or mediate enthusiasm for postwar reforms like coeducation may therefore be understood as attempts to contain the forces of change that they implied. In the next chapter, we will see that because these inherent contradictions between progressive and conservative visions of gender and sexual norms were not reconciled during the Occupation period, they returned to haunt the subsequent two postwar decades as debates about coeds ruining the nation.

# CHAPTER 6

# *"Coeds Ruining the Nation"*

## Coeducation and Moral Panic

ON JUNE 26, 1956, in the course of a campaign junket in Tokushima prefecture on behalf of fellow Liberal Democratic Party (LDP) candidates for the approaching Upper House elections, Minister of Education Kiyose Ichirō declared his intention to "reexamine" the coeducational system, vaguely noting that it had a "negative effect" on Japanese society and "did not fit with the national character." Two weeks later, on July 10, he elaborated on these remarks, implying that coeducation had been the source of "moral problems" among Japan's youth.[1] Kiyose's claim was particularly puzzling given that a 1952 study sponsored by his own ministry had found that thirty-three out of forty-seven prefectures reported "no connection" between coeducation and moral problems. Furthermore, the majority of prefectures that responded to the study noted that sex-segregated institutions were more likely to experience such problems than coed ones.[2]

By 1954, 63 percent of high schools—the level of education that occasioned the most concern for parents and teachers—had already become coeducational. This figure is impressive because ministry guidelines had given local school districts wide latitude in deciding whether to convert to coeducation at the high school level, effectively making coeducation beyond middle school optional.[3] Therefore, a majority of school districts seem to have accepted the idea of coeducation in high school by this time. By the end of the decade, 80 percent of universities had also become coeducational, and the system had almost completely taken root at the middle school level as well.[4] So at the time Kiyose made his remarks, coeducation was already a fact of life for many students, and according to the minister's own data, by all accounts the "new system" of education seemed to be proceeding quite smoothly.

This stubborn insistence on coeducation as the source of moral problems in Japanese society (in the face of all evidence to the contrary) was not exclusive to Kiyose or to the moment in which he was speaking. As we saw in previous chapters, coeducation had troubled conservative parents, educators, and bureaucrats even prior to its introduction as part of the Occupation-era education reforms articulated in the Fundamental Law of Education of 1947. Many had argued against the practice on the grounds that it was not only dangerous but also "un-Japanese," as Kiyose intimated.

However, what had changed at the time he uttered these remarks was the political context. Japan had regained its sovereignty in 1952, and by 1955 the conservatives would consolidate their power under the LDP. This party would go on to rule Japan almost unobstructed until 1993, ushering in the "economic miracle" of high growth in the 1960s that brought prosperity to the nation and, at its apex, elevated Japan to the status of the world's second-largest economy. The 1950s was a time of assessment of the legacy of Occupation-era reforms, and Kiyose's doubts about coeducation were voiced on the heels of a host of other attempts by the newly empowered conservative party to roll back many of these reforms. For example, at the time the minister made his remarks, the Diet had just voted to rescind the right to publicly elect local board of education members, a clear signal that the MOE would exert more centralized control over the educational system at the national level. There were also fears that the LDP intended to revive the prewar family (*ie*) system.[5] So Kiyose's concerns about coeducation were expressed at a time when conservatives were invigorated by the political shift that had brought them to power and had begun to flex their regulatory muscles.

In this chapter, we will see that such concerns about coeducation persisted well into the postwar period, eventually morphing into a full-blown moral panic over "coeds ruining the nation" that was fed by the mass media in the 1960s. While the precise object of concern shifted, from coeducation during adolescence to the rise of women's universities to the presence of women on elite university campuses, the root cause of this social malaise was the challenge that coeducation continued to pose to the ideology of separate spheres for men and women that had underlined the prewar sex-segregated system of education. As noted in previous chapters, during the Occupation young people had struggled to reconcile mixed messages about gender norms, stemming from the conflict between prewar values that stressed gender-specific societal roles and Occupation-era discourses of "equality of opportunity." These value conflicts were not so much resolved as sublimated in the postwar period into anxieties regarding new social "problems," such as widespread concern about juvenile delinquency and the "threat" of talented female students taking jobs and university placements away from male students who had historically monopolized such opportunities.

In what follows, we will see that these unresolved conflicts perpetuated concerns about moral problems—understood in the sense of premarital sexual experimentation but also transgression of gender norms and roles—well into the postwar period. This raised troubling questions about how to balance women's legal equality with men against the societal demands placed upon women to behave as latter-day "good wives and wise mothers." Furthermore, the object of these concerns expanded well beyond coeducation at the high school level—ostensibly the age of greatest concern to parents and teachers—to encompass all aspects of the postwar educational system, including not only coeducational universities but also those specifically designated for women. In the 1950s, this moral panic focused its attention on the "rise" in juvenile delinquency (attributed to the moral problems supposedly caused by coeducation) and the potential of coeducation to encourage transgression of gender and sexual norms. By the 1960s, the discussion had shifted to concerns about female students "taking over" historically male universities. This phase of the debate was quickly dubbed a controversy over "coeds ruining the nation" (*joshidaisei bōkokuron*), and the issue was eagerly picked up by and amplified through coverage in the mass media.

But regardless of these shifts in focus over time, the underlying concerns remained the same. The coeducational system had facilitated new forms of interaction between young people and new roles for women in Japanese society. This threatened the integrity of the sex-segregated and hierarchical societal structure that was comfortable and familiar to older generations, who worked to contain this process of social change by attempting to reinstate elements of the prewar system. Ultimately, this resulted in an educational system that was coeducational on the surface but continued to exert pressure on women to pursue "careers" as latter-day "good wives and wise mothers" well into the postwar period.

TEENAGE WASTELAND: THE *TAIYŌZOKU* AS EMBODIMENT OF POSTWAR MORAL PROBLEMS

From the beginning of the "new system," educators and government bureaucrats began to fret about the various moral problems that would likely arise when boys and girls, particularly at the high school level, were educated in close proximity to one another. In response to these concerns, the MOE released a set of guidelines as early as 1949—the year of both the introduction of coeducation at the high school level and the release of the film *Blue Mountains*—calling for "purity education" (*junketsu kyōiku*) to counteract the anticipated negative effects of coeducation. This was envisioned as a variety of abstinence education that emphasized virginity for unmarried men and women and chastity after marriage. By 1955, the MOE had further refined its definition of "purity education" to emphasize this decisive break with the outmoded traditions of the prewar era:

> We do not wish purity education to be associated only with preconceptions such as feudalistic chastity and principles of religious abstinence. Purity education means "measures or education to correct the psychological and physical relationships between the two sexes"; it aims at human happiness and healthy social life and should be considered based on scientific rationality.[6]

Parents, women's groups, youth groups, and parent-teacher associations were exhorted to cooperate in disseminating this new postwar version of moral education. This focus on abstinence would continue, in modified form, into the early 1970s, when the Japanese Sex Education Association began to lobby the MOE for a more comprehensive sex education program that would also address the psychological and pleasurable aspects of sex, not merely portray it as a means of reproduction.[7]

The need for "purity education" was rationalized by extensive media coverage spotlighting a "dramatic rise" in juvenile delinquency during the 1950s. A Ministry of Justice (MOJ) study in 1958 found a significant rise in juvenile crime rates in the years following World War II.[8] Particularly disturbing to the authors of the MOJ report was the proportionate rise in the number of violent crimes committed by minors and particularly those with a sexual component; the study found that in 1957, 53 percent of all rapes were committed by juveniles, along with 39 percent of robberies, 29 percent of thefts, and 23 percent of other types of violent crimes (including "violence, bodily injury, threat, [and] extortion").[9]

It is important to note that these MOJ statistics may have been misleading in a number of ways. First, the 1958 study used the year 1941 as a benchmark for measuring postwar increases, meaning that crime rates were indexed at 100 for that year, yielding a relative increase to 274 (or 2.74 times the 1941 figure) by 1957.[10] While it may be statistically true that there were over two and a half times the number of crimes committed by juveniles in that year, this statistic becomes less alarming when taken in historical context. Viewed in another way, juvenile crime rates for 1941 might well be considered to have been unnaturally low, given that Japan at that time was governed by an autocratic system of military rule that placed extraordinary limitations on personal freedoms, effectively coercing citizens to police their own behaviors for fear of dire consequences. As David Ambaras notes, by this time many of the youth in the age ranges most likely to have committed such infractions—the sixteen- to nineteen-year-olds whose behavior caused such consternation in the late 1950s—would already have been conscripted into either the military or the student labor details that absorbed the energies of so many adolescents growing up during this state of total war mobilization.[11] So the "high" rates of delinquency reported in this and subsequent ministry reports may well have been inflated by this standard of comparison. It is also worth mentioning that MOJ statistics on juvenile delinquency also included offenses like traffic accidents, technically also considered to be infractions of the penal code, that may not have resulted from the kind of deliberate adolescent malfeasance typically associated with the term "juvenile delinquency."[12] While the rate of increase of juvenile arrests in Japan during the late 1950s did exceed that of adults,[13] it seems more likely that the furor occasioned by these statistics in the media was out of proportion to whatever actual increase in juvenile crime might have occurred.

Although the mass media and government bureaucracies like the MOE and the MOJ tended to suggest a connection between juvenile crime and the lax morals of the new postwar generation of youth, other commentators took a more sympathetic approach. For example, Nagai Michio was quick to note that rather than providing evidence of the moral bankruptcy of youth, the recent social instability might have more to do with the challenges faced by the generation that grew up during the years of privation immediately following defeat. He reminds his readers that these young people were schooled in the "classrooms" of the *aozora gakkō* (lit. "open-air schools")—the practice of conducting classes outdoors during the Occupation period because of a lack of school facilities. He notes that these students were educated when there were not enough teachers and classrooms to conduct a credible education system of any kind, only to face a world of straitened opportunities for employment and university placement as they matured.[14] He further argues that rather than willfully acting out of caprice, young people are suffering because they are caught between a rapidly changing economy defined by an increasingly mechanized labor market and tough competition for university and jobs, on the one hand, and a host of new freedoms, on the other. Since their opportunities for self-actualization are limited, simply touting the need for "moral education"—the solution proposed by Education Minister Kiyose—would do nothing to resolve the underlying cause of rebellion by youth who lack a positive outlet for their energies.[15]

As Yoshizawa Natsuko notes, with the transition to coeducational environments stressing sexual equality that accompanied the postwar democratic reforms, for the first time young men and women began to perceive themselves as having more in common with one another than they did with adults. This social transformation resulted in the "invention" of the teenager as a form of social identification with its own cultural mores and set of experiences.[16] This oppositional form of identification, whereby teenagers understood themselves to occupy a subject position that was defined against that of adults, seems to have fostered the worldwide culture of adolescent rebellion that flourished in the first few postwar decades. In Japan, this was manifested most visibly in the *taiyōzoku* (lit. "sun-tribe") phenomenon—a boom in novels, films, and popular weekly magazines that celebrated youthful defiance of adult societal norms.

Paralleling the popularity of films like *Rebel Without a Cause* (1955) and *Blackboard Jungle* (1955) in the United States, the *taiyōzoku* phenomenon stoked fears of moral collapse and juvenile depravity in Japan. The term refers to a popular 1955 novel by Ishihara Shintarō, *Taiyō no kisetsu* (Season of the sun), which won the Akutagawa Prize in 1956 and launched its young author, a college student at the time of publication, on a career as a controversial media celebrity (and eventual LDP candidate for the Japanese Diet). The novel details the adventures of a young couple, Eiko and Tatsuya, whose thirst for "speed" and sex led them into risky behavior and affairs with multiple partners, culminating tragically in Eiko's death due to a botched abortion.[17] The novel (and the film made from it) seemed to encapsulate all of the fears and anxieties provoked by the specter of young men and women allowed to socialize freely with one another, and discussion of this phenomenon figured prominently in debates over coeducation in 1956 and 1957.[18]

The connection between the *taiyōzoku* and coeducation seems to have been first suggested by a reporter during a press conference on July 10, 1956, following Kiyose's announcement of his desire to "reexamine" coeducation.[19] Kiyose's response to the reporter's question was vague and noncommittal, but the association seems to have stuck and was picked up by the news cycle, repeated in the columns of opinion leaders and pundits, and debated in the letters to the editor of various newspapers. While conservatives were quick to draw rhetorical linkages between coeducation and the kind of moral depravity depicted in these media products, these arguments did not go uncontested by supporters of coeducation. For example, one female second-year student at a coeducational high school in the Tokyo area, in a letter to the editor of the *Asahi Shinbun* dated July 27, 1956 (evening edition), wrote an impassioned defense of the "new system" as a direct rebuttal of Kiyose's attack on it. In the course of this letter, she explicitly critiques the *taiyōzoku* phenomenon for capriciously stoking fears about moral problems, insisting that such portrayals are representative of only a "tiny fraction" of students. She further suggests that Ishihara and his publishers were simply motivated by profit to produce such narratives:

> Because of Mr. Ishihara's books and movies, adults probably think that our way of living is immoral [*fuketsu*]. That world is just a tiny fraction [of the youth population]. I can only think that Mr. Ishihara is simply writing these things for money. I can say with confidence that the vast majority of us are healthy [*kenzen*]. Those adults who accept things like the selling of sex without love are far, far more impure.[20]

Scholar Ishikawa Hideo, in an article in a research journal published by Tokyo Keizai Daigaku, expressed agreement with this view, noting that in spite of the recent media frenzy over juvenile delinquency and other social problems, the number of cases of love suicides, abortions, and sexual misconduct was actually quite small. Rather, he placed the blame for the recent controversy over coeducation squarely on sensationalized coverage in the mass media:

> In our society today, movies, magazines, and other forms of journalism are overflowing with eroticism. It gives us the feeling that morals have declined. It's common to think that these social conditions have caused scandals among middle and high school students. But the blame for moral corruption is not in the coeducational system, but rather the commercialism of society. . . . I have not seen any evidence to suggest that coeducation has caused impure relationships between the sexes. Rather, coeducation has naturally cultivated an attitude of fairness toward the opposite sex, and we can consider it to provide a basis for the development of healthy opposite-sex relationships, though it goes without saying that this requires careful guidance

and understanding of the actual state of relationships between men and women.[21]

Nevertheless, the notion of a rebellious youth culture run amok remained persuasive in the popular consciousness, thanks to media representations that painted these fearsome trends in lurid tones, creating a moral panic that demanded remediation.

That coeducation was still so easily associated with juvenile delinquency in the minds of the Japanese public well into the 1950s indicates the persistence of prewar ideologies that understood sex-segregated environments as normative and viewed social mixing of the sexes with extreme skepticism. Almost a decade after its implementation, there still seems to have been a prevalent assumption that coeducation facilitated an unseemly degree of intimacy between young people that threatened to foster social degeneracy. This was the case even as the practice of dating was gradually gaining a measure of acceptance in Japanese society. As Mark McLelland notes, because of the intensely sex-segregated nature of Japanese society during the Pacific War and the prevalence of arranged marriage, the idea that young people of the opposite sex might respectably spend time in one another's company for the purpose of romance was anathema to good morals and common sense. Thus, "dating" as understood in the West was a new concept that was introduced during the Occupation period.[22]

As we can see from the continued controversy surrounding coeducation, this idea of socializing with the opposite sex before marriage as a harmless practice did not gain immediate acceptance. However, it did become more common over the course of the 1950s, as increasing numbers of women gained admittance to historically all-male campuses. At the university level this increasingly resulted in classmates marrying one another upon graduation, indicating that coeducational campuses helped to foster the popularity of "love marriages"—where partners became acquainted with one another and chose each other voluntarily—as opposed to arranged marriages, which were typically facilitated by parents with the help of an intermediary. At the same time, though, the stigma attached to coeducation precisely because it facilitated such socializing between the sexes had not entirely dissipated, leading to the persistence of mixed messages regarding sexual norms well into the postwar period.

A 1957 article by Waseda University professor Teruoka Yasutaka, who would

become one of the main progenitors of the debate over "coeds ruining the nation" in the early 1960s, provides an intriguing example of this stubborn determination to link coeducation to moral problems. His essay, "Why Female Students Go to University," was featured as part of a series called "Criticism of
Women Today" in the popular women's journal *Fujin Kōron*. The article might
best be described as a free-range rant on the general subject of young women in
academics based primarily on his own experiences at Waseda. He notes with
disapproval that female students in the early days of coeducation "thought too
much of themselves" and were determined "not to be outdone" by their male
peers. By contrast, while female students now generally out-perform their male
classmates in terms of course grades, they tend to "disappear" into marriage and
motherhood within five years of graduating, so that only the male graduates
manage to establish themselves in careers that actually use the knowledge
gained through university study. He admits that while at first he thought this
was a shame, he has since changed his mind; he now considers it a good thing
that young women are more apt to use their time in college to find a husband:

> Lately female students lack ambition in a positive sense. It may also have
> something to do with the fact that they come from upper-middle-class
> homes, but they're not particularly anxious to find employment, and if the
> right opportunity comes along, they're comfortable with either going to
> work or getting married. I think this is because the anxiousness that comes
> with an inferiority complex and the desire to compete [with men] has disap-
> peared little by little.

> Gradually there are more and more cases where these marriages result from
> love that blooms during their university years.

> It's like a four-year miai [the process of arranging a marriage]; they fall in love
> having already understood their partner's character, intellectual ability,
> tastes, family ties, and financial strength. You might call it an "arranged love
> marriage." It's healthy because once they feel love for one another, they date
> and marry, having met each other's families and gained their approval.
> There's no room for sun-tribe girls at a first-rate university.

> Two or three years ago, we had a female student whom we called a "Japanese
> Marilyn Monroe," who walked around [campus] shaking her hips and jig-

gling her breasts. No respectable male student would go near her, and in the end she was followed around by fake students and went crying to the Student Life Office.[23]

He then returns abruptly to the topic of marriage, noting that young people these days tend to prefer mates their own age, in contrast to his own youth when men tended to prefer wives a few years younger. He attributes this to the fact that this generation of young people have grown up with democratic ideals and naturally seek "a partner [*kyōryokusha*] in the true sense of the word."[24]

The sudden reference to the figure of the "sun-tribe girl" (*taiyō musume*) in the midst of a polemic about the marriage patterns of today's youth is quite jarring and not obviously connected to the remainder of the passage. And yet Teruoka clearly intends to contrast this symbol of female delinquency against the wholesome image of the "healthy" coed whose ambitions are modest and who knows better than to attempt to "compete" with men on their own territory. This juxtaposition of ostensibly opposite terms creates a hierarchical system of value that presupposes there is something very wrong with women who strive for academic success or whose goals include a strong desire to pursue a profession rather than "disappear" into roles as conventional wives and mothers. It is also striking that the "Japanese Marilyn Monroe" of Teruoka's anecdote is connected in his mind with the specter of the delinquent "sun-tribe girl" not because of anything she does but simply because of what she is—a woman who inhabits an obviously female body in an environment whose history as an all-male institution of higher learning renders that body anomalous. Furthermore, although his telling of the story suggests that the young woman was somewhat traumatized by the degree of unwanted male attention she received—what would undoubtedly today be described as sexual harassment—Teruoka seems to take perverse pleasure in recounting this incident, using it humorously to underscore the degree to which she stood out as a woman in an overwhelmingly masculine environment. In likening her to a member of the "sun-tribe," which by this point was a highly pejorative reference, Teruoka not only implies that she does not belong at a storied institution of higher learning like Waseda but also suggests that, like the morally licentious women portrayed in the *taiyōzoku* films and novels, she was probably "asking for it."[25]

That detractors of coeducation were so determined to link the practice to moral problems no doubt explains why the *taiyōzoku* phenomenon held such sway over the Japanese popular culture imaginary in the late 1950s. Its sensational treatment of "associations" between young men and women validated the fears of those who keenly sensed the challenge that coeducation posed to conventional gender and sexual norms and found this prospect threatening. Thus, the popularity of these narratives was not the cause but rather the result of deeper anxieties regarding the legacy of coeducation. As we will see in the next section, these anxieties included the transgression of gender as well as sexual norms.

## "ANDROGYNY" AS RHETORICAL CONTAINMENT OF FEMININE AMBITION

In addition to fears of premarital sexual experimentation among adolescents, accusations that coeducation fostered androgyny also carried over from the Occupation period to the postwar era. The frequent use of this term to describe any example of behavior that failed to conform completely with prewar gender norms may be seen as an attempt to rhetorically contain such challenges to the status quo by portraying them as aberrant and disturbing. That these accusations of androgyny were overwhelmingly leveled at women rather than men—particularly during this period, when women were increasingly narrowing the academic gap between the sexes and gaining admittance to prestigious university campuses and other previously all-male spaces—indicates a concerted attempt to contain feminine aspirations by circumscribing ambitious young women within the realm of the abnormal.

For example, echoing Teruoka's remarks above, psychologist Hatano Isoko took up this problem of androgyny in a 1955 roundtable discussion on university entrance exams in *Fujin Kōron* that also dealt with issues related to coeducation. While she says she agrees with the system of coeducation in principle, she has observed that it results in the "masculinization" of girls who become socialized to compete with men. This is implied to be problematic not just in and of itself but also because it opens up the possibility of girls besting boys in competition for entrance to prestigious schools. Hatano is particularly concerned that in doing so, girls might learn that boys are "unreliable" (*tanomoshiku nai*): "Since it's a coeducational system it's fine for them to strive to imitate boys' good points, but I don't agree that they should become overly ambitious [*gattsukiya*]."[26] While this statement is made in the course of a critique of the university entrance exam system, which Hatano feels puts undue pressure on students of both sexes, the language employed here suggests a rather conventional definition of gender difference that reinstates prewar expectations of gendered educational outcomes.

The use of the word "unreliable" is particularly revealing, since here she seems to be implying that girls *should* rely upon boys to outstrip them intellectually. On the other hand, girls are criticized for harboring the same kind of ambitions, which are implicitly coded as "masculine" and therefore inappropriate for their gender. Her concern about boys being demystified in the process of competition for school placements seems to indicate a kind of nostalgic desire to perpetuate the gender distinctions created by the prewar sex-segregated system, wherein girls were supposed to look up to boys as academically superior. Failure to internalize this asymmetrical view of sex difference is thus posited as a failure to differentiate properly as a fully gendered subject. It is particularly interesting that in spite of her avowed concern for the effect of coeducation on girls, it is masculinity that is portrayed as vulnerable. This implies that the mere experience of "losing" in academic competition to a girl threatens to emasculate by stripping away the mantle of intellectual superiority (see chap. 3).

While this concern with androgyny was prevalent in debates over coeducation in middle school and high school, it also permeated discourses concerned with higher education for women as well. Women who see higher education as a path to employment and financial independence receive the greatest degree of criticism for being "mannish" and allowing their academic ambitions to compromise their femininity. For example, in a 1958 article in *Fujin Kōron*, Ozaki Moriteru characterizes female students seeking career-track employment as competing with men in a way that makes them unfeminine (*otoko masari*) and renders them "lacking in sex appeal."[27] Likewise, in the midst of an attack on women's universities as "bridal schools" (see chap. 3), Nakaya Ken'ichi diverts from his main subject to criticize women from coeducational institutions who pursue post-graduation employment for their failure to conform to gender norms. In an unfavorable comparison of female students at Tokyo University with their counterparts at women's universities, he characterizes the former as "grade grubbing" and "always conscious of not wanting to be outdone by the men," echoing the negative portrayal of women in competition with men seen in Ozaki above. In contrast to these "mannish" ladies at coeducational schools, who are further described as "dry" and "cold," women's university students are portrayed in gender-appropriate fashion as "bright" and "cheerful."[28]

But although such complaints about coeducation rendering women androgynous might seem to be limited to discourses about female students at coeducational universities, in fact they may also be observed in discussions of the legitimacy and purpose of women's universities as well. In a 1952 essay on female students at women's universities in the mass-circulation journal *Gunzō*, Fukuhara Rintarō, professor of English literature at an unnamed women's university, expresses similar concerns about the products of the postwar coeducational system having been rendered mannish in comparison with prewar female students. He waxes eloquently about the prewar generation of "young women of ability" who nevertheless managed to preserve a "sense of themselves as women." These "bright beauties" of the prewar era, who are romanticized for their affinity for poetry and other ostensibly feminine intellectual pursuits, are depicted as far superior to the postwar generation of women's university students, who are described in implicitly masculine terms as "prosaic," "intellectual," and "shrewd."[29]

Concerns about androgyny were not exclusive to opponents of coeducation. In a 1956 article in the education journal *Kyōiku Gijutsu*, Nagata Shin, president of the Japan Education Association (Nihon Kyōiku Gakkai), ironically winds up reiterating many of the same conventional values regarding gender difference in the course of a defense of coeducation. As a liberal educator dispatched to Europe by the MOE during the Taishō period (1912–26) to study educational practices abroad, Nagata is in an excellent position to attack fears of coeducation as unfounded, based on cross-cultural experience. Using Holland as an example, he demystifies much contemporary speculation about the practice, dismissing notions of the intellectual inferiority of women and concerns that educating the sexes together during puberty invites sexual misconduct. He discounts the idea that coeducation makes students androgynous, but in the course of doing so he tries to reassure his audience that rather than erasing gender differences, the practice actually encourages boys and girls to display the "special characteristics" and "good points" of their own gender.[30] In doing so, Nagata clearly echoes the idealized vision of gender complementarity embraced by many student supporters of coeducation during the Occupation period as a compromise between prewar and postwar ideals of gender relations.

There is a remarkable consistency across the prewar/postwar divide in terms of the way concerns about coeducation were expressed through anxieties regarding the androgynization of youth. By definition, adolescence is a liminal stage of development when young people are neither children nor adults but rather in a process of becoming the latter. However, in these narratives this stage is portrayed as a dangerous time when youth are particularly susceptible to influences that might derail them from internalizing appropriately gendered characteristics. As we saw in previous chapters, opponents of coeducation in particular tended to portray such gendered development as a process that is vulnerable to disruption, with potentially disastrous consequences. Therefore, this process of development must be controlled as much as possible to contain it within socially acceptable bounds, lest it spin irrevocably out of control. Androgyny here is portrayed as an apocalyptic result of adolescent development gone wrong, and according to this logic, coeducation only encourages such outcomes. As we will see, by the time the generation of young women educated entirely under the coeducational system reached university age in the early 1960s, these anxieties had exploded into a full-blown moral panic that sought to redirect the energies of this small number of ambitious women back into the domestic sphere.

## THE RISE OF DEBATES OVER COEDS RUINING THE NATION

Viewed in historical context, it is not surprising that the mass-media discourse on coeds ruining the nation came to a head in the early 1960s. By this time, young women who had begun their elementary school education under the "new system" were just beginning to graduate from high school. In 1960, only 2.5 percent of young women in the age cohort eligible for higher education enrolled in four-year universities, versus 13.1 percent of men, but by 1965 the percentage of women had nearly doubled, to 4.6 percent.[31] While this may still sound like a tiny fraction of women, they were becoming an increasingly visible presence on university campuses, particularly in humanities fields. This made literature professors like Teruoka increasingly sensitive to the prospect of their fields being "invaded" by female interlopers, who they perceived as less serious in their dedication to graduate or professional work than male students.[32]

This generation of girls had grown up in an educational system that at the very least accorded lip service to the goals of democracy and gender equality. Though this message often conflicted with others that persistently envisioned more conventional and gender-specific roles for women, young women who sought the same degree and quality of higher education as their male peers could nevertheless find justification for these aspirations in the postwar democratic reforms. However, this generation also faced unprecedented competition for university entrance and professional opportunities, aggravating resentments over the prospect of women taking men's places away from them. The postwar baby boom had put great pressure not only on the educational system but also on the labor market, as children of this generation left school and attempted to find jobs. Although many factors contributed to these straitened circumstances—in particular, the transition from an elite to a mass model of education that opened the universities to many more male as well as female students[33]—women increasingly were blamed by the mass media for the resultant social and economic dislocations.

In a March 1962 essay that has been widely identified as the catalyst for the debate over coeds ruining the nation,[34] Teruoka blamed the recent influx of female students into the academy for the "dumbing down" of the university as an educational institution. He complained that he felt obligated to dilute the intellectual content of his own lectures, "ignoring academic rigor [to focus on] the realistic and familiar, [which is necessary to prepare] girls to enter the home [as housewives]."[35] Citing what he presents as an alarming set of statistics, he noted that of the 2,508 female students at his home institution during the previous year, 2,300 were majoring in the fields of literature or education; at rival Keio University, 1,116 out of 1,450 were enrolled in literature alone. However, he claimed, "almost none" of these women anticipated a career in their chosen field of study.[36] If this trend is allowed to continue, he argued, an inordinate number of university placements that should rightfully go to male applicants, who can be counted on to serve Japanese society through long careers in the workforce after graduation, will be "lost" to women. Teruoka takes this to be evidence that the university as a whole—and particularly certain fields where women were overrepresented, such as his own field of Japanese literature—was rapidly becoming feminized, imperiling not only the future of these fields of study but also the future of Japanese society writ large.[37]

Thus, while many young women were encouraged to aim higher by discourses extolling democracy and equality, they also had to contend with mass-media attacks on both women's universities and female students enrolled in four-year coeducational universities. Though they might seem like separate arguments, these two strands of discourse—denoted in Japanese as the rhetoric of "women's universities [as] useless" (*joshidaigaku muyōron*) versus "coeds ruining the nation" (joshidaisei bōkokuron)—may actually be seen as two sides of the same coin. Both were based to some degree on conservative presumptions of women's intellectual inferiority, along with a sense of masculinity in crisis that resulted not just from defeat in war but also from a growing sense that women's legal equality with men threatened to erode historically male privileges. In the case of coeducational universities, this was typically phrased in terms of women depriving men of university placements and professional positions. In the case of women's universities, pundits characterized these institutions as inferior in intellectual rigor compared with historically male institutions, based on the fact that many were created out of schools that had legally been defined at the level of "specialty schools" (semmon gakkō) rather than universities prior to 1945.[38]

In both cases, we see prewar discourses of feminine intellectual inferiority retooled for postwar purposes. Conservatives may not have explicitly said in the 1960s that women were less capable of academic success than men—as Teruoka himself noted in the 1957 essay analyzed above, women's classroom performance had already begun to outstrip that of their male classmates. However, they still found ways to imply that women were not as worthy of scholarly investment as men, based on a combination of conventional misogyny and willful blindness to the many ways that society attempted to contain feminine ambition in spite of the postwar promises of equality of opportunity. As the Japanese entered this era of high economic growth, government and corporate interests colluded to reinforce normative gender roles—for example, through pension plans and taxation systems that privileged single-earner households—on the theory that hardworking salarymen would be more willing and able to work long hours of overtime if their wives stayed home to shoulder responsibility for the domestic sphere.[39] Furthermore, education at the primary and secondary levels began to formally and informally guide female students in the direction of marriage and motherhood rather than professional development, for example, by requiring girls (but not boys) to take coursework in home economics.[40] Young women thus received profoundly mixed messages during these two decades as to the degree and purpose of education to which they should aspire.

These mixed messages were encoded into the DNA of arguments against female university students, often producing constitutive contradictions that sound nonsensical in historical perspective. In his various essays on the topic of coeds ruining the nation, Teruoka tends to make self-contradictory complaints about female students at coeducational universities, faulting them for compliance with conventional gender norms even as he ridicules those who transgress those norms. Whereas in the 1957 essay analyzed above he commends women for choosing marriage over career, by 1962 he excoriates them for making the same choice, arguing that they are taking opportunities for higher education away from male students, who he thinks harbor more legitimate ambitions for success in the professional world. On the other hand, he also pokes fun at women with serious academic ambitions, characterizing them as thinking too much of their own abilities and arguing that they drive men away with their attitude of *otoko masari* (defeating men).[41] The persistent concern in Teruoka's essays with the problem of women competing with men on historically male territory indicates that these concerns were based on more than merely a distaste for female transgression of gender norms. By the early 1960s, when women's "invasion" of formerly all-male universities had become more statistically significant, the integrity of the elite university as a gendered space had itself become a subject of intense concern.

Interestingly, while the notion of women intruding on male spaces might have seemed a problem peculiar to newly coeducational elite institutions like Waseda and Tokyo Universities, the rhetoric of female transgression upon male prerogatives was also extended to criticism of women's universities. For example, in a 1955 screed lambasting such institutions that was published in *Bungei Shunjū*, Yoshida Ken'ichi expresses some strongly worded concerns about the quality of the newly christened women's institutions of higher education, which had only recently been elevated to the university level as part of the Occupation's effort to ensure equality of educational opportunity. He clearly considers this entire process to have been illegitimate. He even suggests that such schools may have attained their new status by fraudulent means, such as temporarily borrowing books from other schools to meet the required number of volumes set by the accreditation standards:

> It costs an awful lot of money to make a single university, and even if you make do by elevating higher commercial schools or women's medical colleges, it still requires a lot of money just to raise them to university level. Around Showa 25 or 26 [1950 or 1951] . . . there was a big to-do about libraries having to have 30,000 books or something. There was even talk of schools who borrowed collections [from other schools] on the understanding that

the books would be returned after they passed inspection, though in the end it seems that most schools bought the books outright. I hear that the used bookstores in Kanda made a killing. In other words, it was a tough job just to collect the books for the library, so it seems strange to think about going that far just to increase the number of makeshift universities in that age of burned-out ruins when we barely had clothes on our backs.[42]

While he raises these intimations of foul play only to disavow them in the next breath as gossip, he has nevertheless planted a seed of suspicion in his reader's mind, thus effectively discrediting such schools as undeserving of the status of "university." Naturally, his point of comparison is the prewar all-male elite institution such as Tokyo University, which he implies earned its status at the top of the academic food chain through long years of cultivated excellence. (He omits the fact that such distinctions were decided by legal fiat regardless of the quality of the school, so that the former imperial universities would occupy the highest rung on the status ladder.)

Underlying all this grousing about academic merit or its absence is a clear sense of umbrage at the notion that women's universities might ever be considered equal in status to those historically serving only men. He denigrates the intelligence of female students as well as the quality of the women's universities they attend, characterizing them derisively as institutions "that were formed [hastily] in the postwar era out of dressmaking schools."[43] He further ridicules the desire of women to attend university in the first place, claiming that it stems not from any legitimate desire for professional employment but rather from a vain attempt to aggressively assert their newly granted equality with men. Most of these women, Yoshida argues, are motivated by a simplistic notion of "equal rights" that causes them to insist on doing the same things as men regardless of circumstances:

> The reason why women who have no desire to study anything in particular nevertheless persist in wanting to go to university is nothing more than the fact that men go. They confuse the fact that men go to university with the idea that women too have the right [kenri] to receive a university education. Women-only universities were created because men go to university to ensure that they can get a job, and schools that have strong track records at ensuring employment [for their graduates] are hard to get into.[44]

In fact, the entire notion of women's rights seems to annoy Yoshida. He refers to women's pride in exercising these newly granted rights in pejorative terms on a number of occasions in this brief essay, including a pointed dig at "women who aren't satisfied unless they constantly emphasize to themselves their gratitude for the right to vote that they received as a result of Japan's democratization."[45] The frequency of overt and implicit references to the Occupation in his essay is telling. The elevation of women's colleges to university status, for example, is dismissed with the explanation that "it was an Occupation order, so it couldn't be helped,"[46] implying a pervasive sense of resentment, even emasculation, at the fact that women are now extended rights and privileges historically granted only to men.

## CONSEQUENCES OF THE POSTWAR BACKLASH

It is clear that this backlash against the notion of equality of educational opportunity had a measurable effect on the choices that young women made about their own futures. Numerous articles published during the late 1950s and early 1960s attest to the power of this discourse of coeds ruining the nation to pressure women to pursue the more conventional path of wife-and-motherhood. For example, in a 1958 article titled "Obstacles to Women's Liberation" in the journal *Intellect* (*Shisō*), Tanaka Sumiko clearly describes the primary "obstacle" of the title to be men's conventionally gendered expectations of women.[47] While women's postwar roles have changed, she argues, with many more women working outside the home, men remain "tyrants" in both the home and the workplace, which helps explain why many women therefore "choose" more conventional roles in spite of having ostensibly been liberated by postwar democratic reforms. At the same time, these reforms have encouraged women to aim higher by seeking financial independence and the satisfaction of meaningful careers, thus producing intense frustration in those who are forced to compromise their dreams in this way. Five years before Betty Friedan's seminal work of feminist analysis, *The Feminine Mystique*, Tanaka decries the "problem with no name" so eloquently identified by Friedan, albeit from a socialist-feminist analytical perspective.

Tanaka further notes that because many women are forced to yield their career goals to domestic roles within the home, those who do persist in pursuing roles outside the home must face lowered expectations about their own level of commitment to their jobs. Since the prevalent expectation is that they will put marriage and motherhood first, many employers assume that they will be a bad investment and refuse to hire them in the first place or else fail to invest in their careers. She offers the example of women in high-status occupations with so much experience that if they were men, they would be in management, but instead they are relegated to support roles no matter how much education or experience they have.[48]

While Tanaka does not mention this specifically, at this time it was also standard practice in most industries to specify in employment announcements that open positions for professional (rather than clerical) workers were for men only. In her memoirs, Yoshitake Teruko shares the following demoralizing experience of searching for employment after graduating from Keio University in the mid-1950s:

> I was with an upperclassman from the theater club, K, who was a graduate student, and we were diligently looking at the job posters. . . . While K was intently taking down job application information and writing it in his notebook, I was standing there becoming increasingly irritated. An assistant film director was an artistic position. However, in all the film companies, artistic positions were classified as "women ineligible," which would be written in big, bold letters. It was not only film companies. In fact, among all the job announcement posters that were hanging up on two different bulletin boards, more than two-thirds of the positions were women ineligible.

> Fortunately, one film company, Toei, had not plastered "women ineligible" across all their job categories. So, feeling that I was placing all my hopes for the future on this one company, I applied to take the entrance examination. At the test site for an artistic position, there were some twenty women assembled. But when it came to the second round of interviews, I was the only female remaining. My name was called right about in the middle, so I did as I was asked and sat in the chair in front of me. I sat there very nervously as they hurled one question after another at me.

> However, these questions had absolutely no connection with either film, my view of work, or my understanding of human nature. Rather, in the end, they all had to do with private matters about my relationships with members of the opposite sex. There was even one guy who kept asking rather suggestive questions without the slightest trace of embarrassment, such as:

"What kind of men do you like?"

"Is there a type of man that you like among this group?"

"Do you have a boyfriend?"

One fat guy sitting right in the middle who was laughing as he spoke said to me quite frankly, "Actually, in our company, since way back, artistic positions have only been filled by males, so we did not think we needed to go to the trouble of writing 'women ineligible' all over our job announcements."[49]

Likewise, as late as 1963, Kyoto University graduate Kanō Mikiyo recalls women of her cohort struggling to find any employment whatsoever, in spite of the otherwise excellent employment opportunities that their male classmates faced, thanks to high economic growth and the boom years just prior to the Tokyo Olympics.[50]

These concerns are echoed by the young women surveyed in a 1956 article by Hayashi Susumu in the magazine *Chisei*, titled "What are Female University Students Thinking?"[51] Based on quantitative analysis of personal testimonies written by 135 young women ages eighteen to twenty-four, Hayashi concludes that social pressure to conform to gender stereotypes influences the way girls envision their own futures. He notes that while fully 60 percent of his subjects imagined themselves holding a profession in the future, only 20 percent anticipated remaining in these positions ten years later.[52] According to Hayashi, this indicates not only that most of these young women still perceived work outside the home as a temporary stage of life preceding the (implicitly more important) stage of full-time wife-and-motherhood but also that society was unlikely to support women who dream of financial independence through lifetime commitment to a profession.[53] Hayashi further argues that women are sheltered by the current system, only interacting with the world "in parentheses" (i.e., in a qualified way), which makes it doubly hard for them to envision a life outside of conventional roles. Based on the responses of the female students surveyed, he concludes that women's choices about education and employment are profoundly shaped by messages received from parents and society, which convince them that marriage is the only means to a woman's happiness.

He further notes that many of these young women perceive marriage as an "escape" from the contradictory expectations placed on women by an educational system that simultaneously assures them that they are equal to men and yet encourages them to aspire to a gender-appropriate life course. While on some level they may want independence from the family structure and recognize the tensions within that structure, they find the difficulty of supporting themselves more daunting. Marriage thus provides them an easy out, in spite of requiring them to relinquish "control over their destinies."[54] At the same time, these contradictions produce frustration and ambivalence in the girls forced to make such choices. Fully 60 percent expressed a desire to balance work with family, and nearly all respondents to the question "How do you view the current social circumstances?" expressed some type of dissatisfaction with the way society is structured, with 60 percent agreeing that the structure of society must be fundamentally changed.[55] So while on one level these female students may have made conventional choices about their goals and aspirations, they were also clearly aware of the degree to which their decisions were shaped by social context and were to some extent critical of this pressure to yield to a gender-appropriate life script.

But while most young women continued to prioritize marriage and motherhood in the 1950s, an intrepid minority sought to capitalize on the promises of the new constitution by preparing for professional career paths that had previously been foreclosed to them. A roundtable discussion among some of these students, published in *Fujin Kōron* in March 1959, provides an instructive range of commentary about the opportunities that were now available to those with lofty ambitions, as well as the problems and pitfalls they encountered as they groped for ways to realize these dreams. Aside from male moderator Nakano Yoshio, identified here as a "[social] critic" (*hyōronka*) by the magazine's editorial staff, all the participants in this discussion—Takemori Setsuko, Noguchi Hisa, Yoshimura Setsuko, and Kumada Yūko—are young female *rōnin*, or students who have graduated high school but are still trying to secure entrance to their university of choice. All four seem to be aiming straight for the top of the academic food chain; it is implied that they are holding out for admission to Tokyo University, although the girls[56] seem a bit bashful about admitting this outright to Nakano when asked.[57] This seems to suggest that for all their drive and motivation to succeed, they are nevertheless keenly aware that this determination places them on the wrong side of conventional gender norms that understand such ambition as a decidedly masculine trait.

That these young women understand their aspirations to be unusual for their sex is evident in the subsequent dialogue, in terms of both the kind of goals they articulate for themselves and the way they describe peers and elders responding to these goals. In contrast to the female students targeted by coeds ruining the nation pundits—that is, those students who crowd into programs like literature and are accused of turning such departments into prestigious avenues of "bridal training"—all of the female participants in this roundtable plan to major in science or social science.[58] Furthermore, most seem to see an elite university education as a necessary stage of preparation for a professional career rather than for an advantageous marriage—another accusation frequently hurled by conservative pundits at female university students. For example, Takemori expresses the desire to go into the medical profession and become "like [Albert] Schweitzer," helping people in remote areas in Asia or the Amazon.[59] Although the other girls encourage her in this dream, Takemori seems rather self-conscious about it, noting that others might think her "strange"—an apparent admission of the conflict this poses with the conventional feminine script of marriage and motherhood.[60]

Noguchi seems more confident in her expression of desire for self-actualization, declaring herself to be "proud to be a *rōnin*,"[61] but she too acknowledges the conflict that society perceives between feminine professional ambition and more normative roles for women. While most of the girls seem to have identified specific professions of interest, Noguchi takes a more philosophical and comprehensive attitude toward education, understanding it as a search for a "theme" by which to live her life. In this sense, advanced study at an elite institution of higher learning seems, from Noguchi's perspective, more akin to a personal quest for knowledge of the human condition in general and herself in particular, and she is quite eloquent in her expression of her desire for a meaningful life of the mind.

However, Noguchi admits that her intellectual ambitions made her stand out in an uncomfortable way as distinctly different from most of her female peers. She describes her middle school teachers as treating her like a "strange woman" (*okashii onna*) for wanting to go on to university and says they assumed therefore that she had no thought of marriage. When moderator Nakano makes the same assumption, she challenges this perspective:

> I think it's strange to think [of marriage and employment] as separate. People tend to associate [women's desire to] go to university with not getting mar-

ried and living an active life as some sort of eminent female scholar, but it's not that I've decided not to get married, and I don't think of myself as particularly elite [*erai*], nor am I living with an excessive sense of my own importance. The reason why I want to go to university is because I need a purpose [*tēma*, lit. "theme"] to live by. I can't stand the idea of just walking ever closer to death without some sort of purpose.[62]

Although Yoshimura backs her up here, considering it strange for people to make such assumptions—from her perspective it is "taken for granted" (*atarimae*) that girls in this day and age advance to high school and even university[63]—Noguchi's reference to the image of the "female scholar" suggests some sensitivity to the way highly educated women are portrayed in contemporary society. Evidently the term *joshi* (女史), commonly employed in reference to women of distinction with a high level of education or expertise, has something of a negative connotation for these young women. They speak of a "*joshi* type" as if it suggests someone who puts on airs or considers herself to be superior to others, and Noguchi states that she consciously tries not to behave that way. Kumada adds, "Generally when a woman tries to do anything in the company of men she's immediately called a *joshi*," indicating that such women are perceived as harboring ambitions or self-regard inappropriate to their gender.[64] This exchange suggests a heightened degree of sensitivity to the way educated women were perceived as aberrant, even as more and more young women implicitly challenged conventional structures of gender difference by attaining such distinctions, which historically had been reserved for men.

The sensitivities articulated by these young women betray the influence of the coeds ruining the nation discourse that permeated the mass media of the time. They criticize women's universities as institutions of inferior quality that promote outmoded gender stereotypes. They further suggest such institutions place inordinate emphasis on "feminine" fields of study like literature and home economics while devoting scant resources to subjects like the sciences and social sciences. Echoing many of the claims made by Teruoka and colleagues discussed above, Yoshimura states that even those departments in which women's universities are said to excel, like literature, do a poor job of preparing their students to work in these fields. She further suggests that students at such institutions have weak motivation to learn and only superficial interest in their courses of study; because they have little interest in a professional career in the field, they lack the dedication to truly master the material.[65] Noguchi concurs with this assessment:

> I read this in a magazine somewhere, but it said that the kind of people who gather there [i.e., in women's universities] are really "young lady" types [ojōsan], and there are a lot of them who are living without any particular purpose. And the teachers there—even though they would give classes for the purpose of academic inquiry in boys' schools, when they teach at girls' schools they wonder why the students even bother to come and are afraid to teach the same thing that they do at boys' schools. A scholar of literature wrote that, it was quite a while ago, but it made sense to me.[66]

It is difficult to guess which scholar Noguchi might be referencing with this statement, given that a number of muyōron pundits had been making these claims since the early 1950s.[67] However, it is interesting that these women seem generally to agree that the "fault" for these lowered expectations lies with female students and not with the attitudes of their professors or with the conservative values that structured the environment surrounding them.

These speakers also express resentment at the way their own choices to resist gender norms are made more difficult by the willingness of so many other young women to conform to gendered expectations. For example, when Kumada explicitly critiques the media hype over "female university students," Noguchi counters with the argument that the choices of "irresponsible" women only add fuel to these debates. By this she seems to mean women who have no other ambition than to marry and who see education as a form of "bridal training." All the girls seem to be in agreement about their opposition to this way of thinking. Takemori attributes it to a lack of self-awareness, and Noguchi describes them as lacking a sense of purpose. Yoshimura contributes a story about a friend who converted one of these "traditional" Japanese ladies to her more progressive style of self-awareness, only to be told by this girl that she was happier when she did not have to think so much.[68] These casual remarks and anecdotes hint at the struggles faced by ambitious young women in legitimizing their unconventional choices, suggesting that battling normative ideals of gender often pitted the nonconformists against other women who chose to comply with those norms. While the female students discussed above all perceived conventional gender roles to be restrictive in some way, it is also clear from their remarks that those conventions still held powerful sway, demonstrating that they left an indelible mark even on those who sought to challenge them.

## CONCLUSION

As we have seen in this chapter, Occupation-era criticisms of coeducation persisted well into the postwar era, in the form of accusations of moral problems (transgression of both gender and sexual norms) as well as intimations of feminine intellectual inferiority. Mixed messages about gender roles for women also continued to haunt the postwar ideological landscape, simultaneously justifying and stigmatizing women's intellectual and professional ambitions. Japanese society prior to 1945 had been structured according to a strictly sex-segregated system that presumed complementary roles for men and women in society, even as women often worked outside the home for part of their adult lives. The Occupation-era educational reforms had attempted to dismantle this system by offering women equal (in the sense of "same") opportunities. However, the persistence of prewar ideologies of gender resulted in the acceptance of coeducation only to the extent that it could be co-opted to produce an idealized model of gender complementarity that had much in common with the prewar sex-gender system.

Once the Occupation ended and Japanese conservatives regained power, the structure of coeducation was preserved on the surface, but the contents of education (and the ideologies surrounding it) increasingly emphasized gender-specific outcomes for boys and girls that were more or less consonant with the goals of the prewar educational system. The postwar backlash against coeducation, culminating in the early 1960s debates over coeds ruining the nation, may thus be understood as one of a host of containment strategies to confine women's ambitions within a version of the prewar "good wife and wise mother" ideology that had been updated for the postwar context.

Ideologies of gender complementarity persisted not merely because older generations of Japanese clung stubbornly to the past but because they were useful to rebuilding the Japanese economy, providing a foundation for high economic growth well into the postwar period. Salarymen were able to devote their energies wholeheartedly to serving "Japan Inc." as corporate warriors only because their wives could be counted on to stabilize the domestic front through service as latter-day "good wives and wise mothers." The furor over coeds ruining the nation reached a fever pitch in the early 1960s because these "coeds" challenged conventional gender roles and norms and threatened to take away historically male privileges, but also— and perhaps most importantly—because their challenge to those norms threatened the very foundations of the postwar recovery, built as it was on a perhaps untenable tension between conventional ideals of gender and postwar promises of equality.

# Conclusion

WE BEGAN THIS BOOK with the case of Miss Doi, who was struggling between postwar exhortations to exercise her new right to equality with men and more conventional expectations of feminine docility. Let us now return to the question that opened our discussion: What "lessons" might the Miss Dois of Japan have learned about gender equality as a result of this coeducational experiment, and how did this impact relationships between men and women in the years and decades to come? If Miss Doi did indeed master the art of being "polite when associating with the opposite sex and not . . . careless in [her] speech," she may well have embraced a more conventional path, becoming a latter-day "good wife and wise mother" whose equality of educational opportunity was leveraged to nurture the next generation. But for those of her cohort who did not choose this path—and particularly for the small minority of academically inclined young women who earned admission to historically all-male universities—how did they navigate the minefield of conflicting ideologies regarding the form this equality should take? Or perhaps more importantly, what do the experiences of these women tell us about the ways contemporary Japanese discourses of gender and sexuality were (and were not) shaped by Occupation-era challenges?

We have seen that the prewar educational system trained women separately for gender-specific service to the family and nation, through reproduction of the next generation of Japanese subjects and through labor in the public and private sphere that was supportive of yet separate from the work of men. After Japan lost the war in 1945, the Allied Occupation reformed the nation's educational system, making coeducation the norm through the middle school level and common in high schools and universities. This new system was underwritten by an ideology of equality-as-sameness that clashed with the prewar logic of separate spheres for men and women. Young people who were in school when this shift occurred were thus forced to negotiate an uneasy truce between these seemingly incommensurate worldviews. For many, this contradiction would be resolved through an embrace of coeducation as a means of cultivating democratic values such as cooperation between boys and girls, while simultaneously training them to perform different yet complementary roles in society.

While girls struggled at first because of inferior academic preparation for the "new system," they soon caught up with their male peers and even began to exceed them in terms of classroom performance in the years that followed. However, intimations of feminine intellectual inferiority continued to haunt higher education for women well into the postwar period. Concerns about moral problems also persisted and were stoked by sensationalistic coverage of coeducation in the mass media, culminating in debates over coeds ruining the nation. Although the rampant sexual experimentation feared by parents and teachers failed to materialize, this moral panic seems to have been fueled as much by the specter of transgression of gender norms as by fears of sexual impropriety. This was frequently articulated during the Occupation period as androgyny—the possibility that girls might adopt masculine characteristics and (to a lesser extent) that boys' masculinity might be eroded through association with the feminine. But what it really signified was the concern that girls might begin to encroach upon male territory, usurping university placements and professional careers that had previously been the sole bastion of men. This explains why Japanese society remained enthralled with the specter of coeds ruining the nation well into the 1960s even as the number of women in elite universities and high-powered career tracks remained pitifully small. In fact, most young women who pursued higher education at this time opted for the more "ladylike" route to junior college, followed by lower-level clerical positions upon graduation.[1]

That the coeducational system was frequently portrayed in Japanese media as unprecedented and diametrically opposed to "traditional" Japanese values, in spite of prewar advocacy of the practice by progressive Japanese educators, perhaps speaks to what Jan Bardsley has described as a "vested interest in believing in the newness of the postwar" as a historical moment of discontinuity.[2] And yet the ideology of gender complementarity that underwrote this system may be seen in many ways as continuous with prewar ideologies of gender such as good wife, wise mother. Both exhorted women to contribute to the nation through labor construed as supportive to men's activities in the public sphere—whether domestically (for example, through housework and childcare) or through paid labor understood as supplementary to family budgets and therefore not intended to earn a living wage.

It is clear that many in Japanese society hoped to preserve the absolute differentiation between gender roles and behaviors that characterized the prewar sex-segregated system of society—particularly conservative politicians whose close cooperation with business leaders produced the "economic miracle" of the 1960s. Coeducation had opened up a space for ambitious and intelligent women to envision futures other than the prewar "good wife and wise mother" model of femininity. Putting that genie back in the bottle was a crucial goal of conservatives intent on preserving the basis of the postwar economic recovery, built as it was on an ideology of harmonious gender complementarity. The LDP, the conservative party that ruled Japan uninterrupted throughout this period of growth, thus worked closely with industry to craft social policies that kept women at home so that their husbands could devote themselves wholeheartedly to careers as corporate warriors. This prompted government attempts to reify ideological distinctions between masculine and feminine roles in the postwar decades by, for example, requiring girls to take home economics courses, counseling them to desire futures as latter-day good wives and wise mothers, and crafting pension and tax systems that effectively penalized families with two full-time earners. So while pundits continued to stress that these gender-specific roles were "natural," they also sought to reinforce them through social and educational policies designed to inculcate conventional gender norms.

One thing that is striking about these assumptions of the "naturalness" of gender, upon which much of the postwar Japanese sex-gender system was based, is the way gender norms are assumed to be simultaneously innate *and* prone to disruption. We can see this in the way androgyny was said to result from mutual influence when boys and girls spent too much time in one another's company during the liminal stage of adolescence. In these accounts, androgyny is described as unnatural and disturbing, something to be carefully policed and quickly rectified, whereas expressions of conventionally masculine or feminine behavior are understood to be natural when performed by someone inhabiting the "correctly" sexed body. In other words, according to this logic, male bodies are expected to produce masculine behaviors, and female bodies are expected to produce feminine behaviors, with little to no overlap between these realms of comportment. And yet if this is the case—if bodies naturally produce the behavior associated with their gender—how can such expressions of gender be vulnerable to disruption?

Put differently, why might it be necessary to segregate the sexes to prevent such mutual influence or to reinforce correct expressions of gender identity through training considered appropriate to each sex?

As we saw in chapter 4, many elements of the prewar Japanese sex-gender system were actually inspired by Western theories of gender essentialism, such as those that underlined Stanley Hall's influential 1904 study *Adolescence*. However, rather than being superseded by egalitarian models of gender that emphasized "sameness"—the need for men and women to have the same rights and opportunities in modern society—this presumption of gender essentialism seems to have been *incorporated into* Occupation-era discourses of equality of opportunity. This hybrid structure of difference-within-equality persists to some extent even to the present day and appears to have produced a Japanese model of gender as *kata*—a form that is grounded in biological reality but that must also be mastered through repetitive practice, as in martial arts or tea ceremony.[3] Gender here is understood simultaneously as an essence (*honshitsu*) that originates in the sexed body *and* as a set of disciplinary practices that must continually be honed to achieve a more perfect version of itself. In some ways this resembles Judith Butler's notion of gender as performative, but without the subversive intent.[4] According to this way of thinking, gender reaffirms the natural order of things and staves off social disorder; thus, it is necessary for individuals to perfect the forms of appropriately gendered behavior to ensure a stable and principled society.

While the furor over coeds ruining the nation seems to have died down in the late 1960s and the "women's lib" movement of the 1970s challenged many of the assumptions of this system of essentialized gender difference, its legacy persists to this day. Many of the most virulent public controversies in recent decades have turned on unresolved tensions between the harmonious complementarity and equality-as-sameness models of gender difference, such as debates over the framing of the Equal Employment Opportunity Law in the 1980s and the Basic Law for a Gender Equal Society in the 1990s.[5] This is evident most recently in the current prime minister Abe Shinzō's call for Japanese women to "shine" in the public sphere while taking on ever more responsibility for the care of aging parents and the reproduction of the next generation. In a speech to the United Nations on September 26, 2013, Abe proposed "womenomics" as a key to Japan's economic recovery from a prolonged recession and a stubbornly low birthrate. Acknowledging the challenges Japanese women face in balancing the demands of professional careers with expectations that they shoulder the lion's share of responsibility for housework and childcare, Abe "pledged to create 'an environment in which women find it comfortable to work and . . . be active in society.'"

But as Ayako Kano and Vera Mackie have pointed out,[6] these pledges remain hollow in the face of his own party's stubborn insistence on protecting "traditional" Japanese values, including conventional gender roles based on a presumption of gender essentialism. As Kano and Mackie note, while "deep-seated gendered inequalities still exist in contemporary Japanese society, and nearly all aspects of government policy could benefit from adopting a more gender-sensitive outlook," Abe's proposed half-measures to deal with the problem promised little in the way of an actual solution. They questioned the prime minister's credentials as a self-declared "feminist":

> Abe's task force considered instilling the idea of a "proper childbearing age" into all women through the distribution of "women's notebooks." This has been criticized as being intrusive. Abe also proposed extending women's childcare leave to three years to encourage women to withdraw from the workforce and be full-time carers of their infants. This has been criticized as unrealistic and likely to lead only to further discrimination against women in the workplace.

Thus, by exhorting women to "shine" in the public sphere and simultaneously do more to remedy Japan's low birthrate, Abe sought to enhance women's economic contributions to the state while preserving the system of gender inequality that rendered them problematic in the first place.

As Mary Brinton and Dong-Ju Lee have argued, the persistence of gender essentialism has in fact been an important contributor to the low birthrate in Japan (and elsewhere).[7] Japanese women choose not to have children precisely because they continue to be expected to shoulder the majority of domestic tasks and cannot reconcile these with their professional responsibilities. Conservative claims that women are "selfishly" choosing careers over children thus mask the stubborn reality that gender essentialism produces gender inequality, which itself forces women to make a Manichean choice between work and family. Furthermore, even when fathers wish to take on an equal portion of childcare responsibilities, the world of work is still structured so that they cannot do so without adversely impacting their careers. This problem of course also affects women and is exacerbated by the lack of political will to invest in expanding the highly regulated system of licensed day care centers to accommodate the large number of working families even today. Thus, the convoluted set of ideologies surrounding the promises of "equal opportunity" for women that plagued coeducation during the Occupation period continues to inform present-day debates over gender and sexuality in Japanese society, to the detriment of its economic and demographic security.

# Notes

## Introduction

1. Doi Sachiko, untitled, in "Tokushū: Danjo kyōgaku—Kamiukena kōtō gakkō ni okeru danjo kyōgaku ni tsuite," *Ehime kyōiku*, August 1949, 22.

2. It is well known that many of the masterpieces of classical Japanese literature were the work of women writers. To cite just two of the most famous examples from the Heian period, see Murasaki Shikibu, *The Tale of Genji* (*Genji monogatari*), available in multiple English translations, most recently by Dennis C. Washburn (New York and London: W.W. Norton, 2015), and Sei Shōnagon, *The Pillow Book* (*Makura no sōshi*), trans. Ivan Morris (New York: Columbia University Press, 1967).

3. From the Kamakura period (1185–1333), see, for example, Nakanoin Masatada no Musume, *The Confessions of Lady Nijō* (*Towazugatari*), trans. Karen Brazell (Stanford, CA: Stanford University Press, 1976). More recent scholarship has also documented the literary activities of women in the Edo period (1600–1868); see, for example, the essays in P. F. Kornicki, Mara Patessio, and G. G. Rowley, eds., *The Female as Subject: Reading and Writing in Early Modern Japan* (Ann Arbor: Center for Japanese Studies, University of Michigan, 2010).

4. Martha Tocco, "Made in Japan: Meiji Women's Education," in *Gendering Modern Japanese History*, ed. Barbara Molony and Kathleen Uno (Cambridge, MA, and London: Harvard University Press, 2005), 40.

5. Herbert Passin, *Society and Education in Japan* (New York: Teachers·College, Columbia University, 1965), 31.

6. Martha Tocco notes, "Geography, region, and locale . . . often proved to be more of an impediment [to women's education] than did social class." See Tocco, "Made in Japan," 41.

7. For an engaging window into the cultural context of these interactions between aristocratic men and women, see Ivan I. Morris, *The World of the Shining Prince: Court Life in Ancient Japan* (New York: Kodansha International, 1994).

8. Brazell, in Nakanoin Masatada no Musume, *Confessions of Lady Nijō,* xv.

9. See, for example, the essays collected in Ruch's important edited collection *Engendering Faith: Women and Buddhism in Premodern Japan* (Ann Arbor: Center for Japanese Studies, University of Michigan, 2002). Griffiths also discusses the freedom of movement of itinerant nuns in mixed-gender groups in her book *Tracing the Itinerant Path: Jishū Nuns of Medieval Japan* (Honolulu: University of Hawai'i Press, 2016).

10. Tocco, "Made in Japan," 40–41.

11. John F. Embree, *Suye Mura: A Japanese Village* (Chicago and London: University of Chicago Press, 1939), 193–95. See also the book Wiswell coauthored with Robert J. Smith, *The Women of Suye Mura* (Chicago: University of Chicago Press, 1982). Of particular interest for this discussion is the practice of "night crawling" (*yobai*), whereby young men would "have a go at slipping into a house at night with a view to having intercourse with a daughter of the house or a female servant" (115).

12. Sonia Ryang, *Love in Modern Japan: Its Estrangement from Self, Sex, and Society* (London and New York: Routledge, 2006), 5.

13. Hirota Masaki, "Notes on the 'Process of Creating Women' in the Meiji Period," trans. Suzanne O'Brien, in *Gender and Japanese History*, vol. 2, *The Self and Expression/Work and Life*, ed. Wakita Haruko, Anne Bouchy, and Ueno Chizuko (Osaka: Osaka University Press, 1999), 209.

14. Kathleen Uno, "Womanhood, War, and Empire: Transmutations of 'Good Wife, Wise Mother' before 1931," in *Gendering Modern Japanese History*, ed. Barbara Molony and Kathleen Uno (Cambridge, MA, and London: Harvard University Press, 2005), 497.

15. Kyoko Hirano, *Mr. Smith Goes to Tokyo: Japanese Cinema under the American Occupation, 1945–1952* (Washington, DC, and London: Smithsonian Institutional Press, 1992), 16.

16. On Occupation-era pulp magazines (*kasutori zasshi*) devoted to erotica, see Mark McLelland, *Love, Sex, and Democracy in Japan during the American Occupation* (New York: Palgrave Macmillan, 2012); on early postwar "literature of the flesh" (*nikutai bungaku*), see Douglas Slaymaker, *The Body in Postwar Japanese Fiction* (London and New York: RoutledgeCurzon, 2004).

17. Michiko Suzuki, *Becoming Modern Women: Love and Female Identity in Prewar Japanese Literature and Culture* (Stanford, CA: Stanford University Press, 2010), 114.

18. Tsutsumi Ayako, quoted in Tessa Morris-Suzuki, *Shōwa: An Inside Story of Hirohito's Japan* (New York: Schocken Books, 1985), 142.

19. *Aoi sanmyaku* was first serialized in the mass-circulation newspaper *Asahi shinbun* from June to October 1947, before being republished as a single-volume

novel in 1949, the same year the film version was released. Kamei Shunsuke, "The Kiss and Japanese Culture after World War II," *Comparative Literature Studies* 18, no. 2, East-West Issue (June 1981): 120.

20. For more on this linkage between government and corporate interests, see Andrew Gordon, "Managing the Japanese Household: The New Life Movement in Postwar Japan," in *Gendering Modern Japanese History*, ed. Barbara Molony and Kathleen Uno (Cambridge, MA: Harvard University Press), 425.

21. Mire Koikari, *Pedagogy of Democracy: Feminism and the Cold War in the U.S. Occupation of Japan* (Philadelphia, PA: Temple University Press, 2008), 22.

22. Fukaya Masashi, *Ryōsai kenbo shugi no kyōiku* (Tokyo: Reimei shobō, 1998), 11.

23. By invoking the notion of "disciplinary power," I reference the work of Michel Foucault, but only in a qualified sense, given that Foucault tends not to speak of power in ideological terms. See Michel Foucault, *Discipline and Punish: The Birth of the Prison*, trans. Alan Sheridan, 2nd ed. (New York: Vintage Books, 1995). Warren Montag suggests that Foucault's avoidance of the term "ideology" may actually have been a way of distinguishing his own philosophy from that of Louis Althusser, given that he seems to have gone to great pains to take issue with many aspects of Althusserian models of ideology even as he appears to have built on those theories in other respects. See Warren Montag, *Althusser and His Contemporaries: Philosophy's Perpetual War* (Durham, NC, and London: Duke University Press, 2013), 161–62.

24. See chapter 1 for more on this point.

25. As noted on its website, "The Gordon W. Prange Collection is the most comprehensive archive in the world of Japanese print publications issued during the early years of the Occupation of Japan, 1945–1949." It houses all materials collected by the members of the Civil Censorship Detachment of SCAP from October 1945 to November 1949, when Japanese publishers were required to submit publications for censorship by the Occupation bureaucracy. It is therefore an invaluable source of data for scholars interested in Japanese responses to the social transformations of the Occupation period. For more information on the Prange Collection, see http://www.lib.umd.edu/prange.

26. For an overview of claims made about coeducation at the moment of its introduction to colleges and universities in the United States, see the introduction to Leslie Miller-Bernal and Susan L. Poulson, eds., *Going Coed: Women's Experiences in Formerly Men's Colleges and Universities, 1950–2000* (Nashville, TN: Vanderbilt University Press, 2004). See also Patricia A. Palmieri, "From Republican Motherhood to Race Suicide: Arguments on the Higher Education of Women in the United States, 1820–1920," in *Educating Men and Women Together: Coeduca-*

*tion in a Changing World*, ed. Carol Lasser (Urbana: University of Illinois Press, 1987). We can also see echoes of the Japanese experience in Jane Bernard Powers, *The "Girl Question" in Education: Vocational Education for Young Women in the Progressive Era* (London and Washington, DC: Falmer Press, 1992); and David Tyack and Elisabeth Hansot, *Learning Together: A History of Coeducation in American Schools* (New Haven, CT, and London: Yale University Press, 1990).

27. I use this term advisedly, understanding the sexual connotation that it carries, precisely because—as I demonstrate in the chapters that follow—coeducation was viewed with skepticism precisely because of the eroticism it connoted for many.

## Chapter 1

1. General Headquarters, Supreme Commander for the Allied Powers, Civil Information and Education Section, Education Division, *Education in Japan* (Tokyo: February 15, 1946), 42–43. This study was compiled by SCAP in preparation for reform of the Japanese educational system during the Allied Occupation of Japan (1945–52).

2. See the introduction for more on these points.

3. Tocco, "Made in Japan," 39. "Tokugawa" here denotes the same era referred to elsewhere in this book as "Edo."

4. Koikari, *Pedagogy of Democracy*, 33.

5. "Co-Education—Staff Studies," GHQ/SCAP Records, RG 331, National Archives and Records Service, Box 5391, Folder 12. This report is unsigned and undated, but based on internal evidence, it seems to have been written after the U.S. Education Mission to Japan concluded its business in March 1946 but before the Japanese Education Committee began negotiations to implement its recommendations in September of that year.

6. "Co-Education—Staff Studies," 2–3.

7. "Co-Education—Staff Studies," 3.

8. "Co-Education—Staff Studies," 4.

9. See, for example, Barbara Rose, *Tsuda Umeko and Women's Education in Japan* (New Haven, CT: Yale University Press, 1992); Ann M. Harrington, "Women and Higher Education in the Japanese Empire (1895–1945)," *Journal of Asian History* 21, no. 2 (1987): 169–86; Sally Hastings, "Women Educators of the Meiji Era and the Making of Modern Japan," *International Journal of Social Education* 6, no. 1 (Spring 1991): 83–94; Margaret Mehl, "Women Educators and the Confucian Tradition in Meiji Japan (1868–1912): Miwada Masako and Atomi Kakei," *Women's History Review* 10, no. 4 (2001): 579–602.

10. The first national education law, known as the Gakusei, was issued in August 1872 with the lofty goal of extending the benefits of education to all Japanese subjects. It was modeled on the highly centralized French educational system and intended to promote the edification of individual citizens so that they might contribute to the national goal of modernization. The administrative structure rhetorically enacted by the document might best be described as aspirational, as it envisioned a vast and complex network of school districts and institutions that had yet to be constructed. It divided the country into 8 "university districts" (*daigakku*), meaning that students in each geographical division would be eligible to attend a university that would hopefully be created in that district in the near future. Each university district was further subdivided into 32 "middle school districts" (*chūgakku*), which were in turn composed of 210 elementary school districts. The proposed system would therefore have required the creation of a total of 53,760 elementary schools, a rather utopian goal for the cash-strapped Meiji regime that was not attained by the time the Gakusei was first revised in 1879. For a detailed discussion of the creation and revision of the early Meiji educational system, see Benjamin Duke, *The History of Modern Japanese Education: Constructing the National School System, 1872-1890* (New Brunswick, NJ: Rutgers University Press, 2009).

11. Initially only four years of elementary school was compulsory; this was raised to six in 1907.

12. Herbert Passin provides a helpful chart of these institutions (including those for girls) in his *Society and Education in Japan*, 308.

13. Hashimoto Noriko, *Danjo kyōgakusei no shiteki kenkyū* (Tokyo: Ōtsuki shoten, 1992), 33.

14. See E. Patricia Tsurumi, "The State, Education, and Two Generations of Women in Meiji Japan, 1868-1912," *U.S.-Japan Women's Journal*, no. 18 (2000): 3-26.

15. In English, see the pamphlet by C. Tsune Gauntlett, "Dr. Yoshioka Yayoi: A Brief Sketch of Her Life" (Tokyo, 1934).

16. Passin, *Society and Education in Japan*, 105. Passin translates *semmon gakkō* as "college," but because "college" and "university" are frequently used interchangeably in colloquial English, I have chosen to use the literal translation of the term to highlight the institution's legal subordination to universities in Japan at this time.

17. Koyama Shizuko, *Ryōsai Kenbo and the Educational Ideal of "Good Wife, Wise Mother" in Modern Japan* (Boston, MA: Brill, 2013), 38.

18. Koyama, *Ryōsai Kenbo*, 43.

19. The persuasiveness of this model of gender complementarity is evident in

the fact that it was still touted toward the end of the twentieth century by some Japanese feminists. See, for example, Sumiko Iwao, *The Japanese Woman: Traditional Image and Changing Reality* (New York: Free Press, 1993).

20. Koyama, *Ryōsai Kenbo*, 45–46.

21. Koyama, *Ryōsai Kenbo*, 47.

22. Koyama, *Ryōsai Kenbo*, 48.

23. Passin, *Society and Education in Japan*, 97.

24. See the essay collection *Modern Girls on the Go: Gender, Mobility, and Labor in Japan*, ed. Alisa Freedman, Laura Miller, and Christine R. Yano (Stanford, CA: Stanford University Press, 2013), for more information on each of these emergent occupations.

25. Koyama Shizuko, "Domestic Roles and the Incorporation of Women into the Nation-State: The Emergence and Development of the 'Good Wife, Wise Mother' Ideology," trans. Vera Mackie, in *Gender, Nation, and State in Modern Japan*, ed. Andrea Germer, Vera Mackie, and Ulrike Wohr (London and New York: Routledge, 2014), 94.

26. Koyama, "Domestic Roles," 95.

27. Sally Ann Hastings, "Women's Professional Expertise and Women's Suffrage in Japan, 1868–1952," in *Gender, Nation, and State in Modern Japan*, ed. Andrea Germer, Vera Mackie, and Ulrike Wohr, 181.

28. Much English-language scholarship has already been produced on the diverse range of feminist activists and organizations prior to 1945. For information on conservative women educators, see Sally Hastings, "Women Educators of the Meiji Era and the Making of Modern Japan," *International Journal of Social Education* 6, no. 1 (Spring 1991), 83–94; and Margaret Mehl, "Women Educators and the Confucian Tradition in Meiji Japan (1868–1912): Miwada Masako and Atomi Kakei," *Women's History Review* 10, no. 4 (2001): 579–602. For an overview of the debates on "motherhood protection," which offer a cross-section of competing views on women's roles inside and outside the home, see Laurel Rasplica Rodd, "Yosano Akiko and the Taishō Debate over the 'New Woman,'" in *Recreating Japanese Women, 1600–1945*, ed. Gail Lee Bernstein (Berkeley: University of California Press, 1991); and Ayako Kano, *Japanese Feminist Debates: A Century of Contention on Sex, Love, and Labor* (Honolulu: University of Hawai'i Press, 2016). There is a wealth of published scholarship on the Seitō society and its contributors; see, for example, Jan Bardsley, *The Bluestockings of Japan: New Woman Essays and Fiction from Seitō, 1911–1916* (Ann Arbor: University of Michigan, Center for Japanese Studies, 2007), and Rebecca L. Copeland and Melek Ortabasi, eds., *The Modern Murasaki: Writing by Women of Meiji Japan* (New York: Columbia University Press, 2006). For information on the New Women's Society, see Akiko Tokuza, *The Rise*

*of the Feminist Movement in Japan* (Tokyo: Keio University Press, 1999). For a sampling of prewar feminist thought, see Sharon Sievers, *Flowers in Salt: The Beginnings of Feminist Consciousness in Japan* (Stanford, CA: Stanford University Press, 1983). Finally, Vera Mackie's comprehensive *Feminism in Modern Japan: Citizenship, Embodiment, and Sexuality* (Cambridge and New York: Cambridge University Press, 2003) provides excellent context for and discussion of Japanese feminist activity from the Meiji period to the present day.

29. For more information, see chapter 3 of Tachibanaki Toshiaki, *Josei to gakureki: Joshi kōtō kyōiku no ayumi to yukue* (Tokyo: Keisō shobō, 2011).

30. Hashimoto, *Danjo kyōgakusei no shiteki kenkyū*, 135.

31. Hashimoto, *Danjo kyōgakusei no shiteki kenkyū*, 137.

32. Hashimoto, *Danjo kyōgakusei no shiteki kenkyū*, 152.

33. Hashimoto, *Danjo kyōgakusei no shiteki kenkyū*, 139–41.

34. Hashimoto, *Danjo kyōgakusei no shiteki kenkyū*, 148, 156.

35. Hashimoto, *Danjo kyōgakusei no shiteki kenkyū*, 130–31.

36. For a lengthy discussion of the arguments presented for and against coeducation in the prewar period from the perspective of a supporter of coeducation, see Koizumi Ikuko, *Danjo kyōgakuron* (1931; reprint, Tokyo: Nihon Tosho Sentā, 1984). For a brief explication of this text in English, see Julia C. Bullock, "Coeducation in the Age of 'Good Wife, Wise Mother': Koizumi Ikuko's Quest for 'Equality of Opportunity,'" in *Rethinking Japanese Feminisms*, ed. Julia C. Bullock, Ayako Kano, and James Welker (Honolulu: University of Hawai'i Press, 2017).

37. Hashimoto, *Danjo kyōgakusei no shiteki kenkyū*, 202.

38. Hashimoto, *Danjo kyōgakusei no shiteki kenkyū*, 204.

39. Hashimoto, *Danjo kyōgakusei no shiteki kenkyū*, 209.

40. Hashimoto, *Danjo kyōgakusei no shiteki kenkyū*, 212.

41. Hashimoto, *Danjo kyōgakusei no shiteki kenkyū*, 213.

42. Hashimoto, *Danjo kyōgakusei no shiteki kenkyū*, 213.

43. Sasaki Keiko, "Dentōteki kihan kara dakkyaku shita shinchūkansō no joseitachi: Senzenki Nihon ni okeru joshi kōtō kyōiku kakudai no mekanizumu," in *Josei to kōtō kyōiku—kikai kakuchō to shakaiteki sōkoku*, ed. Kagawa Setsuko and Kawamura Sadae (Kyoto: Shōwadō, 2008), 196–97.

44. These proposals, and transcripts of the discussions of the committee that debated them, are collected in Toshiaki Okubo and Tokiomi Kaigō, *Kyōiku Shingikai Shimon Dai 1-gō Tokubetsu Iinkai Seiri Iinkai Kaigiroku*, vol. 8 (Tokyo: Senbundō Shoten, 1970–1971).

45. Toshiaki Okubo and Tokiomi Kaigō, *Kyōiku Shingikai Shimon Dai*, 41.

46. Toshiaki Okubo and Tokiomi Kaigō, *Kyōiku Shingikai Shimon Dai*, 38–43.

47. Toshiaki Okubo and Tokiomi Kaigō, *Kyōiku Shingikai Shimon Dai*, 38.

48. Toshiaki Okubo and Tokiomi Kaigō, *Kyōiku Shingikai Shimon Dai*, 38–39.

49. Toshiaki Okubo and Tokiomi Kaigō, *Kyōiku Shingikai Shimon Dai*, 261–66. For the text of the proposed Joshi Daigaku Rei, see 260.

50. Uemura Chikako, *Josei kaihō o meguru senryō seisaku* (Tokyo: Keisō shobō, 2007).

51. Uemura, *Josei kaihō*, 24–25.

52. For example, Joseph Trainor actively aided Donovan and colleagues during discussions over the wording of the FLE in negotiating with the MOE for more explicit assurances of "equality of opportunity in education" for women. See Uemura, *Josei kaihō*, chap. 7.

53. Ethel Weed, in a February 12, 1947, letter to Mary Beard, as quoted in Mire Koikari, *Pedagogy of Democracy*, 92.

54. Uemura, *Josei kaihō*, 184.

55. Gary H. Tsuchimochi, *Education Reform in Postwar Japan: The 1946 U.S. Education Mission* (Tokyo: University of Tokyo Press, 1993), 133–34.

56. Uemura, *Josei kaihō*, 143.

57. As quoted in Kyoko Inoue, *MacArthur's Japanese Constitution: A Linguistic and Cultural Study of Its Making* (Chicago and London: University of Chicago Press, 1991), 240–41.

58. It is significant that the proposed "gender equality" provisions of the new constitution caused the most consternation among Diet members, where they threatened to nullify the power of the male head of household over the other members of the family. See Inoue, *MacArthur's Japanese Constitution*, 253–54.

59. Inoue, *MacArthur's Japanese Constitution*, 268.

60. Takemae Eiji, *Inside GHQ: The Allied Occupation of Japan and Its Legacy* (New York: Continuum, 2002), xlii.

61. Monbusho, *Monbu gyōsei shiryō*, vol. 1 (Tokyo: Kokushokan gyōkai, 1997), 59.

62. Monbusho, *Monbu gyōsei shiryō*, 59.

63. Monbusho, *Monbu gyōsei shiryō*, 59–60.

64. There is also evidence to indicate that some private all-male institutions of higher learning may have begun admitting women before this time. For example, Hashimoto Noriko notes that Tōyō University began admitting women "with the tacit approval of the Ministry of Education" as early as 1916. Because this occurred prior to the 1918 promulgation of the Daigaku Rei, which provided a framework for elevating such schools to university status, they would technically have been classed as "specialty schools" (*semmon gakkō*) at the time. Hashimoto, *Danjo kyōgakusei no shiteki kenkyū*, 121.

65. Monbusho, *Monbu gyōsei shiryō*, 83.

66. Monbusho, *Monbu gyōsei shiryō*, 79.

67. Kurosawa Hidefumi, *Sengo kyōiku no genryū o motomete: Maeda Tamon no kyōiku rinen* (Tokyo: Naigai Shuppan, 1982), 193.

68. Monbusho, *Monbu gyōsei shiryō*, 130–36, contains the full text of this proclamation.

69. Monbusho, *Monbu gyōsei shiryō*, 131.

70. Monbusho, *Monbu gyōsei shiryō*, 134–35.

71. Takemae, *Inside GHQ*, 352.

72. Tsuchimochi, *Education Reform in Postwar Japan*, 76.

73. Uemura, *Josei kaihō*, 119–20.

74. Uemura, *Josei kaihō*, 118–19.

75. United States Education Mission to Japan, *Report of the U.S. Education Mission to Japan* (Washington, DC: United States Government Printing Office, 1946), 26.

76. United States Education Mission to Japan, *Report*, 24.

77. United States Education Mission to Japan, *Report*, 50.

78. United States Education Mission to Japan, *Report*, 33.

79. For example, "A system of education for life in a democracy will rest upon the recognition of the worth and dignity of the individual.... These ends cannot be promoted if the work of the school is limited to prescribed courses of study and to a single approved textbook in each subject. The success of education in a democracy cannot be measured in terms of uniformity and standardization." United States Education Mission to Japan, *Report*, 8–9.

80. United States Education Mission to Japan, *Report*, 33.

81. United States Education Mission to Japan, *Report*, 13.

82. United States Education Mission to Japan, *Report*, 33.

83. United States Education Mission to Japan, *Report*, 25.

84. United States Education Mission to Japan, *Report*, 26.

85. United States Education Mission to Japan, *Report*, 26.

86. Mark Taylor Orr, "Education Reform Policy in Occupied Japan" (PhD diss., University of North Carolina, 1954), 131.

87. Orr, "Education Reform Policy," 131–32.

88. Takemae, *Inside GHQ*, 369.

89. Hashimoto Noriko, *Danjo kyōgakusei no shiteki kenkyū* (Tokyo: Ōtsuka Shoten, 1992), 269.

90. Hashimoto, *Danjo kyōgakusei no shiteki kenkyū*, 269.

91. Hashimoto, *Danjo kyōgakusei no shiteki kenkyū*, 271.

92. Hashimoto, *Danjo kyōgakusei no shiteki kenkyū*, 273.

93. Hashimoto, *Danjo kyōgakusei no shiteki kenkyū*, 274.

94. Hashimoto, *Danjo kyōgakusei no shiteki kenkyū*, 274.
95. Hashimoto, *Danjo kyōgakusei no shiteki kenkyū*, 274.
96. Hashimoto, *Danjo kyōgakusei no shiteki kenkyū*, 270.
97. Hashimoto, *Danjo kyōgakusei no shiteki kenkyū*, 275.
98. Hashimoto, *Danjo kyōgakusei no shiteki kenkyū*, 275–76.
99. Hashimoto, *Danjo kyōgakusei no shiteki kenkyū*, 274–75.
100. Hashimoto, *Danjo kyōgakusei no shiteki kenkyū*, 275.

## Chapter 2

1. "Danjo kyōgaku kyōsei sezu; Shiritsu gakkō ni yon sentakuken," *Kahoku shinpō*, February 6, 1947, 2.
2. "Joshi wa mina rakudai: 'Danjo kyōgaku' ikkagetsugo no seiseki,'" *Ōita gōdō shinbun*, June 11, 1948, 2.
3. "Momoiro gassen o nakusu ni wa shakai ga umidasu nikutai no yūgi," *Sasebo jiji shinbun*, September 9, 1948, 2.
4. "Sesō o kiru: Honsha shakaibu dai-issen kisha zadankai," *Chūgoku shinbun*, September 7, 1949, 2.
5. I opted to do both quantitative and qualitative analysis for this chapter because the corpus was much larger than that analyzed in chapters 3 through 5. Quantitative analysis consisted of sorting all articles by location of origin and date of publication, as well as coding for the degree of support or opposition expressed for or against coeducation and the perspective of the author (i.e., was this an op-ed; a letter to the editor from a parent, teacher, or member of the community; a piece of "objective" journalism, etc.). I then searched for correlations between these factors to detect trends in responses to coeducation according to geographical location, publication date, and author's subject position vis-à-vis debates over coeducation. Qualitative analysis consisted of a close reading of all articles on coeducation in a single newspaper over time and analysis of specific claims made about coeducation, noting not merely the degree of support or opposition but also what arguments were made and how they were phrased.
6. See "Kōshanan de danjo kyōgaku," November 4, 1947, 2; "Shasetsu: Danjo kyōgaku no mondaiten," February 25, 1949, 1; "Danjo kyōgaku no kōkō jūyon," February 27, 1949, 3; "Shō-chū-kōkō no saihaichi keikaku kimaru: Kōkō ni mo tsūgaku settei, danjo kyōgaku wa myōnendo kara kanzen jisshi," May 12, 1949, 2; and "Sukusuku nobiru danjo kyōgaku: Chijimatta gakuryokusa, nayami no tane wa kōgai de no kōsai," October 9, 1949, 2.
7. "Seika ageru danjo kyōgaku no jitsu zairyō fusoku mo gojo de kaishō," *Chūgoku shinbun*, May 18, 1949, 2.

8. "Danjo kyōgaku e zenshin: 'Sōgō kōkōsei' tsūgaku no fuben mo kaishō," *Kahoku shinpō*, December 20, 1948, 3.

9. "Jiyūtō: Niigata Ichi-shi no danjo kyōgaku mondai," *Niigata nippō*, February 27, 1948, 2.

10. "Dai-ichi Shihan Danjo Kyōgaku kimaru," *Niigata nippō*, April 10, 1948, 2.

11. "Shinsei kōkō no kōsō: Nijū kōchō ni kiku," *Ōita gōdō shinbun*, April 15, 1948, 2.

12. "Zōkin motte tereru otoko gakusei: Me made somete danjo kyōgaku wa yoki mono," *Ōita gōdō shinbun*, May 11, 1948, 2.

13. According to Uemura Chikako, on the heels of this change in policy, instructions to begin implementing coeducation at the elementary level—the stage of education that was met with the least degree of objection by the public—were handed down to local educational authorities. Thus, in some areas coeducation was well underway in elementary schools even before the FLE was approved by the Diet in March 1947; Uemura, *Josei kaihō*, 145. This was the case in Hiroshima, for example, where a visiting Red Cross official in January 1947 noted with approval that coeducation seemed to be progressing smoothly in area elementary schools; "Danjo kyōgaku wa yoku dekite imasu," *Chūgoku shinbun*, January 14, 1947, 2.

14. See, for example, coverage in the *Chūgoku Shinbun* and the *Kahoku Shinbun* on October 27, 1946. Both stories were featured prominently on the front page.

15. These were Yamagata, Niigata, Shizuoka, Toyama, Yamaguchi, Matsue, Saga, Fukuoka, and the No. 5 Higher School in Kumamoto.

16. "Danjo kyōgaku o kataru," *Niigata nippō*, May 24, 1947, 2.

17. See Donald Roden, *Schooldays in Imperial Japan: A Study in the Culture of a Student Elite* (Berkeley: University of California Press, 1980).

18. "Joshi wa mina rakudai: 'Danjo kyōgaku' ikkagetsugo no seiseki,'" *Ōita gōdō shinbun*, June 11, 1948, 2.

19. "Sukusuku nobiru danjo kyōgaku: Chijimatta gakuryokusa, nayami no tane wa kōgai de no kōsai," *Hokkaidō shinbun sapporoban*, October 9, 1949, 2.

20. "Danjo kyōgaku no jittai: Yamanoborichū no baai," part 1, *Sasebo jiji shinbun*, September 21, 1948, 2. Part 2 of this article appeared in the next day's paper on the same page.

21. Amazaki Yoshio, "Danjo kyōgakuron—toku ni kōkō no," part I, *Sasebo jiji shinbun*, October 1, 1948, 2.

22. Amazaki Yoshio, "Danjo kyōgakuron—toku ni kōkō no," part II, *Sasebo jiji shinbun*, October 2, 1948, 2.

23. "Danjo kyōgaku wa tanoshi: Ōita Ichi undōkai," *Ōita gōdō shinbun*, October 10, 1949, 2.

24. While the Prange Collection database revealed twelve articles from this newspaper on "danjo kyōgaku," it is worth noting that its collection of this newspaper only begins with issue no. 303 (October 10, 1947), fully one year after its holdings for most other newspapers. So it is quite likely that the *Sasebo jiji shinbun* published many more articles on this topic in the three-year period covered by this sample that are not represented here.

25. "Momoiro gassen o nakusu ni wa shakai ga umidasu nikutai no yūgi," *Sasebo jiji shinbun*, September 9, 1948, 2.

26. "Danjo nana-sai sei o onajū sezu—bōkun otoko, yoku warau onna: Danjo kyōgaku saitenbo," *Sasebo jiji shinbun*, February 1, 1948, 2.

27. See, for example, "Sukusuku nobiru danjo kyōgaku: Chijimatta gakuryokusa, nayami no tane wa kōgai de no kōsai," *Hokkaidō shinbun sapporoban*, October 9, 1949, 2; "Fūki wa shinpai muyō: Ebetsu kōkō waki ai ai no danjo kyōgaku," *Hokkaidō shinbun* (Sapporo kinkōban), June 17, 1948, 2; "'Danjo kyōgaku' ni tsuite," *Chūgoku shinbun*, September 17, 1949, 2; "Hanashikago: Appare danjo kyōgaku," *Niigata nippō*, March 18, 1947, 2; "Danjo kyōgaku wa tanoshi: Ōita Ichi undōkai," *Ōita gōdō shinbun*, October 10, 1949, 2.

28. "Otona kaomake kodomo gikai," *Sasebo jiji shinbun*, June 17, 1948, 2. Remarks of this type were actually a common refrain in the early postwar era, sometimes serving as a source of humor; see, for example, "Chijin no kyōgen," January 26, 1948, 2, in the same paper.

29. Sarah Kovner documents this impact on local populations in her important book on the subject, *Occupying Power: Sex Workers and Servicemen in Postwar Japan* (Stanford, CA: Stanford University Press, 2012).

30. "Sesō o kiru: Honsha shakaibu dai-issen kisha zadankai," *Chūgoku shinbun*, September 7, 1949, 2.

31. "'Danjo kyōgaku' ni tsuite," *Chūgoku shinbun*, September 17, 1949, 2.

32. "Shūdan iede ga oshieru mono: Yugamerareta seishun no seitai—Danjo kyōgaku de kyōka," *Niigata nippō*, June 15, 1948, 2.

33. "Sukusuku nobiru danjo kyōgaku: Chijimatta gakuryokusa, nayami no tane wa kōgai de no kōsai," *Hokkaidō shinbun sapporoban*, October 9, 1949, 2.

34. "Danjo kyōgaku ze ka hi ka: Tōronkai," *Chūgoku shinbun*, March 15, 1949, 2. The article seems to have paraphrased the remarks of the speakers, so the material in quotation marks here is a direct quote from the article, though not necessarily the speaker.

35. "Danjo kyōgaku o kataru," *Niigata nippō*, May 24, 1947, 2.

36. "Danjo kyōgaku wa sansei: 6-3-3-sei ni tai suru iken," *Ōita gōdō shinbun*, January 24, 1947, 2.

37. "Zōkin motte tereru otoko gakusei: Me made somete danjo kyōgaku wa yoki mono," *Ōita gōdō shinbun*, May 11, 1948, 2.

38. "'Danjo kyōgaku' ni tsuite: Hotondo ga kyōgaku ōka," *Chūgoku shinbun*, September 17, 1949, 2. These complaints too were commonplace in the articles surveyed; see, for example, "Danjo kyōgaku no jittai: Yamanoborichū no baai," part 2, *Sasebo jiji shinbun*, September 22, 1948, 2.

39. Donald Roden, "Taishō Culture and the Problem of Gender Ambivalence," in *Culture and Identity: Japanese Intellectuals during the Interwar Years*, ed. J. Thomas Rimer (Princeton, NJ: Princeton University Press, 1990).

40. Roden, "Taishō Culture," 41–42.

### Chapter 3

1. Frederik L. Schodt, *Manga! Manga! The World of Japanese Comics* (Tokyo: Kodansha International, 1983), 61.

2. Peter Duus, "Presidential Address: Weapons of the Weak, Weapons of the Strong—The Development of the Japanese Political Cartoon," *Journal of Asian Studies* 60, no. 4 (November 2001), 965.

3. Schodt, *Manga! Manga!* 41.

4. Schodt, *Manga! Manga!* 42.

5. Rei Okamoto provides a detailed analysis of political cartoons during the height of the war, including their censorship and use in propaganda by the Japanese authorities, in her PhD dissertation, "Pictorial Propaganda in Japanese Comic Art, 1941–1945: Images of the Self and the Other in a Newspaper Strip, Single-Panel Cartoons, and Cartoon Leaflets" (Temple University, 1999).

6. Brigitte Koyama-Richard, *One Thousand Years of Manga* (Paris: Flammarion, 2007), 133.

7. *Sazae-san* was a four-panel comic strip featuring the plucky heroine Sazae and her extended family. It ran first in a local Kyūshū newspaper before being picked up for serialization in the national paper *Asahi shinbun*. Appearing in print from 1946 to 1974, the comic offers a warmly humorous window into Japanese society from wartime recovery to postwar prosperity. It was also made into a highly successful animated television show that is still on air today. The comic strip is available in English translation by Jules Young as *The Wonderful World of Sazae-san* (Tokyo: Kodansha International, 1997).

8. Brigitte Koyama-Richard, *One Thousand Years of Manga* (Paris: Flammarion, 2007), 139.

9. Koyama-Richard, *One Thousand Years of Manga*, 133.

10. See chapter 4 for a fuller discussion of this point. Specifically with regard to censorship of cartoons, we see an interesting example of this tolerance of caricatures of coeducation in the publication *Shin Manga*. While a cartoon poking fun at coeducation ("Danjo kyōgaku igo," *Shin manga*, June 1946, discussed below) was allowed to be published unaltered, censorship records reflect that another cartoon in the same magazine depicting Occupation soldiers fraternizing with local women required significant editing, with Civil Censorship Detachment censors mandating that the offending depictions be removed before the magazine could be published.

11. On the influence of Chic Young's *Blondie* on postwar Japanese culture, see also John Dower, *Embracing Defeat: Japan in the Wake of World War II* (New York: W.W. Norton, 1999), 252.

12. Sabine Frühstück, *Colonizing Sex: Sexology and Social Control in Modern Japan* (Berkeley: University of California Press, 2003), 51.

13. "Ichikō" refers to the No. 1 Higher School for boys, the most prestigious such institution in the nation. See Roden, *Schooldays in Imperial Japan*, 152–53.

14. Okada Jun, "Danjo kyōgaku hantai," *Yomimono chūgoku*, October 1949, 18–19.

15. "Danjo kyōgaku: Ze ka hi ka?"

16. Shioda Eijirō, "Danjo kyōgaku no han," *Hōpu*, August 1946, 35.

17. See Dower, *Embracing Defeat*, 111, for an image of this kind of childish play.

18. Kogane Haruo, "Honshi ōbō shinjin manga: Danjo kyōgaku," *Shin sekai*, February 1947, 53.

19. "Saikin otoko no seito de, kyōkasho o wasureru mono ga ōku nattchiyatte ne."

20. Ueki Bin, "Gendai fūkei 1: Danjo kyōgaku," *Toppu* 1, no. 2 (July 1946): 7.

21. "Mozomozo shite iru no de, ara, shirami ga aru no jya nai kashira? to, isasaka kanojo wa shinkei o tsukarasete imashita ga, aa, sono jittai wa, bokkon azayaka ni, 'Anata o ai shite imasu.'"

22. Kobayashi Genzaburō, "Danjo kyōgaku igo," *Shin manga*, June 1946, unpaginated.

23. This is also suggested by the date of the publication (1946), since many universities became coeducational in the spring of this year, but the vast majority of high schools did not convert to the "new system" until 1948 at the earliest.

24. "Omae o mukashi ni kuraberu to zuibun sumāto ni natta ne."

25. Wakatsuki Saburō, "Danjo kyōgaku," *Sakura*, May 1947, 10.

26. "Segare, chikagoro nesshin ni gakkō ni iku yō ni natta wai."

27. See Vera Mackie, *Feminism in Modern Japan: Citizenship, Embodiment, and*

*Sexuality* (Cambridge and New York: Cambridge University Press, 2003), 21–24, for a brief explanation of this system.

28. Kakimoto Hachirō, "Danjo kyōgaku ibun," *Baton*, November 1947, 25.

29. Katō Yoshirō, "Danjo kyōgaku," *Repōto* 3, no. 7 (July 1948): 31.

30. "Gakkō o yoso ni kyōgakudai hayari."

31. Yokoyama Yasuzō, "Danjo kyōgaku no hanayome gakkō," *Yomimono kurabu* 1, no. 1 (July 10, 1946): 18.

32. "Yūtō sotsugyō shōsho."

33. Takie Sugiyama Lebra, *Japanese Women: Constraint and Fulfillment* (Honolulu: University of Hawai'i Press, 1984), 58–59; italics in original.

34. I base this on the venue of publication; the aforementioned periodicals are all mass-market regional or national magazines that featured the work of professional authors and journalists, with the exception of one (*Shin sekai*) that appears to have solicited contributions from readers.

35. N.S.-sei, "Danjo kyōgaku no urei," *Tomoshibi*, no. 1 (December 1948), unpaginated. The title of the cartoon literally translates as "The Sorrows of Coeducation."

## Chapter 4

1. Senryūshi Tōrō, "Danjo kyōgaku," *Kōyū*, no. 1 (March 1948): 16. "Tōrō" is evidently this young man's given name or an alias. "Senryūshi" is not a family name but rather an epithet that means something like "a practitioner of *senryū*," a comic poetic form related to the haiku that dates to the Edo period (1600–1868).

2. I distinguish here both from "mass media," with large circulation figures and ad revenues, and from the kind of *mini-komi* (lit. "mini-communication") publications employed by the "women's lib" movement of the 1970s and other activist circles for dissemination of explicitly political discourse. By contrast, these "small media" publications seem intended primarily as a community-building exercise, providing an outlet for amateur artistic expression and a forum for discussion of local concerns but mostly without the "call to arms" style of activist rhetoric employed by political organizers. These publications seem to have been encouraged by Occupation authorities as a tangible demonstration of the free speech rights that they were attempting to promote to a newly democratized Japanese populace. On the other hand, everything published during this period was carefully scrutinized by Occupation censors, who deleted material that ran afoul of censorship guidelines, which forbade criticism of the Occupiers or their Allies, dissemination of information that would paint the Occupiers in a nega-

tive light (such as GI patronage of Japanese prostitutes), and expressions of militarist or imperialist ideologies. See Jay Rubin, "From Wholesomeness to Decadence: The Censorship of Literature under the Allied Occupation," *Journal of Japanese Studies* 11, no. 1 (Winter 1985): 84–87, for a brief discussion of SCAP censorship protocols.

3. There were 21 accounts by high school students (out of 37) in this sample. Of the remainder, 12 were of university age and 4 were middle school students.

4. Of the 37 files analyzed here, 20 were written by males and 13 by females; the sex of the remaining 4 authors was unclear. Even when articles were unsigned, the sex of the author in most cases could be determined by use of personal pronouns or other internal references that clarified group affiliation (e.g., "we girls"). There were 4 unsigned articles in this sample, with 3 clearly written by female authors; the sex of the fourth author was indeterminate from the contents. There were also 4 articles where authorship was attributed with initials rather than full names; only one of these authors was recognizably male.

5. Careful review of the surviving censorship documents that accompany many of these files in the Prange Collection reveals that while Occupation censors were highly sensitive to speech that painted the Occupiers or their Allies in a negative light (such as sexual liaisons between GIs and native women), they did not tend to strike criticism of coeducation from published materials. I was able to find only one example of a deletion of such views, in an essay penned by a foreign professor at Jōchi Daigaku (otherwise known as Sophia University) who directly countered Occupation claims that coeducation helped to promote democratic values; H. Herwegh, "Danjo kyōgaku ni tsuite—hatashite sore wa minshushugi-teki yōsei to shite teinin sareru ka," *Josei kaizō*, April 1947, 22–27. Interestingly, Japanese writers who made similar claims seem to have been permitted to do so. In his study of the "perverse press" in Occupied Japan, Mark McLelland argues that Civil Censorship Detachment employees tended not to censor material on grounds of obscenity unless they directly implicated members of Allied nations in such immoral behavior; McLelland, *Love, Sex, and Democracy*, 63. Based on my research, the same hands-off approach seems to have been taken with regard to criticism of coeducation. So while we must not discount the role of censorship in analyzing materials published during this time, particularly in terms of the possibility of self-censorship in anticipation of Occupation oversight, we also must not assume that students writing in support of coeducation were simply parroting the views of the Occupiers.

6. Fujita, "Watashi wa danjo kyōgaku o kaku miru," *Gyōbō*, no. 4 (January 1948): 2–4. No first name is given.

7. Kuji Arashi, "Danjo kyōgaku ni tsuite," *Suzuran*, no. 6 (January 1949), 20.

Publication of this newsletter is credited to the "Shibutami Gakusei-kai Bungei-bu" (Shibutami Student Association Arts Division) of Shibutami village, Iwate prefecture. It is unlikely that such a rural area could have supported a university, so this student is likely either of middle school or high school age.

8. Kanei Akito, "Danjo kyōgaku ni tsuite," *Aozora*, March 10, 1947, unpaginated.

9. Aoyanagi Noriko, "Zuisō: Danjo kyōgaku no kansō," *Manabiya no kane*, no. 3 (November 1948), 27–28.

10. Aoyanagi, "Zuisō: Danjo kyōgaku no kansō," 27.

11. Tashiro Teruko, "Ronzetsu: Danjo kyōgaku ni natte," *Sazanami*, no. 1 (December 1948): 27–28.

12. Fukuda Hiroshi, "Danjo kyōgaku seido o kōtei suru," *Kakurei*, no. 23 (February 1947): 32–33.

13. Takahashi Keiichi, "Danjo kyōgaku to warera no kakugo," *Kakurei*, no. 23 (February 1947): 34–35.

14. Of the thirty-seven narratives analyzed in this chapter, nineteen made some reference to "moral problems" or to the need for sex education, but only two of these agreed that this was actually a problem.

15. Takashita Iku, "Danjo kyōgaku ni tsuite aru joshi gakusei wa daisansei!" *Taremizu bunka* 2, no. 5 (May 1949), unpaginated.

16. "Jiyū nōto: Danjo kyōgaku no sono go," *Aozora*, no. 21 (August 1949): 15–16.

17. Daitō Shōjiki, "Danjo kyōgaku ron," *Kōyū kaishi*, October 1948, 10–12.

18. Fukuda Hiroshi, "Danjo kyōgaku seido o kōtei suru." *Kakurei*, no. 23 (February 1947): 32–33.

19. Takagi Takeshi, "Danjo kyōgaku ni tsuite," *Muhyō*, no. 1 (December 1948): 5–6.

20. Takagi Takeshi, "Danjo kyōgaku ni tsuite," 5–6.

21. Tenaka Kazuko, "Danjo kyōgaku," *Wakakusa*, no. 1 (March 1949): 24.

22. G. Stanley Hall (1846–1924) was a famous educational philosopher and child development specialist who authored the oft-cited book *Adolescence: Its Psychology and Its Relations to Physiology, Anthropology, Sociology, Sex, Crime, Religion, and Education* (New York: D. Appleton, 1904), which pioneered the study of this stage of physical, psychological, and sexual growth as a separate phase of human development. His work was well known in Japan and often cited by critics of co-education in support of the existence of innately gendered qualities that justified separate spheres for men and women in society.

23. Fukuda Hiroshi, "Danjo kyōgaku seido o kōtei suru," *Kakurei*, no. 23 (February 1947): 32–33.

24. Daitō Shōjiki, "Danjo kyōgaku ron," *Kōyū kaishi*, no. 1 (October 1948): 10–12.

25. Fujishima Hiromichi, "Danjo kyōgaku ni tsuite," *Nami*, no. 1 (March 1949): 21–22.

26. Only four (out of thirty-seven) of the student accounts in this sample made such an argument.

27. Saga Tadao, "Danjo kyōgaku hiteiron," *Kakurei*, no. 23 (February 1947): 35–37. Because several male students from the same high school also argued in favor of coeducation in the same publication, it should not be presumed that this author's opposition to the practice was strictly a product of local conservatism.

28. Ten writers in this sample made some version of this argument.

29. Yoshida Michiko, "Danjo kyōgaku o omou," *Yakusōshi*, no. 1 (March 1949): 32.

30. As discussed by Suzuki in *Becoming Modern Women*.

## Chapter 5

1. The remaining article appeared in a pedagogical journal.

2. The word seems to have been used exclusively at this time to refer to heterosexual social interaction. I have yet to find an example of it being used to describe same-sex relations in the pages of these publications.

3. It should be noted that based on the student comments in these roundtable discussions, young people evidently arrived at the coeducational classroom with a diverse array of experiences (or lack thereof) with the opposite sex. Some could rely on relationships with opposite-sex siblings to guide their interactions with classmates; others had attended elementary schools where boys and girls were taught together at least some of the time, in spite of the famous dictum that "boys and girls should not sit together after the age of seven." Still others had spent their entire lives in sex-segregated environments and could only speak about coeducation in the abstract when asked their opinion on the topic. (Not surprisingly, this group was most likely to echo their parents' concerns about "moral problems.") Furthermore, while students at the compulsory level of education generally started the "new system" in the spring of 1947, high schools were given wide latitude to decide when and to what degree to implement coeducation, with some integrating in 1948 or 1949 and others later, sometimes much later. Finally, even after many high schools in theory began to implement "coeducation," this seems to have meant different things in different localities, with some integrating nearly every class and others dividing students into different "tracks," some of which had gendered implications (for example, a "home economics" course versus a "general" college prep course). So while this chapter is primarily concerned with trends in responses by the first cohort of students to

actually experience coeducation, it should be kept in mind that students as a whole expressed a variety of opinions regarding coeducation based on varying degrees of experience with the practice. For an example of this range of student experiences, see "Zadankai: Atarashii danjo kōsai," *Kindai* 3 (June 1949): 2–9.

4. "Zadankai: Danjo kyōgaku ni tsuite," *Hana no kyōshitsu* 1, no. 2 (September 1948): 4–7. A literal translation of the title of this magazine, *Flower Classroom*, would give the erroneous impression that it is targeted at *ikebana* (flower arranging) students, but in fact as noted below its target audience is female high school students. I believe the "flower" in the title is meant symbolically to connote something bright, cheerful, and implicitly feminine.

5. This slogan adorns the cover of the September 1948 issue.

6. Tokorosawa Ayako, "Aki o mukaete," *Hana no kyōshitsu* 1, no. 2 (September 1948), 1.

7. "Zadankai: Danjo kyōgaku ni tsuite," *Hana no kyōshitsu* 1, no. 2 (September 1948), 4–7.

8. "Zadankai: Danjo kyōgaku ni tsuite," 4.

9. "Zadankai: Danjo kyōgaku ni tsuite," 6.

10. "Zadankai: Danjo kyōgaku ni tsuite," 6–7.

11. This rendering of her name may be the result of a typo. There is no "Takasaka" included in the list of participants on p. 4. There is, however, a Miyasaka Kazue, who is identified as a second-year student at Yashiro Minami High School.

12. "Zadankai: Danjo kyōgaku ni tsuite," 5.

13. "Zadankai: Danjo kyōgaku ni tsuite," 4–5.

14. "Zadankai: Danjo kyōgaku ni tsuite," 5.

15. "Zadankai: Danjo kyōgaku ni tsuite," 5.

16. "Zadankai: Danjo kyōgaku ni tsuite," 7.

17. "Zadankai: Danjo kyōgaku ni tsuite," 7.

18. "Zadankai: Atarashii danjo kōsai," *Kindai* 3 (June 1949): 2–9.

19. "Zadankai: Atarashii danjo kōsai," 9.

20. "Zadankai: Atarashii danjo kōsai," 2.

21. "Zadankai: Atarashii danjo kōsai," 2–3.

22. "Zadankai: Atarashii danjo kōsai," 5.

23. "Zadankai: Atarashii danjo kōsai," 9.

24. "Zadankai: Atarashii danjo kōsai," 3.

25. "Zadankai: Atarashii danjo kōsai," 4.

26. "Zadankai: Atarashii danjo kōsai," 4.

27. "Zadankai: Atarashii danjo kōsai," 5.

28. For other examples of adult commentary intruding upon or clashing with student accounts of coeducation, in addition to the roundtable from *Ansaazu*

discussed below, see the following articles: Makino Tsuneo, Kawazumi Masahiko, and Kedōin Yoshiaki, "Gakusei to ren'ai," *Gen'ya* 1, no. 2 (February 1947): 25–27; "Zadankai: Shokugyō fujin o kakomu shinsei kōkō danjo gakusei," *Shisutaa*, no. 2 (April 1949): 28–37; and Miyamoto Yuriko et al., "Seishun o kataru," *Gakusei hyōron*, September 1947, 2–12.

29. "Danjo kyōgaku de yokatta koto iya datta koto," *Akatombo*, July 1, 1948, 10–18.

30. Most described "last year" (meaning fifth grade) as their first year of coeducation, but at least one student mentioned an integrated fourth-year class as well. This may reflect an unusual degree of mobility by these students and their families; for example, at least one student appears to have moved to Tokyo recently from the countryside. This would make sense if understood against the backdrop of extreme social chaos that was characteristic of Japan in the first few postwar years, as children returned to the cities from the rural villages that had sheltered them from wartime bombing, and some families were reunited as loved ones returned from the front, while others attempted to move on from the loss of male breadwinners and family homes by consolidating households with extended family members.

31. Three out of thirteen of the groups featured in this article are mixed sex. The three include one boy-girl pair, one group of two boys and one girl, and one group of two girls and one boy. In all cases, the girls are active and vigorous participants in the discussions, with one girl admitting her own tendency to become involved in verbal altercations with boys ("Danjo kyōgaku de yokatta koto iya datta koto," 12) and another berating a male conversation partner in rough language for playing pranks on girls (15–16). The boys too are open about their feelings and shortcomings and admit their part in mixed-sex conflict (one admits to making girls cry, for example; 15).

32. "Danjo kyōgaku de yokatta koto iya datta koto," 10.

33. "Danjo kyōgaku de yokatta koto iya datta koto," 10–11.

34. "Danjo kyōgaku de yokatta koto iya datta koto," 11.

35. "Danjo kyōgaku de yokatta koto iya datta koto," 11–12.

36. "Danjo kyōgaku de yokatta koto iya datta koto," 11.

37. "Danjo kyōgaku de yokatta koto iya datta koto," 17.

38. In addition to the conversation between Hayashi and Ōnishi, discussed above, a female student elsewhere suggests that girls should take the high ground when faced with the mistreatment by the boys and links this to the national interest in fostering more harmonious relationships between the sexes as follows: "I think that's a good idea for rebuilding Japan. So no matter how much the boys bully us, we girls shouldn't get mad but instead make the boys into good people"; "Danjo kyōgaku de yokatta koto iya datta koto," 14.

39. "Gendai joshi gakusei zadankai: Kanojotachi wa nani o kangaete iru ka," *Ansaazu*, February 1, 1948, 56–61.

40. "Gendai joshi gakusei zadankai," 56.

41. "Gendai joshi gakusei zadankai," 61. The term *pan-pan* might best translate here as streetwalker; as many scholars of this period have noted, the *pan-pan* was a ubiquitous figure of early postwar Japanese society who was both admired for her moxie (and ability to turn her assets into ready cash) and reviled as a constant reminder of the status of Japan as a defeated nation. See, for example, John Dower, *Embracing Defeat*, and Kovner, *Occupying Power*.

42. "Gendai joshi gakusei zadankai," 61.

43. "Zadankai: Shokugyō fujin o kakomu shinsei kōkō danjo gakusei," *Shisutaa*, no. 2 (April 1949): 28–37.

44. The "career women" represent a diverse array of industries—teaching, insurance, retail, public service, medicine, banking, and police work. One of the journalists represents the magazine that published the roundtable; the other two work for a local newspaper (*Kyoto Nichinichi Shinbun*) and radio station (Kyoto Hōdō Kyoku).

45. あなたは卒業後にどの職域を選ぶか！

46. "Zadankai: Shokugyō fujin o kakomu shinsei kōkō danjo gakusei," *Shisutaa*, no. 2 (April 1949): 29.

47. "Zadankai: Shokugyō fujin o kakomu shinsei kōkō danjo gakusei," 29.

48. Koizumi Ikuko, an early proponent of coeducation, argued forcefully against such commonplace gender stereotypes in her seminal manifesto advocating coeducation, *Danjo kyōgakuron* (On coeducation). For a brief explication of this text in English, see Julia C. Bullock, "Coeducation in the Age of 'Good Wife, Wise Mother': Koizumi Ikuko's Quest for 'Equality of Opportunity,'" in *Rethinking Japanese Feminisms*, ed. Julia C. Bullock, Ayako Kano, and James Welker (Honolulu: University of Hawai'i Press, 2017).

49. "Zadankai: Shokugyō fujin o kakomu shinsei kōkō danjo gakusei," *Shisutaa*, no. 2 (April 1949): 31.

## Chapter 6

1. Hashimoto, *Danjo kyōgakusei no shiteki kenkyū*, 367; Nagata Shin, "Danjo kyōgaku mondai o megutte," *Kyōiku Gijutsu* 11, no. 7 (1956): 16–17.

2. Nagata, "Danjo kyōgaku mondai o megutte," 16.

3. Koyama Shizuko, *Sengo kyōiku no jendā chitsujo* (Tokyo: Keisō shobō, 2009), 27–29.

4. Hashimoto, *Danjo kyōgakusei no shiteki kenkyū*, 365.

5. Hashimoto, *Danjo kyōgakusei no shiteki kenkyū*, 367.

6. Kawahara Yukari, "Politics, Pedagogy, and Sexuality: Sex Education in Japanese Secondary Schools," PhD diss., Yale University, December 1996, 31.

7. Kawahara, "Politics, Pedagogy, and Sexuality," 29–32.

8. Ministry of Justice, *Juvenile Delinquency in Japan: Characteristics and Preventive Measures* (Tokyo: Ministry of Justice, 1958). By law, a "juvenile" was defined as a person under twenty years of age.

9. Ministry of Justice, *Juvenile Delinquency in Japan*, 3.

10. Ministry of Justice, *Juvenile Delinquency in Japan*, 2.

11. This is described in chapter 6 of David Ambaras, *Bad Youth: Juvenile Delinquency and the Politics of Everyday Life in Modern Japan* (Berkeley: University of California Press, 2006), 166–98.

12. This is made clear in a subsequent MOJ report, entitled *The Present State of Juvenile Delinquency and Counter-Measures in Japan* (Tokyo: Ministry of Justice, 1965). Thus, for example, while this report recorded a 77.7 percent increase in the total number of crimes from 1959 to 1963, 84.5 percent of these were traffic violations (1). Factoring these out yielded an actual decrease in the crime rate during this period.

13. Hideo Fujiki, "Recent Trends of Juvenile Crime in Japan," *Journal of Criminal Law, Criminology, and Political Science* 53, no. 2 (June 1962): 219.

14. Nagai Michio, "Roku san sei kyōiku ga unda wakamonotachi," *Shinchō* 54, no. 3 (March 1957): 99.

15. Nagai, "Roku san sei kyōiku ga unda wakamonotachi," 103.

16. Yoshizawa Natsuko, "Sei no daburu sutandaado o meguru kattō 'Heibon' ni okeru 'wakamono' no sekushuariti," in *Kindai Nihon bunkaron 8: Onna no bunka*, ed. Aoki Tamotsu et al. (Tokyo: Iwanami shoten, 2000), 207–8.

17. For an analysis of the novel and of Ishihara's colorful literary and political career, see Ann Sherif, "The Aesthetics of Speed and the Illogicality of Politics: Ishihara Shintarō's Literary Debut," *Japan Forum* 17, no. 2 (July 1, 2005): 185–211.

18. See, for example, Itō Noboru, "Yōjinbukai 'kyōgakuron': Kiyose bunshō to no ichimon ittō," *Shūkan Asahi*, July 29, 1956, 18–19; Nagata, "Danjo kyōgaku mondai o megutte"; Ishikawa Hideo, "Danjo kyōgaku no mondai," *Tokyo Kei Daigaku Kaishi*, no. 16 (1957), 1–56; Nagai, "Roku san sei kyōiku ga unda wakamonotachi"; and Teruoka Yasutaka, "Joshigakusei wa nani yue daigaku ni iku," *Fujin Kōron* 42, no. 1 (January 1957): 138–40.

19. Nagai, "Roku san sei kyōiku ga unda wakamonotachi," 17.

20. As quoted in Ishikawa, "Danjo kyōgaku no mondai," 2.

21. Ishikawa, "Danjo kyōgaku no mondai," 32.

22. McLelland, *Love, Sex, and Democracy*, 3.

23. Teruoka, "Joshigakusei wa nani yue daigaku ni iku," 139–40. "Fake students" refers to the then-common practice of young men who were not formally enrolled at prestigious schools like Waseda posing as students to sneak into lectures by famous professors (and occasionally take advantage of other campus perquisites, such as the opportunity to socialize with pretty coeds).

24. Teruoka, "Joshigakusei wa nani yue daigaku ni iku," 140.

25. Teruoka, "Joshigakusei wa nani yue daigaku ni iku," 140.

26. Itō Noboru, Hatano Isoko, et al., "Zadankai: Nyūgaku shiken bōkokuron," *Fujin Kōron* 40, no. 1 (January 1955): 178.

27. Ozaki Moriteru, "Tōdai hanayome gakkōron," *Fujin Kōron*, December 1958, 139.

28. Nakaya Ken'ichi, "Joshi daigaku muyōron," *Shinchō* 54, no. 3 (March 1957): 93.

29. Fukuhara Rintarō, "Joshigakusei," *Gunzō* 7, no. 5 (May 1952): 46–47.

30. Nagata, "Danjo kyōgaku mondai o megutte," 14.

31. The percentage of men also rose, to 20.7 percent; Kumiko Fujimura-Fanselow, "College Women Today: Options and Dilemmas," in *Japanese Women: New Feminist Perspectives on the Past, Present, and Future*, ed. Kumiko Fujimura-Fanselow and Atsuko Kameda (New York: Feminist Press, 1995), 127.

32. Teruoka Yasutaka, "Joshigakusei yo ni habakaru: kanojora no mokuteki wa nani ka," *Fujin Kōron* 47, no. 3 (March 1962): 278.

33. Edward R. Beauchamp, in "Introduction: Japanese Education since 1945," in Edward R. Beauchamp and James M. Vardaman Jr, eds., *Japanese Education Since 1945: A Documentary Study* (Armonk, NY, and London: M.E. Sharpe, 1994), 14.

34. See, for example, Koyama Shizuko, *Sengo kyōiku no jendā chitsujo*, chap. 4; and Kanō Mikiyo, "Jibunshi no naka no 'Joshi gakusei bōkokuron,'" in *Jūgoshi nōto sengohen 6: Kōdō seichō no jidai*, 111.

35. Teruoka, "Joshigakusei yo ni habakaru," 277.

36. Teruoka, "Joshigakusei yo ni habakaru," 279.

37. Teruoka, "Joshigakusei yo ni habakaru," 280.

38. These were legally defined as inferior in status to universities, which in the prewar period were largely restricted to male students; see chapter 1 for details.

39. Andrew Gordon demonstrates the active participation of both state bureaucracies and corporate leadership in this effort in his essay "Managing the Japanese Household: The New Life Movement in Postwar Japan," in *Gendering Modern Japanese History*, ed. Barbara Molony and Kathleen Uno (Cambridge, MA: Harvard University Press, 2005).

40. Hashimoto, *Danjo kyōgakusei no shiteki kenkyū*, 394.

41. Teruoka, "Joshigakusei yo ni habakaru," 280–81.

42. Yoshida Ken'ichi, "Joshidai wa bokumetsu subeki ka?" *Bungei shunjū* 33, no. 22 (December 1955): 242–43.

43. Yoshida Ken'ichi, "Joshidai wa bokumetsu subeki ka?" 246.

44. Yoshida Ken'ichi, "Joshidai wa bokumetsu subeki ka?" 244.

45. Yoshida Ken'ichi, "Joshidai wa bokumetsu subeki ka?" 246.

46. Yoshida Ken'ichi, "Joshidai wa bokumetsu subeki ka?" 243.

47. Tanaka Sumiko, "Fujin kaihō no kabe," *Shisō*, no. 414 (December 1958): 1964–68.

48. Tanaka, "Fujin kaihō no kabe," 1964.

49. As translated by Ronald P. Loftus in his book *Changing Lives: The "Postwar" in Japanese Women's Autobiographies and Memoirs* (Ann Arbor, MI: Association for Asian Studies, 2013), 68–70.

50. See her article, "Jibunshi no naka no 'joshigakusei bōkokuron,'" 110.

51. Hayashi Susumu, "Joshidaisei wa nani o kangaeteiru ka," *Chisei* 3, no. 8 (July 1956): 96–100.

52. Hayashi, "Joshidaisei wa nani o kangaeteiru ka," 96. Hayashi cites the pamphlet *Mirai no jigazō* (Future self-portrait) as the source of this information. Unfortunately, he provides no other publication information.

53. Hayashi, "Joshidaisei wa nani o kangaeteiru ka," 96.

54. Hayashi, "Joshidaisei wa nani o kangaeteiru ka," 97–98.

55. Hayashi, "Joshidaisei wa nani o kangaeteiru ka," 100.

56. I use this term advisedly and with no intention of disrespect, as the age of majority in Japan is twenty and these speakers appear to be recent high school graduates, so are probably still legally underage.

57. Nakano Yoshio et al., "Zadankai: Joshidaigaku wa gomen da—Onna rōnin ooi ni kataru," *Fujin Kōron*, March 1959, 98.

58. Nakano Yoshio et al., "Zadankai: Joshidaigaku wa gomen da," 96–101.

59. Nakano Yoshio et al., "Zadankai: Joshidaigaku wa gomen da," 100–101.

60. Nakano Yoshio et al., "Zadankai: Joshidaigaku wa gomen da," 100.

61. Nakano Yoshio et al., "Zadankai: Joshidaigaku wa gomen da," 97.

62. Nakano Yoshio et al., "Zadankai: Joshidaigaku wa gomen da," 96–97.

63. Nakano Yoshio et al., "Zadankai: Joshidaigaku wa gomen da," 97.

64. Nakano Yoshio et al., "Zadankai: Joshidaigaku wa gomen da," 101.

65. Nakano Yoshio et al., "Zadankai: Joshidaigaku wa gomen da," 100.

66. Nakano Yoshio et al., "Zadankai: Joshidaigaku wa gomen da," 98.

67. See for example Fukuhara, "Joshigakusei," discussed above.

68. Nakano Yoshio et al., "Zadankai: Joshidaigaku wa gomen da," 101.

### Conclusion

1. Fujimura-Fanselow, "College Women Today: Options and Dilemmas," 127. On junior colleges as training women for "ladylike" careers, see Brian J. McVeigh, *Life in a Japanese Women's College: Learning to Be Ladylike* (London and New York: Routledge, 1997).

2. Jan Bardsley, *Women and Democracy in Cold War Japan* (London and New York: Bloomsbury, 2014), 106.

3. For a discussion of *kata* in the context of the kabuki theater, see Maki Isaka, *Onnagata: A Labyrinth of Gendering in Kabuki Theater* (Seattle and London: University of Washington Press, 2016), 146–47.

4. Judith Butler, *Gender Trouble: Feminism and the Subversion of Identity* (New York: Routledge, 2006).

5. Ayako Kano provides a thorough and cogent discussion of these controversies in her book *Japanese Feminist Debates: A Century of Contention on Sex, Love, and Labor* (Honolulu: University of Hawai'i Press, 2016). For more on the Equal Employment Opportunity Law, see Barbara Molony, "Japan's 1986 Equal Employment Opportunity Law and the Changing Discourse on Gender," *Signs* 20, no. 2 (Winter 1995): 268–302. On the backlash against the Basic Law for a Gender Equal Society, see Tomomi Yamaguchi, "The Mainstreaming of Feminism and the Politics of Backlash in Twenty-First Century Japan," in *Rethinking Japanese Feminisms*, ed. Julia C. Bullock, Ayako Kano, and James Welker (Honolulu: University of Hawai'i Press, 2017).

6. Ayako Kano and Vera Mackie, "Is Shinzo Abe Really a Feminist?" *East Asia Forum*, November 9, 2013, accessed April 16, 2017. http://www.eastasiaforum.org/2013/11/09/is-shinzo-abe-really-a-feminist/.

7. Mary Brinton and Dong-Ju Lee, "Gender-Role Ideology, Labor Market Institutions, and Post-Industrial Fertility," *Population and Development Review* 42, no. 3 (2016): 405–33.

# Works Cited

Althusser, Louis. *Lenin and Philosophy and Other Essays*. Trans. Ben Brewster. New York and London: Monthly Review Press, 1971.

Amazaki, Yoshio. "Danjo kyōgakuron—toku ni kōkō no." Part I. *Sasebo jiji shinbun*, October 1, 1948. Gordon W. Prange Collection, University of Maryland Libraries.

Amazaki, Yoshio. "Danjo kyōgakuron—toku ni kōkō no." Part II. *Sasebo jiji shinbun*, October 2, 1948. Gordon W. Prange Collection, University of Maryland Libraries.

Ambaras, David. *Bad Youth: Juvenile Delinquency and the Politics of Everyday Life in Modern Japan*. Berkeley: University of California Press, 2006.

Aoyanagi, Noriko. "Zuisō: Danjo kyōgaku no kansō." *Manabiya no kane*, no. 3 (November 1948): 27–28. Gordon W. Prange Collection, University of Maryland Libraries.

Bardsley, Jan. *The Bluestockings of Japan: New Woman Essays and Fiction from Seitō, 1911–1916*. Ann Arbor: University of Michigan, Center for Japanese Studies, 2007.

Bardsley, Jan. *Women and Democracy in Cold War Japan*. London and New York: Bloomsbury, 2014.

Beauchamp, Edward R., and James M. Vardaman Jr., eds. *Japanese Education since 1945: A Documentary Study*. Armonk, NY, and London: M.E. Sharpe, 1994.

Brinton, Mary, and Dong-Ju Lee. "Gender-Role Ideology, Labor Market Institutions, and Post-Industrial Fertility." *Population and Development Review* 42, no. 3 (2016): 405–33.

Bullock, Julia C. "Coeducation in the Age of 'Good Wife, Wise Mother': Koizumi Ikuko's Quest for 'Equality of Opportunity.'" In *Rethinking Japanese Feminisms*, ed. Julia C. Bullock, Ayako Kano, and James Welker, 89–102. Honolulu: University of Hawai'i Press, 2017.

Butler, Judith. *Gender Trouble: Feminism and the Subversion of Identity.* New York: Routledge, 2006.

"Chijin no kyōgen." *Sasebo jiji shinbun,* January 26, 1948. Gordon W. Prange Collection, University of Maryland Libraries.

"Co-Education—Staff Studies." GHQ/SCAP Records. RG 331, National Archives and Records Service, Box 5391, Folder 12.

Copeland, Rebecca L., and Melek Ortabasi, eds. *The Modern Murasaki: Writing by Women of Meiji Japan.* New York: Columbia University Press, 2006.

"Dai-ichi Shihan danjo kyōgaku kimaru." *Niigata nippō,* April 10, 1948. Gordon W. Prange Collection, University of Maryland Libraries.

Daitō, Shōjiki. "Danjo kyōgaku ron." *Kōyū kaishi,* October 1948. Gordon W. Prange Collection, University of Maryland Libraries.

"Danjo kyōgaku de yokatta koto iya datta koto." *Akatombo,* July 1, 1948. Gordon W. Prange Collection, University of Maryland Libraries.

"Danjo kyōgaku e zenshin: 'Sōgō kōkōsei' tsūgaku no fuben mo kaishō." *Kahoku shinpō,* December 20, 1948. Gordon W. Prange Collection, University of Maryland Libraries.

"Danjo kyōgaku kyōsei sezu: Shiritsu gakkō ni yon sentakuken." *Kahoku shinpō,* February 6, 1947. Gordon W. Prange Collection, University of Maryland Libraries.

"'Danjo kyōgaku' ni tsuite." *Chūgoku shinbun,* September 17, 1949. Gordon W. Prange Collection, University of Maryland Libraries.

"'Danjo kyōgaku' ni tsuite: Hotondo ga kyōgaku ōka." *Chūgoku shinbun,* September 17, 1949. Gordon W. Prange Collection, University of Maryland Libraries.

"Danjo kyōgaku no jittai: Yamanoborichū no baai." Part 1. *Sasebo jiji shinbun,* September 21, 1948. Gordon W. Prange Collection, University of Maryland Libraries.

"Danjo kyōgaku no jittai: Yamanoborichū no baai." Part 2. *Sasebo jiji shinbun,* September 22, 1948. Gordon W. Prange Collection, University of Maryland Libraries.

"Danjo kyōgaku no kōkō jūyon." *Hokkaidō shinbun,* February 27, 1949. Gordon W. Prange Collection, University of Maryland Libraries.

"Danjo kyōgaku o kataru." *Niigata nippō,* May 24, 1947. Gordon W. Prange Collection, University of Maryland Libraries.

"Danjo kyōgaku wa sansei: 6-3-3-sei ni tai suru iken." *Ōita gōdō shinbun,* January 24, 1947. Gordon W. Prange Collection, University of Maryland Libraries.

"Danjo kyōgaku wa tanoshi: Ōita Ichi undōkai." *Ōita gōdō shinbun,* October 10, 1949. Gordon W. Prange Collection, University of Maryland Libraries.

"Danjo kyōgaku wa yoku dekite imasu." *Chūgoku shinbun,* January 14, 1947. Gordon W. Prange Collection, University of Maryland Libraries.

"Danjo kyōgaku ze ka hi ka: Tōronkai." *Chūgoku shinbun*, March 15, 1949. Gordon W. Prange Collection, University of Maryland Libraries.

"Danjo nana-sai sei o onajū sezu—bōkun otoko, yoku warau onna: Danjo kyōgaku saitenbo." *Sasebo jiji shinbun*, February 1, 1948. Gordon W. Prange Collection, University of Maryland Libraries.

Doi, Sachiko. Untitled. In "Tokushū: Danjo kyōgaku—Kamiukena kōtō gakkō ni okeru danjo kyōgaku ni tsuite." *Ehime kyōiku*, August 1949, 18–23. Gordon W. Prange Collection, University of Maryland Libraries.

Dower, John. *Embracing Defeat: Japan in the Wake of World War II.* New York: W.W. Norton, 1999.

Duke, Benjamin. *The History of Modern Japanese Education: Constructing the National School System, 1872–1890.* New Brunswick, NJ: Rutgers University Press, 2009.

Duus, Peter. "Presidential Address: Weapons of the Weak, Weapons of the Strong—The Development of the Japanese Political Cartoon." *Journal of Asian Studies* 60, no. 4 (November 2001): 965–97.

Embree, John F. *Suye Mura: A Japanese Village.* Chicago and London: University of Chicago Press, 1939.

Foucault, Michel. *Discipline and Punish: The Birth of the Prison.* Trans. Alan Sheridan. 2nd ed. New York: Vintage Books, 1995.

Foucault, Michel. *The History of Sexuality.* Vol. 1, *An Introduction.* Trans. Robert Hurley. New York: Vintage Books, 1990.

Freedman, Alisa, Laura Miller, and Christine R. Yano, eds. *Modern Girls on the Go: Gender, Mobility, and Labor in Japan.* Stanford, CA: Stanford University Press, 2013.

Frühstück, Sabine. *Colonizing Sex: Sexology and Social Control in Modern Japan.* Berkeley: University of California Press, 2003.

Fujiki, Hideo. "Recent Trends of Juvenile Crime in Japan." *Journal of Criminal Law, Criminology, and Political Science* 53, no. 2 (June 1962): 219–21.

Fujimura-Fanselow, Kumiko. "College Women Today: Options and Dilemmas." In *Japanese Women: New Feminist Perspectives on the Past, Present, and Future,* ed. Kumiko Fujimura-Fanselow and Atsuko Kameda, 125–54. New York: Feminist Press, 1995.

Fujishima, Hiromichi. "Danjo kyōgaku ni tsuite." *Nami*, no. 1 (March 1949): 21–22. Gordon W. Prange Collection, University of Maryland Libraries.

Fujita. "Watashi wa danjo kyōgaku o kaku miru." *Gyōbō*, no. 4 (January 1948): 2–4. Gordon W. Prange Collection, University of Maryland Libraries.

Fukaya Masashi. *Ryōsai kenbo shugi no kyōiku.* Tokyo: Reimei shobō, 1998.

"Fūki wa shinpai muyō: Ebetsu kōkō waki ai ai no danjo kyōgaku." *Hokkaidō shinbun* (Sapporo kinkōban), June 17, 1948. Gordon W. Prange Collection, University of Maryland Libraries.

Fukuda, Hiroshi. "Danjo kyōgaku seido o kōtei suru." *Kakurei*, no. 23 (February 1947): 32–33. Gordon W. Prange Collection, University of Maryland Libraries.

Fukuhara, Rintarō. "Joshigakusei." *Gunzō* 7, no. 5 (May 1952): 46–48.

Gauntlett, C. Tsune. "Dr. Yoshioka Yayoi: A Brief Sketch of Her Life." Tokyo, 1934.

"Gendai joshi gakusei zadankai: Kanojotachi wa nani o kangaete iru ka." *Ansaazu*, February 1, 1948. Gordon W. Prange Collection, University of Maryland Libraries.

General Headquarters, Supreme Commander for the Allied Powers, Civil Information and Education Section, Education Division. *Education in Japan.* Tokyo: February 15, 1946.

Gordon, Andrew. "Managing the Japanese Household: The New Life Movement in Postwar Japan." In *Gendering Modern Japanese History*, ed. Barbara Molony and Kathleen Uno, 423–60. Cambridge, MA: Harvard University Asia Center, 2005.

Griffiths, Caitilin J. *Tracing the Itinerant Path: Jishū Nuns of Medieval Japan.* Honolulu: University of Hawai'i Press, 2016.

Hall, G. Stanley. *Adolescence: Its Psychology and Its Relations to Physiology, Anthropology, Sociology, Sex, Crime, Religion, and Education.* New York: D. Appleton, 1904.

"Hanashikago: Appare danjo kyōgaku." *Niigata nippō*, March 18, 1947. Gordon W. Prange Collection, University of Maryland Libraries.

Harrington, Ann M. "Women and Higher Education in the Japanese Empire (1895–1945)." *Journal of Asian History* 21, no. 2 (1987): 169–86.

Hasegawa, Machiko. *The Wonderful World of Sazae-san.* Trans. Jules Young. Tokyo: Kodansha International, 1997.

Hashimoto, Noriko. *Danjo kyōgakusei no shiteki kenkyū.* Tokyo: Ōtsuki shoten, 1992.

Hastings, Sally. "Women Educators of the Meiji Era and the Making of Modern Japan." *International Journal of Social Education* 6, no. 1 (Spring 1991): 83–94.

Hastings, Sally Ann. "Women's Professional Expertise and Women's Suffrage in Japan, 1868–1952." In *Gender, Nation, and State in Modern Japan*, ed. Andrea Germer, Vera Mackie, and Ulrike Wohr, 180–97. London and New York: Routledge, 2014.

Hayashi, Susumu. "Joshidaisei wa nani o kangaeteiru ka." *Chisei* 3, no. 8 (July 1956): 96–100.

Herwegh, H. "Danjo kyōgaku ni tsuite—hatashite sore wa minshushugiteki yōsei to shite teinin sareuru ka." *Josei kaizō*, April 1947. Gordon W. Prange Collection, University of Maryland Libraries.

Hirano, Kyoko. *Mr. Smith Goes to Tokyo: Japanese Cinema under the American Occu-*

*pation, 1945–1952.* Washington, DC, and London: Smithsonian Institutional Press, 1992.

Hirota Masaki. "Notes on the 'Process of Creating Women' in the Meiji Period." Trans. Suzanne O'Brien. In *Gender and Japanese History.* Vol. 2. *The Self and Expression/Work and Life,* ed. Wakita Haruko, Anne Bouchy, and Ueno Chizuko, 197–219. Osaka: Osaka University Press, 1999.

Inoue, Kyoko. *MacArthur's Japanese Constitution: A Linguistic and Cultural Study of Its Making.* Chicago and London: University of Chicago Press, 1991.

Isaka, Maki. *Onnagata: A Labyrinth of Gendering in Kabuki Theater.* Seattle and London: University of Washington Press, 2016.

Ishikawa, Hideo. "Danjo kyōgaku no mondai." *Tokyo Kei Daigaku Kaishi,* no. 16 (1957), 1–56.

Itō, Noboru. "Yōjinbukai 'kyōgakuron': Kiyose bunshō to no ichimon ittō." *Shūkan Asahi,* July 29, 1956.

Itō, Noboru, Hatano Isoko, et al. "Zadankai: Nyūgaku shiken bōkokuron." *Fujin Kōron* 40, no. 1 (January 1955): 172–79.

Iwao, Sumiko. *The Japanese Woman: Traditional Image and Changing Reality.* New York: Free Press, 1993.

"Jiyū nōto: Danjo kyōgaku no sono go." *Aozora,* no. 21 (August 1949): 15–16. Gordon W. Prange Collection, University of Maryland Libraries.

"Jiyūtō: Niigata Ichi-shi no danjo kyōgaku mondai." *Niigata nippō,* February 27, 1948. Gordon W. Prange Collection, University of Maryland Libraries.

"Joshi wa mina rakudai: 'Danjo kyōgaku' ikkagetsugo no seiseki.'" *Ōita gōdō shinbun,* June 11, 1948. Gordon W. Prange Collection, University of Maryland Libraries.

Kakimoto, Hachirō. "Danjo kyōgaku ibun." *Baton,* November 1947. Gordon W. Prange Collection, University of Maryland Libraries.

Kamei Shunsuke. "The Kiss and Japanese Culture after World War II." *Comparative Literature Studies* 18, no. 2, East-West Issue (June 1981): 114–23.

Kanei, Akito. "Danjo kyōgaku ni tsuite." *Aozora,* March 10, 1947. Gordon W. Prange Collection, University of Maryland Libraries.

Kano, Ayako. *Japanese Feminist Debates: A Century of Contention on Sex, Love, and Labor.* Honolulu: University of Hawai'i Press, 2016.

Kano, Ayako, and Vera Mackie. "Is Shinzo Abe Really a Feminist?" *East Asia Forum,* November 9, 2013. Accessed April 16, 2017. http://www.eastasiaforum. org/2013/11/09/is-shinzo-abe-really-a-feminist/.

Kanō, Mikiyo. "Jibunshi no naka no 'joshigakusei bōkokuron.'" In *Jūgoshi nōto sengohen 6: Kōdo seichō no jidai,* 110–18. Tokyo: Inpakuto shuppankai, 1992.

Katō, Yoshirō. "Danjo kyōgaku." *Repōto* 3, no. 7 (July 1948): 31. Gordon W. Prange Collection, University of Maryland Libraries.

Kawahara, Yukari. "Politics, Pedagogy, and Sexuality: Sex Education in Japanese Secondary Schools." PhD diss., Yale University, December 1996.

Kobayashi, Genzaburō. "Danjo kyōgaku igo." *Shin manga*, June 1946. Gordon W. Prange Collection, University of Maryland Libraries.

Kogane, Haruo. "Honshi ōbō shinjin manga: Danjo kyōgaku." *Shin sekai*, February 1947. Gordon W. Prange Collection, University of Maryland Libraries.

Koikari, Mire. *Pedagogy of Democracy: Feminism and the Cold War in the U.S. Occupation of Japan*. Philadelphia, PA: Temple University Press, 2008.

Koizumi, Ikuko. *Danjo kyōgakuron*. 1931. Reprint, Tokyo: Nihon Tosho Sentā, 1984.

Kornicki, P. F., Mara Patessio, and G. G. Rowley, eds. *The Female as Subject: Reading and Writing in Early Modern Japan*. Ann Arbor: Center for Japanese Studies, University of Michigan, 2010.

"Kōshanan de danjo kyōgaku." *Hokkaidō shinbun*, November 4, 1947. Gordon W. Prange Collection, University of Maryland Libraries.

Kovner, Sarah. *Occupying Power: Sex Workers and Servicemen in Postwar Japan*. Stanford, CA: Stanford University Press, 2012.

Koyama, Shizuko. "Domestic Roles and the Incorporation of Women into the Nation-State: The Emergence and Development of the 'Good Wife, Wise Mother' Ideology." Trans. Vera Mackie. In *Gender, Nation, and State in Modern Japan*, ed. Andrea Germer, Vera Mackie, and Ulrike Wohr, 85–100. London and New York: Routledge, 2014.

Koyama, Shizuko. *Ryōsai Kenbo and the Educational Ideal of "Good Wife, Wise Mother" in Modern Japan*. Boston, MA: Brill, 2013.

Koyama, Shizuko. *Sengo kyōiku no jendā chitsujo*. Tokyo: Keisō Shobō, 2009.

Koyama-Richard, Brigitte. *One Thousand Years of Manga*. Paris: Flammarion, 2007.

Kuji, Arashi. "Danjo kyōgaku ni tsuite." *Suzuran*, no. 6 (January 1949): 20. Gordon W. Prange Collection, University of Maryland Libraries.

Kurosawa, Hidefumi. *Sengo kyōiku no genryū o motomete: Maeda Tamon no kyōiku rinen*. Tokyo: Naigai Shuppan, 1982.

Lebra, Takie Sugiyama. *Japanese Women: Constraint and Fulfillment*. Honolulu: University of Hawai'i Press, 1984.

Loftus, Ronald P. *Changing Lives: The "Postwar" in Japanese Women's Autobiographies and Memoirs*. Ann Arbor, MI: Association for Asian Studies, 2013.

Mackie, Vera. *Feminism in Modern Japan: Citizenship, Embodiment, and Sexuality*. Cambridge and New York: Cambridge University Press, 2003.

Makino, Tsuneo, Kawazumi Masahiko, and Kedōin Yoshiaki. "Gakusei to ren'ai." *Gen'ya* 1, no. 2 (February 1947): 25–27. Gordon W. Prange Collection, University of Maryland Libraries.

McLelland, Mark. *Love, Sex, and Democracy in Japan during the American Occupation*. New York: Palgrave Macmillan, 2012.

McVeigh, Brian J. *Life in a Japanese Women's College: Learning to Be Ladylike*. London and New York: Routledge, 1997.

Mehl, Margaret. "Women Educators and the Confucian Tradition in Meiji Japan (1868–1912): Miwada Masako and Atomi Kakei." *Women's History Review* 10, no. 4 (2001): 579–602.

Miller-Bernal, Leslie, and Susan L. Poulson, eds. *Going Coed: Women's Experiences in Formerly Men's Colleges and Universities, 1950–2000*. Nashville, TN: Vanderbilt University Press, 2004.

Ministry of Justice. *Juvenile Delinquency in Japan: Characteristics and Preventive Measures*. Tokyo: Ministry of Justice, 1958.

Ministry of Justice. *The Present State of Juvenile Delinquency and Counter-Measures in Japan*. Tokyo: Ministry of Justice, 1965.

Miyamoto Yuriko et al. "Seishun o kataru." *Gakusei hyōron*, September 1947. Gordon W. Prange Collection, University of Maryland Libraries.

Molony, Barbara. "Japan's 1986 Equal Employment Opportunity Law and the Changing Discourse on Gender." *Signs* 20, no. 2 (Winter 1995): 268–302.

"Momoiro gassen o nakusu ni wa shakai ga umidasu nikutai no yūgi." *Sasebo jiji shinbun*, September 9, 1948. Gordon W. Prange Collection, University of Maryland Libraries.

Monbusho. *Monbu gyōsei shiryō*. Vol. 1. Tokyo: Kokushokan gyōkai, 1997.

Montag, Warren. *Althusser and His Contemporaries: Philosophy's Perpetual War*. Durham, NC, and London: Duke University Press, 2013.

Morris, Ivan I. *The World of the Shining Prince: Court Life in Ancient Japan*. New York: Kodansha International, 1994.

Morris-Suzuki, Tessa. *Shōwa: An Inside Story of Hirohito's Japan*. New York: Schocken Books, 1985.

Murasaki Shikibu. *The Tale of Genji*. Trans. Dennis C. Washburn. New York and London: W.W. Norton, 2015.

Nagai, Michio. "Roku san sei kyōiku ga unda wakamonotachi." *Shinchō* 54, no. 3 (March 1957): 98–104.

Nagata, Shin. "Danjo kyōgaku mondai o megutte." *Kyōiku Gijutsu* 11, no. 7 (1956): 10–17.

Nakano, Yoshio, et al. "Zadankai: Joshidaigaku wa gomen da—Onna rōnin ooi ni kataru." *Fujin Kōron*, March 1959.

Nakanoin Masatada no Musume. *The Confessions of Lady Nijō*. Trans. Karen Brazell. Stanford, CA: Stanford University Press, 1976.

Nakaya, Ken'ichi. "Joshi daigaku muyōron." *Shinchō* 54, no. 3 (March 1957): 90–94.

N.S.-sei. "Danjo kyōgaku no urei." *Tomoshibi*, no. 1 (December 1948). Gordon W. Prange Collection, University of Maryland Libraries.

Okada, Jun. "Danjo kyōgaku hantai." *Yomimono chūgoku*, October 1949. Gordon W. Prange Collection, University of Maryland Libraries.

Okamoto, Rei. "Pictorial Propaganda in Japanese Comic Art, 1941–1945: Images of the Self and the Other in a Newspaper Strip, Single-Panel Cartoons, and Cartoon Leaflets." PhD diss., Temple University, 1999.

Okubo, Toshiaki, and Tokiómi Kaigō. *Kyōiku Shingikai Shimon Dai 1-gō Tokubetsu Iinkai Seiri Iinkai Kaigiroku.* Vol. 8. Tokyo: Senbundō Shoten, 1970–71.

Orr, Mark Taylor. "Education Reform Policy in Occupied Japan." PhD diss., University of North Carolina, 1954.

"Otona kaomake kodomo gikai." *Sasebo jiji shinbun*, June 17, 1948. Gordon W. Prange Collection, University of Maryland Libraries.

Ozaki, Moriteru. "Tōdai hanayome gakkōron." *Fujin Kōron,* December 1958.

Palmieri, Patricia A. "From Republican Motherhood to Race Suicide: Arguments on the Higher Education of Women in the United States, 1820–1920." In *Educating Men and Women Together: Coeducation in a Changing World*, ed. Carol Lasser, 49–64. Urbana: University of Illinois Press, 1987.

Passin, Herbert. *Society and Education in Japan.* New York: Teachers College, Columbia University, 1965.

Powers, Jane Bernard. *The "Girl Question" in Education: Vocational Education for Young Women in the Progressive Era.* London and Washington, DC: Falmer Press, 1992.

Rodd, Laurel Rasplica. "Yosano Akiko and the Taishō Debate over the 'New Woman.'" In *Recreating Japanese Women, 1600–1945*, ed. Gail Lee Bernstein, 175–98. Berkeley: University of California Press, 1991.

Roden, Donald. *Schooldays in Imperial Japan: A Study in the Culture of a Student Elite.* Berkeley: University of California Press, 1980.

Roden, Donald. "Taishō Culture and the Problem of Gender Ambivalence." In *Culture and Identity: Japanese Intellectuals during the Interwar Years*, ed. J. Thomas Rimer, 37–55. Princeton, NJ: Princeton University Press, 1990.

Rose, Barbara. *Tsuda Umeko and Women's Education in Japan.* New Haven, CT: Yale University Press, 1992.

Rubin, Jay. "From Wholesomeness to Decadence: The Censorship of Literature under the Allied Occupation." *Journal of Japanese Studies* 11, no. 1 (Winter 1985): 71–103.

Ruch, Barbara, ed. *Engendering Faith: Women and Buddhism in Premodern Japan.* Ann Arbor: Center for Japanese Studies, University of Michigan, 2002.

Ryang, Sonia. *Love in Modern Japan: Its Estrangement from Self, Sex, and Society.* London and New York: Routledge, 2006.

Saga, Tadao. "Danjo kyōgaku hiteiron." *Kakurei,* no. 23 (February 1947), 35–37. Gordon W. Prange Collection, University of Maryland Libraries.

Sasaki, Keiko. "Dentōteki kihan kara dakkyaku shita shinchūkansō no joseitachi: Senzenki Nihon ni okeru joshi kōtō kyōiku kakudai no mekanizumu." In *Josei to kōtō kyōiku—kikai kakuchō to shakaiteki sōkoku,* ed. Kagawa Setsuko and Kawamura Sadae, 196–223. Kyoto: Shōwadō, 2008.

Schodt, Frederik L. *Manga! Manga! The World of Japanese Comics.* Tokyo: Kodansha International, 1983.

Sei Shōnagon. *The Pillow Book.* Trans. Ivan Morris. New York: Columbia University Press, 1967.

"Seika ageru danjo kyōgaku no jitsu zairyō fusoku mo gojo de kaishō." *Chūgoku shinbun,* May 18, 1949. Gordon W. Prange Collection, University of Maryland Libraries.

Senryūshi Tōrō. "Danjo kyōgaku." *Kōyū,* no. 1 (March 1948): 16. Gordon W. Prange Collection, University of Maryland Libraries.

"Sesō o kiru: Honsha shakaibu dai-issen kisha zadankai." *Chūgoku shinbun,* September 7, 1949. Gordon W. Prange Collection, University of Maryland Libraries.

"Shasetsu: Danjo kyōgaku no mondaiten." *Hokkaidō shinbun,* February 25, 1949. Gordon W. Prange Collection, University of Maryland Libraries.

Sherif, Ann. "The Aesthetics of Speed and the Illogicality of Politics: Ishihara Shintarō's Literary Debut." *Japan Forum* 17, no. 2 (July 1, 2005): 185–211.

"Shinsei kōkō no kōsō: Nijū kōchō ni kiku." *Ōita gōdō shinbun,* April 15, 1948. Gordon W. Prange Collection, University of Maryland Libraries.

Shioda, Eijirō. "Danjo kyōgaku no han." *Hōpu,* August 1946. Gordon W. Prange Collection, University of Maryland Libraries.

"Shō-chū-kōkō no saihaichi keikaku kimaru: Kōkō ni mo tsūgakku settei, danjo kyōgaku wa myōnendo kara kanzen jisshi." *Hokkaidō shinbun,* May 12, 1949. Gordon W. Prange Collection, University of Maryland Libraries.

"Shūdan iede ga oshieru mono: Yugamerareta seishun no seitai—Danjo kyōgaku de kyōka." *Niigata nippō,* June 15, 1948. Gordon W. Prange Collection, University of Maryland Libraries.

Sievers, Sharon. *Flowers in Salt: The Beginnings of Feminist Consciousness in Japan.* Stanford, CA: Stanford University Press, 1983.

Slaymaker, Douglas. *The Body in Postwar Japanese Fiction.* London and New York: RoutledgeCurzon, 2004.

"Sukusuku nobiru danjo kyōgaku: Chijimatta gakuryokusa, nayami no tane wa kōgai de no kōsai." *Hokkaidō shinbun sapporoban*, October 9, 1949. Gordon W. Prange Collection, University of Maryland Libraries.

Suzuki, Michiko. *Becoming Modern Women: Love and Female Identity in Prewar Japanese Literature and Culture*. Stanford, CA: Stanford University Press, 2010.

Tachibanaki, Toshiaki. *Josei to gakureki: Joshi kōtō kyōiku no ayumi to yukue*. Tokyo: Keisō shobō, 2011.

Takagi, Takeshi. "Danjo kyōgaku ni tsuite." *Muhyō*, no. 1 (December 1948): 5–6. Gordon W. Prange Collection, University of Maryland Libraries.

Takahashi, Keiichi. "Danjo kyōgaku to warera no Kakugo." *Kakurei*, no. 23 (February 1947): 34–35. Gordon W. Prange Collection, University of Maryland Libraries.

Takashita, Iku. "Danjo kyōgaku ni tsuite aru joshi gakusei wa daisansei!" *Taremizu bunka* 2, no. 5 (May 1949). Gordon W. Prange Collection, University of Maryland Libraries.

Takemae, Eiji. *Inside GHQ: The Allied Occupation of Japan and Its Legacy*. New York: Continuum, 2002.

Tanaka, Sumiko. "Fujin kaihō no kabe." *Shisō*, no. 414 (December 1958): 1964–68.

Tashiro, Teruko. "Ronzetsu: Danjo kyōgaku ni natte." *Sazanami*, no. 1 (December 1948): 27–28. Gordon W. Prange Collection, University of Maryland Libraries.

Tenaka, Kazuko. "Danjo kyōgaku." *Wakakusa*, no. 1 (March 1949): 24. Gordon W. Prange Collection, University of Maryland Libraries.

Teruoka, Yasutaka. "Joshigakusei wa nani yue daigaku ni iku." *Fujin Kōron* 42, no. 1 (January 1957): 138–40.

Teruoka, Yasutaka. "Joshigakusei yo ni habakaru: kanojora no mokuteki wa nani ka." *Fujin Kōron* 47, no. 3 (March 1962): 277–81.

Tocco, Martha. "Made in Japan: Meiji Women's Education." In *Gendering Modern Japanese History*, ed. Barbara Molony and Kathleen Uno, 39–60. Cambridge, MA, and London: Harvard University Press, 2005.

Tokorosawa, Ayako. "Aki o mukaete." *Hana no kyōshitsu* 1, no. 2 (September 1948): 1. Gordon W. Prange Collection, University of Maryland Libraries.

Tokuza, Akiko. *The Rise of the Feminist Movement in Japan*. Tokyo: Keio University Press, 1999.

Tsuchimochi, Gary H. *Education Reform in Postwar Japan: The 1946 U.S. Education Mission*. Tokyo: University of Tokyo Press, 1993.

Tsurumi, E. Patricia. "The State, Education, and Two Generations of Women in Meiji Japan, 1868–1912." *U.S.-Japan Women's Journal*, no. 18 (2000): 3–26.

Tyack, David, and Elisabeth Hansot. *Learning Together: A History of Coeducation in American Schools*. New Haven, CT, and London: Yale University Press, 1990.

Ueki, Bin. "Gendai fūkei 1: Danjo kyōgaku." *Toppu* 1, no. 2 (July 1946): 7. Gordon W. Prange Collection, University of Maryland Libraries.

Uemura, Chikako. *Josei kaihō o meguru senryō seisaku.* Tokyo: Keisō Shobō, 2007.

United States Education Mission to Japan. *Report of the U.S. Education Mission to Japan.* Washington, DC: United States Government Printing Office, 1946.

Uno, Kathleen. "Womanhood, War, and Empire: Transmutations of 'Good Wife, Wise Mother' before 1931." In *Gendering Modern Japanese History*, ed. Barbara Molony and Kathleen Uno, 493–519. Cambridge, MA, and London: Harvard University Press, 2005.

Wakatsuki, Saburō. "Danjo kyōgaku." *Sakura*, May 1947. Gordon W. Prange Collection, University of Maryland Libraries.

Wiswell, Ella Lury, and Robert J. Smith. *The Women of Suye Mura.* Chicago: University of Chicago Press, 1982.

Yamaguchi, Tomomi. "The Mainstreaming of Feminism and the Politics of Backlash in Twenty-First Century Japan." In *Rethinking Japanese Feminisms*, ed. Julia C. Bullock, Ayako Kano, and James Welker, 68–85. Honolulu: University of Hawai'i Press, 2017.

Yokoyama, Yasuzō. "Danjo kyōgaku no hanayome gakkō." *Yomimono kurabu* 1, no. 1 (July 10, 1946): 18. Gordon W. Prange Collection, University of Maryland Libraries.

Yoshida, Ken'ichi. "Joshidai wa bokumetsu subeki ka?" *Bungei shunjū* 33, no. 22 (December 1955): 242–46.

Yoshida, Michiko. "Danjo kyōgaku o omou." *Yakusōshi*, no. 1 (March 1949): 32. Gordon W. Prange Collection, University of Maryland Libraries.

Yoshizawa, Natsuko. "Sei no daburu sutandaado o meguru kattō 'Heibon' ni okeru 'wakamono' no sekushuariti." In *Kindai Nihon bunkaron 8: Onna no bunka*, ed. Aoki Tamotsu et al., 201–25. Tokyo: Iwanami shoten, 2000.

"Zadankai: Atarashii danjo kōsai." *Kindai* 3 (June 1949): 2–9. Gordon W. Prange Collection, University of Maryland Libraries.

"Zadankai: Danjo kyōgaku ni tsuite." *Hana no kyōshitsu* 1, no. 2 (September 1948): 4–7. Gordon W. Prange Collection, University of Maryland Libraries.

"Zadankai: Shokugyō fujin o kakomu shinsei kōkō danjo gakusei." *Shisutaa*, no. 2 (April 1949): 28–37. Gordon W. Prange Collection, University of Maryland Libraries.

"Zōkin motte tereru otoko gakusei: Me made somete danjo kyōgaku wa yoki mono." *Ōita gōdō shinbun*, May 11, 1948. Gordon W. Prange Collection, University of Maryland Libraries.

# Index